Claire Austin's
Book of
PERENNIALS

Claire Austin

White Hopton Publications

First Published in 2015 by White Hopton Publications,
Newtown, Powys SY16 4EN.
This revised and updated edition published by White Hopton
Publications in 2020

A CIP catalogue record for this book is available from the
British Library.

ISBN 978-0-9931647-1-2

For the 2020 edition:
Editor Anna Kruger
Indexer Marie Lorimer

2015 edition project managed and edited for White Hopton
Publications by Outhouse Publishing, Winchester SO22 5DS
Project manager Sue Gordon
Editor Anna Kruger
Proofreader Jo Weeks
Indexer Marie Lorimer

Print management by Printhouse www.printhouseltd.co.uk

Printed and bound in Great Britain using materials
accredited by the Forest Stewardship Council by
Pureprint Group
Uckfield, East Sussex TN22 1PL
www.pureprint.com

Front cover The Garden at White Hopton June
Back cover Veronicastrum virginicum 'Fascination'

Claire Austin Hardy Plants,
White Hopton Farm, Wern Lane, Sarn, Newtown SY16 4EN
www.claireaustin-hardyplants.co.uk

Contents

A border filled with a varied selection of hardy perennials at White Hopton Farm, July

Perennials with contrasting colour, form and texture look fabulous together

MY PASSION FOR PERENNIALS

Perennials have been a passion of mine since the early 1980s. During this time I have grown them on my nursery and planted them in seven different gardens. Although not a trained garden designer, I have used perennials to paint the picture each garden demanded. They offer so much: colour, shape, texture, flowers for the house, and they also invite nature in.

My first book about perennials was written in 1999, commissioned as a result of the colourful catalogue we produced for the nursery each year. The catalogue eventually ran to hundreds of pages, which wasn't cost effective. With rising internet sales, our focus has now shifted to selling plants through the website rather than via our catalogue, which is now much smaller.

However, frustrated by my own online research into more unusual perennials and following repeated requests from customers for the old catalogue, as well as for copies of my first book (long out of print), I realised that there was still a need for a practical, highly illustrated guide to perennials. And so I wrote this book, which is designed not as a selling guide but to encourage all gardeners, especially new ones, to try perennials. The range of plants in the Plant Directory is far from exhaustive, but these are all perennials I have grown and found to be reliable. It is a personal selection and I make no apologies for ignoring your favourites. *Solidago*, for example, I have no time for, while treasures such as *Trachystemon* aren't included because they aren't readily available.

The introductory section describes how I grow perennials and combine them in the garden. In my early years of growing perennials, I found inspiration in the pages of Graham Stuart Thomas's book *Perennial Garden Plants* (Dent, 1976). I grew up knowing Graham. He was never without a small notebook, which he carried in his pocket. If he saw anything interesting he would jot it down. My notebook is my camera. All the pictures in this book were taken by me in my gardens – most of them in the garden at White Hopton Farm.

WHY GROW PERENNIALS?

Of all the plant groups, perennials are the most versatile. They grow in all soils from dry to wet, and in conditions from full sun through to shade. In size and shape, they can form a ground-hugging carpet or a clump that is head-high. In terms of flower colour, there are perennials in every shade from white to almost black, and they have a fabulous range of forms and textures. Most importantly, they are usually very easy to grow, filling a border quickly with leaves and flowers from early spring to late autumn. Some are even generous enough to provide flowers in winter. In short, there can be no doubt that perennials deserve pride of place in every garden.

White Hopton Farm garden, August

Perennials have long been a part of the garden picture and many were first grown for their healing powers. During the 19th century as large numbers of people moved to industrial areas and wealth increased, many homes came with small patches of land that could be cultivated. In rural areas, useful and ornamental plants grew side by side in small cottage gardens, while those who lived in the smoke choked cities started to grow plants in pots. Suburban gardeners with homes on the outskirts of towns benefited from larger gardens. Given these social changes, gardening with ornamental plants increased in popularity and from the middle of the 19th century onwards, gardening was no longer the preserve of the very wealthy. Anyone could enjoy it.

NEW PLANT INTRODUCTION

Most plants grown in gardens up until the time of Queen Victoria were native to Britain and Europe. But with the expansion of empires came a corresponding influx of new plant species from all over the globe. By the time of Queen Victoria's death almost all the plants that are familiar to us could be found growing in gardens. When nurserymen began to cultivate these new discoveries new seedlings emerged. These were given names, added to catalogues and sold to gardeners. The world of gardening had become commercial.

THE WRITTEN WORD

Books and magazines on gardening started to appear in the 19th century, their pages filled with new and exciting ideas. By the late 1800s *The Garden* magazine became the most fashionable publication. Featuring articles on garden styles as well as how to grow and look after plants, it offered advice on gardening overseas, growing in the greenhouse, and vegetables. The 'old-fashioned' flower garden was rarely mentioned, yet it was the magazine's founder, William Robinson, who became the champion of traditional cottage-garden perennials. Frustrated by the Victorian craze for rigid displays of bedding plants, which he described 'false and hideous "art"', Robinson published *The English Flower Garden* in 1883. Extolling the virtues of a more naturalistic style of gardening, it became one of the most influential gardening books of the first half of the 20th century. Perennials had been rediscovered.

TWENTIETH CENTURY – THE FIRST HALF

The years that followed the two World Wars saw the introduction of hundreds of new plant cultivars, many of them raised for the cut flower industry. Carefully packed boxes of freshly cut perennials, including asters, pinks, delphiniums and scabious, were sent by train to flower markets such as London's Covent Garden.

RUDBECKIA PURPUREA

Rudbeckia purpurea, now known as *Echinacea purpurea* from *The Garden* magazine April 29, 1893

Border of Delphiniums in the garden at Hall Green, showing effect of grouping hardy flowers instead of "dotting." Engraved from a photograph.

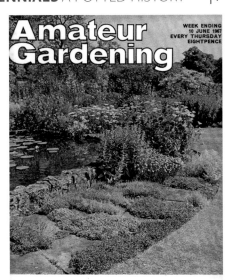

BRITISH PLANT BREEDERS

When gardeners were called on to fight for their country in two World Wars, land was left untended or turned over to vegetable growing. From the mid-1940s, the government actively encouraged people to get back to cultivating plants, especially for the lucrative cut-flower trade.

My father, the rose breeder David Austin, started out in horticulture after the Second World War. He told me that plant breeding and cultivation usually attracted older men who had come out of the army, such as Captain B. H. B. Symons-Jeune. He became famous for raising phloxes, including *Phlox paniculata* 'Bright Eyes' and 'Eventide', which are still available to grow. Bakers of Codsall, Wolverhampton – a nursery where my father worked in his youth – introduced the still-famous Russell Lupins that George Russell had spent more than two decades developing. Asters were, and still are, popular both in borders and as cut flowers. In the 1920s, plants were generally tall and Victor Vokes, an official of the War Graves Commission, turned his attention to breeding a shorter, low-maintenance plant that would be suitable for adorning graves in autumn. He succeeded and his strain of strong-growing Michaelmas daisies include *Aster novi-belgii* 'Little Pink Beauty'. Delphiniums, too, have been popular throughout the 20th century but their heyday was the 1940s and 1950s. Blackmore and Langdon were prolific breeders and in 1945, the Royal Horticultural Society listed 163 varieties of delphinium growing in their gardens at Wisley, Surrey.

The names of famous nurseries are still attached to present-day perennials: *Aster* cultivars from Ernest Ballard (Colwall, Worcestershire), *Papaver* from Amos Perry (Enfield, Middlesex) and *Kniphofia* from Bees (Cheshire). One of the most famous and perhaps the last great breeder of perennials in Britain was Alan Bloom from Bressingham in Norfolk. Blooms initially supplied perennials to other nurseries but by the 1970s, they led the field in mail order. Alan was responsible for raising such lovely perennials as *Bergenia* 'Bressingham White' and *Aconitum* 'Bressingham Spire'.

THE EMERGENCE OF GARDEN CENTRES

Perennials were traditionally sold by nurseries as bare rooted plants during the months of autumn. Visitors were welcome but mail order was a popular method of buying plants. By the mid- to late 1960s, the first garden centres were selling plants grown in black polythene bags. During the 1980s rigid plastic pots were introduced, enabling plants to be sold all year round. The attractive displays led to impulse buying and, as a consequence, to breeders concentrating their efforts on plants that are shorter (so they don't topple over in the pots) and more flamboyant to attract the eye of passing customers.

Nurserymen, Bakers of Codsall advertised delphiniums and the celebrated Russell lupins. Those pictured (right) are seed-grown selections. At the top, the changing covers of gardening magazines from 1937 to 1967

Aster x *frikartii* 'Mönch' was awarded an AGM many years ago. It is still one of the best asters around

In the USA, the common name for *Mertensis virginica* is bluebell. In the UK this is the name for our blue-flowered spring bulb

This is *Geranium* Rozanne ® ('Gerwat'). We know it by its familiar trade name, 'Rozanne'

The term perennial describes any plant that lives for more than two years. It includes trees, shrubs, and bulbs, as well as herbaceous perennials – the subject of this book. In the wild, perennials are found in all parts of the world, although many are not full hardy in this country. While they grow to all sizes, many of the smallest perennials need specific growing conditions, and for gardening purposes these fall into a separate group – alpines. The plants that inspire me, and that feature in this book, are hardy herbaceous perennials. They are very diverse, tolerate a wide range of soils and situations, and are ideal for flower beds or borders.

NAMING PERENNIALS

Latin names have been used for as long as the printed word has existed but in the early centuries of gardening, before widespread literacy, plants were given a name that people could easily remember. Often this 'common' name reflected what the plant was used for. Fleabane, *Pulicaria dysenterica*, is a good example. The strangely scented leaves of this native British flower of wild, damp places were believed to repel fleas. This common name is now applied to all types of *Erigeron,* a family it resembles but is not related to. To avoid any confusion, I feel strongly that plants should be known by their Latin (botanical) name rather than the common name.

Latin names, both for plants and animals, are recognised internationally. The convention is to put the Latin name in italics, such as *Achillea*, followed by the common name in brackets (Yarrow). Latin names are a combination of botanical terminology, and a descriptive or given name, which is within inverted commas, for example *Achillea* 'Terracotta'.

THE RENAMING OF PERENNIALS

Plant names have always changed over time and for a variety of reasons – all of them to do with botanists. Sometimes a group of plants is deemed to contain different species and so the group is split up and renamed. The recent use of DNA profiling has led to a profusion of plants with new names, many of which are so difficult to pronounce I make no apologies for resisting using them.

TRADE NAMES

To confuse things further, but not in this book, some plants have acquired a trade name. This appears after the Latin name, in a different typeface, and has no inverted commas (*see* left). It is then followed by a name that may make no sense. These are given to plants where Plant Varietal Rights (PVR) apply, and where, if you were to propagate it for re-selling, a patent fee would apply. Again I make no apologies for not including these names. They are a selling tool that only serves to bewilder the average gardener.

Once there were hundreds of *Aster* varieties. Without the work of National Collection holders, many more might have disappeared

Sedum 'Mr Goodbud' is now called *Hylotelephium* 'Mr Goodbud'. Until the 1980s *Persicaria* (front) was known as *Polygonum*

AGM

For many years, the Royal Horticultural Society has given plants that reach certain criteria, after extensive trialling, an Award of Garden Merit (AGM for short). Awarded to all types of plants, including perennials, the AGM can be a useful selection tool but it is not foolproof. The list of AGM plants is not exhaustive and the trials are ongoing, so a plant without an AGM may be excellent but has yet to be trialled. Or a cultivar that held an AGM may well have been superseded by a newer variety.

All gardens contain a range of plants. Shrubs, often used as hedging, have woody stems and are particularly useful in winter when there is little showing above ground. Annuals – plants that live for only one year – are ideal for filling gaps quickly but it is perennials that add movement, colour and constant variation to a garden. They also combine perfectly with shrubs, annuals, and early season bulbs such as tulips, (*see* p. 46). However, there is no reason why a garden can't be filled with perennials alone.

PLANNING YOUR GARDEN

When planning a garden, the standard layout is plants in borders surrounded by hedges or fences, paths or grass. The most effective borders look like they are rising naturally from the soil, with plants that vary in heights and spreads. It doesn't matter if the border is seen from one side or all sides; every plant is part of the whole patchwork. Some plants will naturally stand out – usually the tallest and boldest – and one plant will shine for a while before retreating to allow another to carry on the performance.

Perennials, like *Aruncus* and *Nepeta*, will tolerate sun and a semi-shady spot

For a successful border, choose plants that not only grow to different heights, but that also flower for long periods.

When it comes to selecting plants, we are all tempted by a pretty picture. But is it the right plant? There seem to be so many to choose from. Our nursery alone grows over 1000 different perennials. The easiest way might be to simplify the choice and limit the numbers, concentrating on irises, grasses, or perhaps white-flowered plants. That is one option, but given the wealth of perennials out there, why not make a border zing with colour and texture from spring to autumn?

So where do you start? Firstly, don't worry if you put a plant in the wrong place; I've often done this myself. Almost all perennials can be moved at any time as long as the top growth is cut back (to limit the plant's need for water). Secondly, remember that plants need to grow in the right place, so always check the soil type and how much light there is. It's no use putting a beautiful *Trillium* that needs humus-rich ground in dry, sandy soil. It just won't grow.

WHAT MAKES A GOOD PERENNIAL

As you browse through this book, you'll see that perennials come in all colours, shapes and sizes. There are plants for every situation and there are hundreds of them. But how do you select one that suits you, and with limited space and finances will the one you choose do well in your garden? In my experience, a good perennial is one that is easy to grow, easy to maintain, generally pest and disease free and adapted to a variety of situations. Plants that are suited to a specific location, such as *Uvularia*, or are irresistible to slugs, like *Hosta* are still good perennials. You just have to give a little more thought to the question of how and where to grow them.

HARDINESS

As perennials come back year after year, by definition they are hardy. But there are limits to their hardiness. Most of the plants described in this book will survive a temperature down to -15°C, or lower. In 2010 the temperature dipped to -19.5°C at our nursery in mid-Shropshire, yet the vast majority of the plants were fine. However, a few perennials will suffer if the temperature drops below -5°C, especially if the ground is wet. These include *Penstemon* and *Verbena*.

CONSIDERING THE CHOICE

Having decided to grow perennials, the next step is to choose them. For experienced or keen gardeners, this can be a great source of joy; for anyone new to gardening, the sheer choice of plants can be daunting. Below are a few helpful guidelines:

The main things to consider

- What soil type or types do you have in your garden? Be aware that soil in one area may be different to that in other areas
- How much light will the plants get?
- How tall do you want the plants to grow?
- How wide (the spread) do you want them to be?
- When do you want them to flower?
- Which flower colours do you like?

Other things to consider

- How long do you want a plant to stay in flower. Does it matter if the period is fairly short?
- Is it an easy plant to grow?
- Has it got an AGM (*see* p. 53)?
- Do the flowers attract insects?
- Can the flowers be cut for the house?
- How hardy is the plant?

While *Verbena bonariensis* copes well with high winds, it can suffer in cold winters

When I plant up a new garden the first thing I look at is the soil. It is one of the most important elements in the garden, both feeding and watering the plants and so providing them with the energy to grow and thrive. While most perennials grow in any well-drained soil, certain soils can present more of a challenge. If you think your soil falls into this category, it's important to check first to make sure. You can easily tell what sort of soil you have by just grabbing a handful and examining it.

TYPES OF SOIL

Soil is divided into different types and all of them have features that affect the amount of moisture and nutrients available to a plant. A garden often contains a range of soils. Some areas may contain clay; in other parts, the soil may be very dry. This is especially true of new gardens where rubble lies beneath the soil. It is important to remember that no two gardens are alike. These are the most common soil types:

Loam soils

Loam soils are the best of all. They are dark in colour and when rubbed between the fingers crumble easily. They drain well, but do not dry out, which means they are rich in nutrients. They are also easy to dig. Almost all plants will grow in this soil.

Clay soils

Pale and sticky to the touch, clay soils do not drain easily, and are often lumpy, which can make them difficult to dig. Some clay soils are rich in loam. These drain more freely, but still hold water for a long time. Clay and clay-loam mixes are rich in nutrients. These plants happily grow in clay soils:

Aconitum	Helenium
Actaea	Hosta
Aster	Inula
Astrantia	Kirengeshoma
Astilbe	Ligularia
Brunnera	Monarda
Cirsium	Persicaria
Epimedium	Prunella
Eupatorium	Pulmonaria
Geranium	Rudbeckia

Sandy soils

Sandy soils can be brown or red. They are made up of small particles that, when dry, run easily through the fingers. This type of soil is very free draining, so nutrients are quickly leached out, rendering the soil poor. Plants suitable for sandy soils are listed below:

Acanthus	Linaria
Achillea	Lychnis coronaria
Centhranthus	Oenothera
Echinops	Origanum
Eryngium	Salvia
Iris - bearded types	Saxifraga
Knautia	Valeriana
Lamium	Verbascum

Chalk soils

Containing lots of white chalk or flint pieces, these soils are usually pale in colour, are almost always alkaline (*see* right) and often shallow. They are very free-draining so nutrients are quickly washed out. The plants below cope with chalky, alkaline soils:

Achillea	Phlomis
Bergenia	Salvia
Campanula	Sedum
Dianthus	Sidalcea
Eryngium	Verbascum
Euphorbia	Verbena
Origanum	

Aster × *frikartii* 'Flora's Delight' (seen here with *Artemisia*) is happy in chalky soil

Echinacea, *Achillea* and *Helenium* grow well in a very well-drained sandy soil

Persicaria amplexicaulis 'Taurus', *Veronicastrum virginicum* 'Fascination' and *Persicaria polymorpha* will thrive in a clay soil but not in a soil that dries out

DRAINAGE and ACID/ALKALINE SOILS

The majority of plants described in this book will grow in good, well-drained soils. Such soils drain reasonably quickly even after heavy rain, and they contain ample nutrients and a balanced pH. The pH of a soil refers to how acid or alkaline it is. There are very few perennials that require only an acid or alkaline soil. But certain perennials fare better in acid soils than others and these generally grow in soil that remains moist (*see* below). Those that will not thrive in acid soil include bearded irises and *Dianthus*. For perennials that prefer alkaline soils, which contain lots of chalk or flint, *see* Chalk soils, below left.

Moist and wet soils

These are soils that remain wet or moist even during hot summers. They are most likely to be found around or near ponds and streams, and include boggy areas. The plants below thrive in wet soils in sun or partial shade:

Astilbe	*Ligularia*
Hosta	*Lobelia*
Iris ensata	*Lysimachia*
Iris laevigata	*Lythrum*
Iris pseudacorus	*Primula*
Iris sibirica	*Rodgersia*
Kirengeshoma	

Dry soils

A dry soil is most definitely a disadvantage when growing perennials. These soils, which include chalky and sandy soils, are often poor in nutrients. During hot spells they become so dry the plants suffer. Dry soil can also be found beneath trees and shrubs, along the edges of stone and brick walls, and on sloping banks. These plants will tolerate dry soils:

Calamintha	*Eryngium*
Campanula	*Gypsophila*
Coreopsis	*Iris* - bearded types
Dianthus	*Sedum*
Dictamnus	*Stachys byzantina*
Echinops	*Stipa*
Erodium	

Bearded irises thrive in a dry soil

The spring foliage of hostas and irises growing in damp soil in partial shade, with candelabra primulas (rear left)

Iris sibirica 'Silver Edge' is at home in the gravel around our fountain but it can't be grown directly in water

Salvia nemorosa 'Caradonna' and *Scabiosa* 'Butterfly Blue' are sun lovers

The amount of light a garden receives determines which plants will flourish. While many gardens have areas that get lots of sun for most of the day, there will always be spots where the light is limited. To find the aspect of your garden, notice where the sun rises (east) and work round from there. South-facing gardens are always the sunniest and warmest. West, however, is often the best, as gardens with this aspect receive an even amount of light and shade. North-facing gardens can be difficult for plants, especially if the soil is dry, whereas easterly borders can be the coolest. Fortunately, perennials are a diverse group: some thrive
in light shade, very few grow with very little sunlight. Most of the plants in this book will flourish in a sunny position or one that is in shade for part of the day.

HOW MUCH SUN?

The sections below give some guidance on how to judge the amount of sun in your garden. This will vary according to the time of day, or season, and also if the garden is overshadowed by buildings or trees. The sun, of course, is at its highest in summer and at its lowest in winter, when few herbaceous perennials are growing.

Full sun

A site with full sun receives light throughout the day. If the soil is poor, it will dry out quickly, which some plants resent.

Partial shade

These sites get some sunlight for a good proportion of the day, for example from 10am to 4pm. Areas under the eaves of a house and along the margins of tall trees and shrubs will be partially shaded.

This border gets sunlight for just a few hours a day, yet the right choice of plants ensures a good range of colour

Intersectional peony 'Magical Mystery Tour' will take some shade but needs a sunny position to flower at its best. Grey-leaved *Stachys byzantina* (behind) won't tolerate shade

Shade

Full shade does limit a gardener's choices yet there is still a wide range of plants on offer, many of which are spring-flowering. The plants below will grow in a shady spot in soil that does not dry out entirely. Those that will tolerate dry soils have an asterisk*.

Actaea
Aquilegia
Aruncus
Astilbe
Astrantia
Bergenia
Brunnera
Dicentra
Epimedium
Euphorbia - some*
Geranium - some*
Helleborus
Hosta
Iris foetidissima*
Kirengeshoma
Lamium
Lamprocapnos
Linaria
Liriope
Lunaria
Melittis
Omphalodes
Persicaria
Polygonatum*
Primula
Pulmonaria
Symphytum
Tellima*
Trillium
Tricyrtis
Uvularia
Waldsteinia

Astrantia 'Roma' and Alchemilla mollis are happy in shade or partial shade

Paeonia veitchii var. woodwardii will grow at the edge of a woodland, as will Aquilegia vulgaris 'William Guiness'

Shaded by a flowering cherry tree, this border is home to Helleborus argutifoliius and Epimedium × versicolor 'Sulphureum' (back, left). Iris 'Chance Beauty' and Astrantia major 'Sunningdale Variegated' grow along the canopy edge and Geum 'Bell Bank' gets some sun

Growing perennials in some situations can be challenging. If you garden on the side of a hill or mountain, it's wise to choose plants that will tolerate wind and exposure. Coastal plants have to contend with both, as well as gales and salt spray.

HILLSIDE GARDENS

Our garden is relatively low-lying at 300 feet (100 metres) above sea level, compared to plots on the side of hills or mountains. Yet we still get a lot of rain and it can be windy. The obvious plants to grow are those that tolerate wet soil (*see* p. 11) and short plants. However, a few tall varieties with slender stems that bend with the wind cope well. These include *Sanguisorba* and *Valeriana*.

COASTAL GARDENS

Having never gardened down by the sea, I have consulted other specialists' lists of plants that will grow in a salty position. These are their suggestions:

Achillea	Kniphofia
Anemone	Lathyrus
Anthemis	Limonium
Asters - short types	Linaria
Campanula	Mertensia
Catananche	Morina
Centranthus	Oenothera
Crocosmia	Origanum
Dianthus	Penstemon
Echinops	Physostegia
Erigeron	Potentilla
Eryngium	Salvia
Euphorbia	Scabiosa
Geranium	Sedum
Hesperantha	Stachys
Heuchera	Stokesia
Iris	Veronica

GARDENS WITH POOR SOIL

Many new homes have gardens with a layer of poor-quality top soil spread over compacted ground with builders' rubble beneath. When concrete is removed from a garden, you often find an equally unpromising area containing broken bricks and stones. The soil will not only be stony but also lacking in nutrients.

These sites might initially require more input to make the ground workable than an established garden with good soil, but it is still possible to grow perennials. In the list below are suggestion for plants that don't mind poor soil.

Acanthus	Lamium
Centranthus	Salvia
Crocosmia	Sedum
Digitalis	Stachys
Echinops	Stipa
Eryngium	Trifolium
Geranium	Verbascum
Iris - bearded types	Verbena

Stachys byzantina 'Big Ears' and *Sedum telephium* 'Xenox' are wind-proof, and will grow in coastal sites as well as poor soils

One of my previous gardens had very little topsoil yet *Stipa gigantea* thrived

Centranthus is commonly found growing in walls and gardens along the coast

A skilful combination of plants can enhance the natural beauty of the landscape and make it part of the garden

Whether you are creating a new garden or wanting to change an existing border, knowing where to start can be perplexing. I always advise new home owners to hold back and live with the garden for a year to see what emerges. Only then can you decide what to do. If you are new to an area, look at other gardens in the neighbourhood, including the one next door, to see which plants are thriving and seem most suited to the location.

VISITING GARDENS

A trip to another garden, whether a show garden or a small but beautifully planted backyard, can open up creative possibilities and provide inspiration. Visiting gardens through the seasons will also give you an idea of what grows at different times of the year. Every year thousands of private gardens are open through The National Gardens Scheme, not just to inspire gardeners but also to raise funds for nursing and caring charities.

GARDEN AND BORDER STYLES

Over the years thousands of books, articles and blogs have been written about plants and garden design. Although I don't follow any particular style of gardening, choosing plants that combine to create a certain look can be helpful when starting a garden from scratch or creating a new border.

Garden styles, while slow to change, are dictated by the fashion and needs of the day. To help you choose the best and most appropriate plants, the following pages feature a variety of perennials for a range of different styles and situations..

Plastic bottles are creatively re-purposed as plant holders in Sabah, Borneo

A trip to South Africa showed me that *Kniphofia* could grow in very wet soil

The show gardens at RHS Chelsea Flower Show can provide planting inspiration

Creating a garden for children can be fun, even at an exhausting time of life

June Blake's garden in Co Wicklow in 2016 – a beautifully planted space with a wide range of perennials

Strictly speaking, this relaxed style of gardening is what most people would describe as 'cottage garden' but today, that label seems inappropriate. Few people live in cottages and even fewer grow edible plants alongside ornamental ones, which is the true definition of a cottage garden. This informal, sometimes luxuriant, style of planting suits smaller gardens, especially those in rural locations. In larger gardens this look can be achieved by dividing the garden into smaller garden 'rooms'.

The basic aim is to create a garden overflowing with colour, but one where plants are put together loosely without a rigid colour scheme or planting plan. Making an informal flower garden is a process, often with no definite picture in mind and with minimal structure. The garden simply evolves as it is created.

Planting Method

To create an informal flower border, try not to limit the number of plant varieties and aim for a range of colours, tones and shapes in flower and foliage. If, however you want to restrict the colour range, then choose different plants with flowers of similar colour so that texture is maintained in the border.

Very large or dramatic perennials can be grown as a single specimen. Plant others in groups of two or three, but don't be tempted to add more. This can lead to a regimented look and defeat the purpose of the informal, relaxed style.

Tall plants can be put next to shorter ones anywhere in the border. I often place plants with slender, tall spikes of flowers at the front of a border because you can see through them. If the taller plant forms a solid clump and flowers at the same time as those around it, then the shorter plants should sit in front.

This informal border (above) at Montpelier Cottage, Herefordshire was created by Noel Kingsbury and photographed in 2015.

THE DESIGN

- **GOOD** for small gardens in the town and country and for larger gardens divided into smaller gardens by hedging.

- **WHAT TO GROW** Any perennials can be included

- **BORDERS** can be square, circular, oblong, or irregular. These can be edged with box (*Buxus*) for a more tamed appearance. Beds can be cut into the grass, like islands, or set against the edge of the garden. Where space allows, beds of different shapes are preferable so there isn't a uniform design or grid-like structure.

- **OTHER FEATURES** Slabs and bricks can be used along the edges to prevent tumbling plants from shading out and damaging areas of green lawn.

The garden at White Hopton has been described as a 'cottage garden' in style and planting

Originating in the late 19th century, the traditional herbaceous border was designed for larger gardens whose owners could afford full-time gardeners to maintain them. It is a restrained way of creating a garden and time and consideration should be taken when selecting what to grow. The aim of the border is to create a waterfall of colour with tall plants at the back, the shortest at the front. Plant varieties are often repeated in the borders to add rhythm and continuity. They are chosen and placed according to height so that all the plants can be seen. To maintain the border's ordered appearance, avoid thugs and 'tumblers' and choose well-behaved perennials. Generally speaking, this style of border is at its best between June and September.

PLANTS TO GROW

For the back of the border

Aster novi-belgii	Rudbeckia
(Symphyotricum)	Thalictrum
Cephalaria	Verbascum
Delphinium	Veronicastrum

For the middle of the border

Aconitum	Kniphofia
Anemone - Japanese	Lupinus
Campanula lactiflora	Monarda
Echinops	Papaver orientale
Helenium	Phlox
Hemerocallis	Sidalcea

For the Front of the border

Achillea	Geranium
Alchemilla	Nepeta
Anthemis	Persicaria affinis
Aster - short varieties	Salvia
Bergenia	Sedum
Centaurea	Stachys byzantina

THE DESIGN

- **GOOD** for any size of garden
- **PLANTS TO GROW** Tall, medium-sized and short perennials with a long-flowering period
- **BORDERS** Can be any shape with straight or wavy edges. For the best effect, make sure the border has a generous width – ideally enough for three plants deep. If it is too narrow, you will not be able to include enough varieties to make an impact.
- **OTHER FEATURES** Box can be used to create a classic edging to the border. It will also hide the bare stems of some plants.

Planting Method

Starting at the back of the border, place tall plants in groups of three or five in irregular lines, positioning those with tall, slim flower spikes next to others that carry their blooms in clusters. For instance, placing *Aster* next to *Veronicastrum* will create an element of contrast. As you move forwards, place shorter perennials in front of tall ones in the same irregular lines. Position the shortest plants at the front of the border, putting plants with heads of domed flowers together, such as *Geranium*, next to *Sedum*.

Make sure each plant isn't placed too close to its neighbour to avoid an unattractive 'bunched' look. And while the plants grow and mature – which will take a season or two – you can use annuals to fill any gaps at the front of the border.

The more traditional borders in front garden at White Hopton before the lawn was removed

In this 1999 photograph of Wollerton Garden, Shropshire, the traditional long borders are festooned with cottage-style plants such as *Alcea* (Hollyhocks) and *Delphinium*

The gardens at Powis Castle, Welshpool are centuries old. The border in high summer, edged with box, reflects the traditional layout of a formal herbaceous border

Variously known as 'naturalistic' or 'prairie planting' this style of gardening first hit the headlines in the mid 1990s and took its inspiration from the flat landscapes of North America, the Netherlands and Germany. The aim is to create a natural looking garden using rhythm and texture rather than dense blocks of colour. Essentially it is landscaping with plants and suits larger gardens where drifts of plants can create impact. Late and autumn-flowering perennials predominate, interspersed with grasses that won't compete for space until the perennials have filled out. Champions of this planting style have become almost scientific in their approach, writing books and blogs that describe how the plants form communities and interact with each other.

Planting Method

Firstly, you need to select your key plants to create ribbons that weave through the border. Grasses work well, as long as you choose varieties that are strong enough to survive the dense canopy of leaves that some perennials create. Start by positioning grasses in the border, followed by small groups of perennials, ideally in threes or fives, to fill the spaces. Clump-forming perennials are ideal as are those that send the blooms skywards.

Although this style won't have as much impact in a small garden, you can still create a similar effect. Choose shorter perennials that are similar in height, and repeat them through the border .

Scampston Hall, North Yorkshire in 2013 designed by Piet Oudolf, one of the founding fathers of the naturalistic style

THE DESIGN

- **GOOD** for larger gardens with open areas

- **WHAT TO GROW** mainly well-behaved, less vigorous perennials that will seed around, combined with lots of grasses

- **BORDERS** should be large and deep enough to create drifts and swathes of colour and texture

- **OTHER FEATURES** include clipped yew or other shrubs, but generally this style of garden relies on perennial planting

PLANTS TO GROW

Agastache	Persicaria
Astilbe	Rudbeckia
Echinacea - seed	Verbena bonariensis
raised varieties (S)	(S)
Eryngium (S)	Veronicastrum
Eupatorium	
Gaura (S)	**Grasses:**
Helenium (S)	Calamagrostis
Perovskia	Miscanthus
Salvia nemorosa	Molinia (S)
'Caradonna'	Panicum (S)
Salvia verticillata	Stipa
types	
Sedum 'Matrona'	(S) indicates good for
Monarda	smaller gardens

Eryngium planum and *Monarda* combine with fountains of *Molinia* to draw the eye

Drifts of *Echinacea* and *Helenium* backed by *Miscanthus* – all on a grand scale

The majority of people in the UK live in towns and cities, where outside space is at a premium and views are often unattractive. Although urban gardens may be small, you can still create a beautiful space by scaling down some of the ideas on the previous pages and growing perennials in attractive containers. Some lovely perennials will grow in the shade of tall buildings and city gardens can also be more sheltered than those in rural locations.

Planting Method

If your house has a front garden, and you do not have to park a car or bicycle in it, this is the place to start. Curb-side appeal is an advantage for any house. In really tiny spaces, pots of different sizes filled with colourful perennials can be placed in groups either side of the front door. In larger gardens, perennials offer colour and texture, while tumbling plants will soften the edges of paths. For continuity, stick to the same planting theme at the back of the house . Behind the house a seating area, perhaps on a lawn or patio may well dominate the garden, which is likely to be edged by high fences or walls. Between the boundaries and the functional area there should be enough space to create an attractive border, although you will need to limit the number, size and variety of perennials. Urban gardens do, however, have one big advantage over rural ones. Generally, the garden will be warmer and you can grow beautiful plants that would not thrive in colder locations, such as *Francoa* and *Libertia*. Keep the design simple and choose plants for texture rather than flower. Those with handsome foliage are ideal, combined with a few glamorous plants such as *Paeonia*, which also has lovely leaves, to create highlights.

Plantswoman Helen Dillon's old Dublin garden with irises, *Origanum* and *Eryngium*

The big green leaves of shade-loving *Bergenia* contrast beautifully with the silver foliage of *Pulmonaria* 'Diana Clare' and *Pulmonaria* 'Opal'

Euphorbia myrsinites is perfect for disguising edges. Small grasses are ideal for pots

My daughter's first garden in Bristol is designed for family use and to welcome visiting friends but it still has plenty of space for perennials

Many years ago I grew plants for the Botanic Gardens of Wales. It struck me at the time that while the planting scheme included many perennials, there were very few British wild flowers or plants that were close to these wild species. Gardens today contain plants from all over the world, and most autumn-flowering perennials are native to North America but that doesn't mean we need to radically change our choice of plants and include only native species. For me, gardens should have many purposes, just as a home does. One of the most important things a gardener can do is to grow plants that will feed our wildlife, and this means choosing plants with flowers whose nectar is easy for our insects to access and gather. Generally speaking these have flower heads that are made up of many smaller flowers.

Planting Method

The wildlife garden has nature at its heart but the garden itself does not have to look wild and unkempt. However, it's vital to restrain your impulse to be too tidy because allowing perennials to self-seed is key, as is not cutting them back in autumn so enough cover is left for overwintering creatures. After a few years the garden will mature and take on a life of its own but if a plant is beginning to dominate its neighbours then it should be removed to maintain the diversity of the garden. Also, there is no reason why so-called weeds cannot be left to thrive in the border but be aware that some wild flowers are thugs. I discovered this to my cost, having left *Pilosella aurantiaca* (Fox and cubs) to self-seed, with the result that it rampaged through my borders.

PLANTS TO GROW

Plants with an asterisk are not described in the Plant Directory. Some are biennials

Aquilegia	*Persicaria*
Angelica *	*Phuopsis*
Anthriscus	*Pimpinella*
Astrantia	*Sanguisorba*
Centranthus	*Senecio*
Chaerophyllum	*Selinum*
Chamaenerion *	*Succisa*
Digitalis	*Succisella* *
Foeniculum *	*Symphytum*
Galium	*Thalictrum*
Geranium pratense	*Trifolium rubens*
Geum rivale types *	*Valeriana*
Knautia	*Verbascum*
Linaria	*Verbena*
Lythrum	*Veronicastrum*

Although *Linaria purpurea* is a native wild plant, it blends easily with other border plants, such as this pink *Achillea* 'Apfelblute'

Chamaenerion angustifolium 'Album' is a pretty form of our wild Rosebay willowherb

The Field scabious (*Knautia arvensis*) creates a wild look in the border

Dramatic *Anthriscus sylvestris* 'Ravenswing' is a selected form of Cow parsley

Sanguisorba officinalis makes a lovely contrast with white *Selinum wallichianum*

Butterflies and bees are important plant pollinators and their contribution to the garden cannot be underestimated, especially if you grow fruit or vegetables. These small creatures also bring welcome sound and movement to the border. In the UK there are over 250 different types of bees and bumblebees and around 60 different butterflies, plus many more moths, a few of them flying during the day. In my garden it is easy to spot at least seven species of butterflies at any one time, as well as a dozen different bees. Other creatures, such as birds and hedgehogs, also deter pests.

Nectar-rich flowers

To encourage insects into your garden, it is important to grow a wide variety of plants in different parts of your plot. Butterflies and bees are generally attracted to simply shaped, single flowers, like daisies, because the composition allows nectar to be accessed easily. Unlike delicate butterflies and honeybees, which don't touch down to feed for long, big-bodied bumblebees need sturdy flowers to carry their weight.

Other flying creatures

In addition to bees and butterflies, there are many other beneficial insects that you can encourage. The adults and larvae of ladybirds and lacewings eat aphids, as well as other small insects, helping to control unwanted pests. Hoverflies, easily mistaken for bees, are also great pollinators. Sometimes small black beetles, called pollen beetles, can be seen digging into yellow flowers and may help with pollination. The much-feared wasp also loves nectar, and the young of some types will feed on insects.

BIRDS AND SMALL ANIMALS

When a garden is full of flowers, insects will appear, quickly followed by birds, attracted first by the wealth of edible insect life, and later by nutritious seedheads. Frogs, toads, and even hedgehogs are also likely to skulk beneath plants, seeking out succulent slugs, snails, and other delights.

ESSENTIAL BEE- AND BUTTERFLY-ATTRACTING PERENNIALS

Aster	Nepeta
Centaurea	Origanum
Echinacea	Persicaria
Echinops	Pulmonaria
Eupatorium	Sanguisorba
Helenium	Sedum
Monarda	Succisa
Lysimachia	

A bumblebee among stems of *Sanguisorba* 'Pink Tanna'

Eupatorium purpureum covered with large whites and a red admiral butterfly

The cone-like centre of *Eryngium alpinum* consists of very small flowers

A sparrow eating Japanese anemone seedheads left over winter

A baby hedgehog beneath *Aquilegia*

Hummingbird hawkmoths love *Centranthus ruber*

Alchemilla mollis is indispensable in informal arrangements – here with *Achillea*, *Anthemis*, *Phlox* and *Echinacea*

Bearded irises look beautiful in a vase, but remove dark-coloured flowers before they die to avoid inky staining

Cut in July, *Echinops ritro*, *Knautia macedonica*, *Verbena bonariensis* and the lilac flowers of *Hosta* 'Honeybells' create a softly toned arrangement

A vase of peonies, *Achillea millefolium* 'Red Velvet', pale-pink *Astrantia* 'Buckland', blue *Centaurea*, *Veronica spicata*, and yellow-green *Alchemilla mollis*

In years gone by, when all flowers for sale at markets were grown locally, perennials were essential to the trade. Today, when flowers are imported from all over the world, perennials are less popular, but there are many varieties that make beautiful cut flowers for the house.

Cottage-style cutting gardens

The easiest way to grow perennials for cutting, especially in smaller gardens, is in a border with other plants. The flowers of some (but not all) varieties can be removed without spoiling the appearance of the whole plant. They are the sort of 'cut and come again' varieties, but the drawback of this rather uncontrolled approach is that the flower stems may not be very straight or of a uniform size. If this isn't a major concern, plants for cutting can be successfully combined with others that you leave alone.

Formal cutting borders

In larger gardens, you can dedicate an area to growing flowers for cutting, in the same way as you would create a separate plot for vegetables. It's best to arrange the plants in neat rows for easy access. Tie in the flower stems as they grow upwards, as this will keep them perfectly straight. In this more functional area of the garden, appearance is not paramount so you can denude the mother plant by removing the flower stems. I simply use a pair of kitchen scissors to cut flowers from the garden, then immediately plunge the stems into water to seal the ends and prevent the flowers from wilting. The varieties in the list below will last from four to ten days in water.

CUT FLOWERS FOR THE HOUSE

An asterisk indicates a perennial plant best grown in a formal cutting garden or patch. Planted in a border, the plant would soon be denuded of flower and this would leave an unsightly gap.

*Achillea**	*Iris**
Alchemilla	*Knautia*
Aster	*Leucanthemum**
Astrantia	*Liatris**
Centaurea	*Paeonia**
Dianthus	*Persicaria*
*Echinacea**	*Phlox**
*Echinops**	*Sanguisorba*
*Eryngium**	*Scabiosa*
Geum	*Verbena**
Helenium	

Although many gardeners opt for brightly coloured annuals for containers, almost all perennials can be grown in this way. Chosen for their foliage interest, many perennials offer a subtle mix of textures and colours that blends easily into any setting. Perennials also need less feeding and watering, and are easier to maintain than many annual container plantings. Provided you choose a big pot, and provide a little food, a plant can be left for some years. I have, for example, grown hostas and *Hakonechloa* in the same containers for more than three years. After two years it will be necessary to remove the plants and refresh the soil.

Perennials are a diverse bunch and certain plants are ideal for spots where annuals might not thrive. *Bergenia* and *Helleborus*, for example, are both happy in cool, shady areas, and their evergreen leaves create winter interest at a time when it is needed most. Hostas, too, like shade, and growing them in pots is often the best way to prevent marauding slugs from decimating the leaves. Conversely, really hot spots may not suit annuals. If the compost dries out, some annuals will die while certain perennials, such as *Dianthus*, and *Sedum*, can be revived with a good dowsing. Remember that most perennials are big plants so give each its own container. I do, however, tuck *Viola* and *Erigeron karvinskianus*, around the base of broader plants for extra colour.

PLANTS TO GROW

Ajuga	*Heuchera*
Anemanthele	*Hosta*
Aruncus - short types	*Knautia macedonia*
Aster- short types	'Mars Midget'
Bergenia	*Limonium*
Dianthus	*Ophiopogon*
Echinacea	*Origanum*
Erigeron	*Penstemon*
Eryngium planum	*Salvia*
Euphorbia - short	*Saxifraga*
types	*Scabiosa*
Geranium 'Rozanne'	*Sedum* - short types
Geranium	*Stachys byzantina*
sanguineum types	*Trifolium*
Geum	*Verbena*
Hemerocallis	*Veronica*

The low-growing grass *Hakonechloa macra* 'Aureola' looks good until autumn, while black-leaved *Ophiopogon planiscapus* 'Nigrescens' is evergreen

Hostas with leaves of different colours thrive in a shady spot, out of the reach of slugs

Erigeron karvinskianus tumbles over the rim of a pot alongside *Heuchera* 'Palace Purple'

A colourful arrangement of pots at Great Dixter in Kent consisting of annuals, perennials and succulents

I build up my beds and borders in layers, creating the picture as I go, working from front to back. What I am aiming for is a kind of rhythm, which will be created by plants that differ in height, colour, and flowering time. However, knowing where to start can be difficult – like being faced with a blank piece of paper at an exam.

If I am undertaking a big project, such as a whole new border, I plan the scheme out on a piece of paper, drawing a circle for each plant variety. This stops me from repeating plants and making the border too regimented. I tend to group each variety together, and then 'drift' the groups across the soil, making irregular, overlapping shapes and avoiding straight lines. Depending on the style of garden you are aiming for - or even if you don't have a style in mind - designers advise us to plant in groups of three, but as long as you grow sufficient key varieties in large numbers, less-critical varieties can be added in ones or twos. These will balance the border by filling the space between the larger groups and stop it from looking 'blocky.'

KEY PLANTS

The mainstays of the scheme are the plants that flower the longest and provide the most structure. These are your key plants: they tie the border together and allow the eye to drift around the garden so that every inch can be appreciated. To provide the garden with maximum colour, select key plants for each different season.

SHAPES

For me the shape of a perennial and how it grows is more important than flower colour. Perennials come in many different forms and to make choosing easier, they can be divided into different groups; edging, mounding, upright, tall and focal.

COLOUR

Whether from flowers or leaves, colour brings glamour into the garden and is often the first element we notice. I have included suggestions for combining colours, but the plants you choose will inevitably reflect your own personal preferences.

SEASONS

For colour in your garden throughout the year, plan ahead to ensure summer-flowering perennials take over from your key spring plants. You can then keep the show going with others that bloom in autumn.

PATIENCE

However carefully you prepare, things may not go strictly according to plan. In the process of choosing plants, some may not be available, while others not on the list catch your eye. Its inevitable that plants will occasionally die. These can be replaced or, if you let things unfold naturally, more vigorous plants will fill the gaps, as will perennials that have seeded around. This is the beauty of gardening – like nature, it needs to evolve organically. Above all a gardener must learn to be patient because the garden will take a number of years to reach its full potential.

White Hopton Garden May 2012. By 2015 many plants had established well

By early May the garden is just coming alive. One of the first plants to flower is white *Lunaria rediviva*

By early June *Papaver orientale* 'Türkenlouis', peonies and *Geum* are in full flower

Sanguisorba 'Pink Tanna' is quite tall, yet creates a lovely 'see-through' effect

When choosing what to grow along the front of the border, consider what is at its edge. Many of my borders are edged by grass paths and because plants spread, and I don't get round to cutting them back, the grass can die off. Fortunately, it regrows.

The most useful plants for the front, even if you do have grass alongside, are those that spread. They soften harsh lines created by paving slabs, bricks, and timber, and they can be tucked in neatly in front of taller plants, leaving no bare earth. But spreading plants with spreading roots may turn into thugs that rapidly invade their surroundings. The solution, strange though it may seem, is to grow two thugs together. *Stachys byzantina* will romp away, but a good companion like *Persicaria affinis* will keep it in check. There are also neater plants for the front of a border such as *Bergenia* and *Geum*. Slow-growing, they are easily controlled if they get too big.

I don't always use short plants for the front of a border, despite convention. Taller plants, provided they have slender flower stems, can also be grown at the front. They create a transparent 'screen' that allows you to look through to plants growing behind.

EDGING PLANTS

Plants marked with an asterisk can be thugs

*Ajuga**	*Geum*
Alchemilla mollis	*Lamium*
Bergenia	*Origanum*
Campanula - some	*Persicaria affinis**
Epimedium	*Potentilla*
Geranium 'Mavis	*Prunella*
Simpson'	*Sanguisorba*
Geranium 'Rozanne'	*officinalis* 'Red
Geranium ×	Thunder'
riversleaianum	*Saxifraga* × *urbium*
'Russell Prichard'	*Stachys byzantina**
Geranium	*Veronica*
sanguineum types	*Waldsteinia*

Euphorbia seguieriana subsp. *niciciana* is perfect for softening edges

Colour is provided for many months by low, spreading *Geranium wallichianum* 'Rosetta' and *Stachys byzantina*

Plants with evergreen foliage, such as *Ajuga reptans* 'Catlin's Giant' and *Bergenia* , offer interest all year

Stachys byzantina is a classic edging plant that combines well with many low-growing perennials

May is when perennials start to produce mounds of colour. The frothy flowers of *Brunnera macrophylla* 'Hadspen Cream' contrast perfectly with *Centaurea montana* 'Purpurea'

Late evening light in May picks out soft hummocks of perennials

A mound of *Aster pyrenaeus* 'Lutetia' and the gently domed flowers of *Sedum* 'Matrona' draw the eye and both are enhanced by the glowing autumn foliage of *Gillenia trifoliata*

Good for padding, plants that form domed mounds often have small flowers which, from a distance, look like a mass of dots scattered over the leaves. Some carry the flowers in sprays on long stems and create a shape that can be wider than it is high. The leaves are also useful for covering the soil and helping to prevent weeds from emerging. Place them together and mounding plants will compete for room, but unless one is much smaller than the other, each will find its own space.

There are many examples of mounding plants – far too many to list. Those I consider indispensable and have included in all my gardens are:

Alchemilla	*Geum*
Aster	*Nepeta*
Centaurea	*Salvia*
Geranium	*Sedum*

A low mound of *Geranium* 'Dragon Heart' sits in contrast to a river of lemon-coloured perennials

The frothy grass *Anemanthele lessoniana* softens upright *Stachys officinalis* 'Hummelo' and *Hemerocallis* 'Beloved Returns'

Many upright perennials are in full flower by late July including *Echinacea*, *Monarda*, *Helenium*, *Sedum* and *Eupatorium*

While mounding plants fill space from the ground upwards, upright plants create structure. The straight stems are often rigid, and topped with flowers that are held high enough to be seen over other plants. The flowers of tall plants are, I hesitate to say, perhaps more important than the leaves, although the early leaves will add to spring's varied green tapestry. If the plant is set further back in a border, its leaves are often hidden by the time the flowers arrive.

It is important to consider how the flowers are carried on upright plants as this affects the amount of colour on display. Perennials with long spikes of flowers (*Nepeta*) and clusters (*Helenium*) are great for solid colour. If the flower stems carry fewer flowers, the effect is wispy. Perennials with big flowers carried at well-spaced intervals, on the other hand, add accents of colour. A lot of foliage will be visible with these plants so try to arrange them in the border by leaf shape rather than flower colour.

All these plants have upright, straight stems; some are leafy. Some creep, others don't.

Achillea	Geum - some
Aconitum	Helenium
Agastache	Lamprocapnos
Anemone	Lunaria
Aster	Lychnis
Astrantia	Lysimachia
Campanula	Lythrum
Centranthus	Monarda
Echinacea	Phlox
Echinops	Physostegia
Eupatorium	Sidalcea
Euphorbia - some	Stachys - some
Gillenia	Thalictrum

Purple-blue spikes of *Aconitum* 'Spark's Variety' rise up above the loose, lime-yellow heads of *Euphorbia schillingii*

The back of the border is usually reserved for tall, dominant plants. However, some of my borders are surrounded by paths, so I grow tall varieties in the middle where they can be seen from all sides.

Generally late to bloom, the tallest perennials will not reach full height until they are about to flower. To avoid the space looking flat and uninteresting, include earlier-flowering plants or choose tall plants that have particularly lovely leaves. Some are very graceful, carrying their blooms in slender spikes on slim flower stems. These create a 'see-through' effect. Others, such as *Eupatorium*, have dome-shaped flowers and leafy stems, which encourage the eye to drift upwards. Delphiniums and *Verbascum*, on the other hand, carry the flowers down the stems, arresting the gaze and acting rather like a punctuation mark.

TALL PLANTS

Plants with an asterisk are 'see-through'

Actaea	Eupatorium
Aconitum	Helianthus
Aster	Inula magnifica
Calamagrostis	Miscanthus
Campanula	Sanguisorba
Cephalaria	Thalictrum
Cirsium	Valeriana*
Delphinium	Verbascum*
Echinops	Verbena*
Euphorbia - some	Veronicastrum*

Like many short-lived perennials *Verbascum olympicum* will seed about

THE CHELSEA CHOP

If a tall, late-flowering perennial is too high or looking leggy, it can be cut back in spring. Known as the 'Chelsea chop', this method doesn't work for all plants but I have successfully reduced *Aster glehnii* (not listed in the Directory) and *Campanula lactiflora* by half because they screened out other plants. Always cut stems down to a node – the point where leaves emerge. *Sedum* can be cut back by half to stop them flopping owing to the weight of the flowers, although I prefer to grow a variety that does not topple over.

A medley of tall perennials including *Echinops ritro* and *Veronicastrum*

Elegant *Veronicastrum virginicum* 'Fascination' behind *Helenium* in late July

The fluffy arching flower heads of *Sanguisorba hakusanensis* soften the upright spikes of *Persicaria amplexicaulis* 'September Spires' in late August

Plants used as focal points don't have to be big, they just have to stand out from the crowd. A dark background can be used to highlight a particular plant or you can give it a prominent position, such as the corner of a border (*see* right).

It is, however, height or colour that tends to draw the eye. In early summer, colourful irises and peonies – both plants with big flowers – make good focal points. By midsummer, elegant *Thalictrum* towers above its neighbours, while in autumn massive *Eupatorium* takes centre stage, as do tall grasses.

Whatever you grow, only grow one of a kind. I have two varieties of *Thalictrum* that swamp each other, making it difficult to focus on either of these glorious plants. Irises can clash if you aren't careful with colour, so the effect is lost. Be restrained; less is often more.

These are just some of the plants I have used as focal points:

Aconitum	*Persicaria*
Aruncus	*Phlox*
Crambe	*Stemmacantha*
Eupatorium	*Stipa gigantea*
Iris	*Thalictrum*
Paeonia	

Hosta 'Sum And Substance' makes a statement on the corner of a shady border

Sedum 'Mr Goodbud' defines the edge of this border and adds structure

The delicate flowers of graceful *Iris* 'Salamander Crossing' seem to float

Stipa gigantea is a big, but striking plant for a large border

Stemmacantha centaureoides is a handsome and unusual plant for a special place

Thrown into relief by the pale colours and soft-green and grey foliage of surrounding plants, the bold, red flowers of *Paeonia* 'Suruga' make a stunning focal point

The flowers of perennials come in many shapes and sizes, reflecting the different ways the plants create seed to reproduce. Before this process happens, the flowers have to encourage a wide range of pollinating insects to transfer pollen onto the reproductive organs of the flower. Their reward is nutritious, sugar-rich nectar.

The flower shape can affect which insects visit: upward-facing daisies and saucer-shaped flowers, for example, provide a stable platform for butterflies (which cannot enter bell-shaped flowers) as well as smaller bees.

Bigger, sturdier flowers, such as peonies, support the weight of large bumblebees.

The number of flowers a plant produces each year can also affect how long it lives. *Catananche* and *Centranthus* both produce lots of flowers, but neither is long lived. However, they do provide masses of seeds as an insurance policy. Plants with big flowers that produce only a few seeds, such as peonies and irises, live for a long time. Given their natural habitat is harsh, the plants have responded by reserving energy for survival, and not putting it into seed production.

The big, single flowers of *Paeonia* 'Sea Shells' open to reveal lots of yellow stamens

The stiff, spiky ruff (bracts) of *Eryngium alpinum* protects the flower

Irises have sword-like leaves and those of *Iris foetidissima* 'Variegata' are striped white

Delicate and deeply divided, the leaves of *Selinum wallichianum* look like lace

Lupinus foliage is palmate – a large leaf made up of five or more smaller leaves

BOTANICAL TERMS USED

- **BRACTS** are found right at the base of the flower and can look rather like leaves
- **CALYX** is the collective name for the sepals, which wrap around the flower when it is in bud. They are usually green and when the flower is open, they sit at the base
- **STAMENS** are found in the centre of the flower and carry the all-important pollen needed for reproduction

FLOWER SHAPES AND FORMS

Petals come in various arrangements and numbers. These are the forms referred to in this book:

- **Single** flowers have one row of petals
- **Semi-double** flowers have two, perhaps three, rows of petals
- **Double** flowers have lots of petals
- **Bell-shaped** flowers are long or cupped, and can hang down or face upwards
- **Trumpet-shaped** flowers are long and thin, the petals splaying outwards at the end
- **Tubular** flowers are long and thin. They are often carried thickly up flower stems to form a 'poker'
- **Clusters** and **sprays** sit towards the end of the flower stems
- **Heads** and **umbels** are carried at the top of the stem, where several flowers with short stalks grow outwards from a single point
- **Spikes** and **spires** are formed by a series of stalkless flowers carried up a single stem

LEAVES: COLOUR, SHAPE, TEXTURE

With perennials, the shape of leaves, like that of the flowers, also varies greatly. They can be upright, long, and thin; oval or pointed; big or small. Some have serrated edges, others are crinkled or pleated. Smaller leaves are often carried along leaf stems to form a larger leaf, known as pinnate (like a feather), while bigger leaves are usually carried individually.

The leaves of most perennials are green, but the shade can vary from soft to dark. Some are grey, green-blue or yellow, while others look red, purple, or brown; and a few plants have almost black leaves. Variegated leaves come in more than one colour, the green broken with white or cream. The surface of a leaf often tells us where the plant grows naturally. Those with soft, furry, or velvety leaves may come from very dry locations. Really shiny leaves are often more or less evergreen, and are adapted to low light in shady positions.

Size and shape are important considerations when choosing plants, but for most people the colour, shape and size of the flower is the deciding factor. To create an interesting border, it's vital to put flowers of varying shapes and forms together.

DAISIES AND STARS

The most abundant flower form is the daisy or star shape. Smaller flowers, such as those of *Calamintha* are often produced in large numbers, creating fluffy sprays. Bigger daisy flowers, like *Echinacea*, have larger petals and are especially colourful. The flowers of some plants consist of many small daisies that open into tightly knitted, flat heads, like *Achillea*. Taking the eye across, rather than up, they mix well with other shapes.

BELLS AND TRUMPETS

Perennials with bell-shaped flowers, like *Campanula*, are often demure, whatever their size. These don't shout colour from the rooftops, but sit very comfortably among their more brightly coloured neighbours.

SPIKES

Plants that carry the flowers the length of the flower stems, such as *Verbascum* and *Persicaria*, create a vertical exclamation mark, which complements and contrasts with all other flower shapes. The poker-shaped flowers of *Kniphofia* and *Sanguisorba* have the same effect, but the colour is limited to the top of the flower stem.

SAUCERS

Many perennials have flat, saucer-shaped flowers. Often small, some, like *Phlox*, open into tight, colourful heads, while in others, such as *Geranium,* the flowers are more randomly scattered, producing a less colourful, but more textural plant.

BIG FLOWERS

The largest flowers, with the biggest petals, are usually the most colourful. Peonies and irises have generous-sized flowers that come in an amazing range of vibrant as well as gentle tones. While these may be dramatic, blending them with other plants isn't easy because their flowers can easily overpower more delicate ones. The best option is to grow these not in clumps, but as individuals, choosing varieties that will flower before neighbouring border plants begin to bloom.

The upright spikes of *Salvia* × *sylvestris* 'Schneehugel' contrast with the flat heads of *Achillea millefolium* 'Peachy Seduction'

In spring, the blue stars of *Brunnera macrophylla* 'Jack Frost' and the trumpets of *Pulmonaria mollis* are carried in sprays

The slim spikes of *Persicaria amplexicaulis* 'Taurus' won't obscure the domed heads of *Phlox* × *arendsii* 'Luc's Lilac'

Pin-cushion blooms combine with pale-yellow trumpets in this pretty pairing of *Astrantia major* and *Digitalis lutea*

Opening flat, like small saucers, the blooms of *Geranium* 'Blue Cloud' contrast with the poker-like heads of *Sanguisorba* 'Pink Tanna'

Cornflower-like flowers of *Centaurea* 'John Coutts' complement the upright spikes of blue *Campanula persicifolia*

Given the abundant variety of flower, leaf and plant shapes, there are endless ways of combining perennials. One of my basic rules when planting is to place plants with different habits next to each other. Low-growing perennials, which often – but not always – spread, are perfect towards the front. Plants that mound sit well in the middle of the scheme, together with those that carry the flowers on upright stems. Using this approach, the border will knit together, especially as the season advances and perennials grow to reach the optimum height for blooming. Generally speaking, early-flowering perennials will create neat mounds; later, upright and tall plants will dominate. Rarely do I select plants of similar heights as this leads to a rigid, uninteresting border that lacks contrast.

Ball-shaped heads, jagged silver leaves and soft flower spikes combine perfectly in this planting of *Echinops*, *Cynara cardunculus* and *Nepeta* 'Six Hills Giant'

Upright *Lychnis coronaria* with *Campanula lactiflora* 'Loddon Anna'

Fluffy pokers of *Agastache* 'Blue Boa' sit below *Campanula lactiflora* 'Loddon Anna'

Phlox paniculata 'Sweet Summer Dream' with *Campanula lactiflora* 'Loddon Anna'

Lovely contrasting shapes of *Stachys byzantina* 'Big Ears', *Sisyrinchium striatum* and *Geranium* 'Rozanne'

A low carpet of spring-flowering perennials with varied flower forms: *Geranium*, *Sanguisorba menziesii*, *Geum* 'Prinses Juliana', *Achillea* 'Moonshine' and *Centranthus ruber* 'Albus'

This combination of *Salvia nemorosa* 'Ostfriesland', *Sanguisorba tenuifolia* 'Alba' and *Stipa gigantea* balances different heights, textures and colours

Low spreading *Stachys* in front of *Geum* 'Borisii' and *Paeonia* 'Picotee'

Big, blousy flowers of *Paeonia* 'Lilac Time' rise up and draw the eye, adding interest to this early-summer border before other perennials start to bloom

Upright spikes of *Persicaria amplexicaulis* 'White Eastfield' contrast with the daisy flowers of *Anthemis tinctoria* 'E. C. Buxton'

The airy plumes of *Miscanthus* blend well with the flat flower heads of elegant *Verbena bonariensis*

Two woodlanders, *Epimedium* 'Amber Queen' and *Lamprocapnos spectabilis* 'Alba', with delicate yet very different blooms

Colour for me is one of the most important attributes of a flower but I'm not precious about how colours are combined in a border. Most sit happily together, with one exception: I find really vivid pink – the shade of fuchsia- or lipstick-pink – next to bright orange a little uncomfortable, but they should not be dismissed. However, if the orange plant is placed at a distance from the pink one, the two colours don't fight.

Combining colours is a matter of individual taste, so I don't want to be prescriptive. However, when spending money on plants, some gardeners want to be confident that their choices aren't going to clash horribly. If you are unsure, choose plants by colour and tone: rich, strong colours work well together, or opt for soft shades. Selecting just one colour is another option – white being the most common choice.

The lemon flower spikes of *Stachys recta* shine out against a handsome clump of dark-leaved *Sedum*

COLOUR FOR PLANTAHOLICS

I have no discipline when it comes to plants and being a plant collector can be a curse when designing a garden. I can't restrict the variety of plants I grow, and often find it difficult to plant them in garden designer-type drifts of threes or fives. I plant perennials in ones or twos otherwise I would need acres, which would be unmanageable. My solution, which also avoids too many colour clashes, is twofold. Firstly, I graduate colours, so blocks of pastel colours merge gradually with flowers of darker tones. Secondly, I grow different plants with similar-coloured flowers near to each other, such as *Nepeta* 'Six Hills Giant' with *Geranium* 'Orion'. This means I don't have to restrict the number of plants I grow.

Purple-pink spikes of *Salvia nemorosa* 'Amethyst' blend with magenta *Geranium* 'Dragon Heart' and cerise *Lychnis*

In this June border *Geranium* 'Brookside' echoes the blue of the *Nepeta* while white *Gillenia trifoliata* lightens the scheme

By mid August, the blue upright spikes of *Nepeta* 'Six Hills Giant' and *Agastache* 'Blue Fortune' balance and complement the shapes and colours of *Monarda* 'Croftway Pink' and *Helenium* 'Sahin's Early Flowerer'

SOFT COLOURS

The easiest perennials to combine in terms of colour are those with soft pastel flowers. And there are many. Shades of pearly pink, powder-blue, and pure white abound in a variety of flower shapes and forms. You'll never be stuck for a tall, pale-pink, spiky plant, or a low, spreading one. Softly coloured plants are easy on the eye, but they can lack sparkle. Add rich blue, perhaps a hardy geranium or *Salvia*, and the whole scheme will be lifted. To bring the best out of these colours, go further and add soft-yellow flowers, for example *Coreopsis verticillata* 'Moonbeam'. Always remember leaf colour that when creating a softly coloured border. Perennials with silver leaves can add colour all year.

Rhythm is generated by repeating *Stachys byzantina* through this dry border, while *Campanula glomerata* 'Caroline' and *Prunella* add colour and contrasting shapes

A subtle combination of *Astrantia major* and *Veronicastrum virginicum* 'Pink Glow'

The soft-blue flowers of *Geranium* 'Blue Cloud' weave through *Astrantia maxima* and *Senecio polyodon*

Paeonia 'Picotee' takes centre stage in this May border, with lacy *Chaerophyllum hirsutum* 'Roseum' picking up the soft-pink and *Achillea* 'Moonshine' adding grey tones

HOT COLOURS

Perennials with brightly coloured flowers are relatively few in number. Vivid red, rich orange, or sunshine-yellow are not as common in perennials' wild ancestors (from which garden varieties are bred) as softer shades. Late-summer and early autumn borders with really hot, intense colour are difficult to achieve without incorporating tender cannas and dahlias, but perennials such as *Helenium*, *Crocosmia*, *Oenothera* and *Hemerocallis*, offer rich tones and will add a dash of boldness. But be restrained – too many big flowers in strong shades can be jarring. Those with smaller, yet vibrant flowers are useful for blending in smaller groups. I love orange *Geum* with dark purple *Salvia*, and the starry heads of rich-lilac *Aster* with yellow *Rudbeckia*.

The rich colour of *Centranthus ruber* is toned down by the blue flowers of *Geranium* 'Brookside'

Yellow-flowered *Oenothera* 'Summer Sun' has red buds – a colour that matches the flowers of *Potentilla* 'Arc-en-Ciel'

This self-seeded *Lychnis coronaria* happened to emerge near orange-flowered *Helenium* 'Sahin's Early Flowerer'

In late spring, orange *Geum* 'Prinses Juliana' and *Euphorbia griffithii* 'Fireglow' make an exciting combination with *Paeonia* 'Morning Lilac' adding cerise-infused highlights

Red flowers can be difficult to place. Here bold *Crocosmia* 'Lucifer' is complemented by thread-like *Persicaria amplexicaulis* 'Alba'

Lysimachia punctata 'Alexander' echoes the yellow markings and brings out the rich, deep red of *Hemerocallis* 'Ed Murray'

The cascading purple bells of *Campanula* 'Sarastro' add drama to the flat scarlet heads of *Achillea* 'Paprika'

LIMITING COLOURS

At the beginning of the last century, Vita Sackville-West successfully created a white garden at Sissinghurst Castle in Kent. It is described as white, but it is really a white and green garden. Unless planted in large numbers, I rarely include white-flowered perennials in a border as they can be dominant, although the colour is good in a dark spot. Using only one colour, perhaps blue or pink, would not only limit the choice of plants, it could also look and feel bland. One option is to go for two different flower colours: pink and blue; white and yellow; or red and purple. These combinations, though rather restricting in terms of plant varieties, can be quite stunning.

A cool, white combination of *Gillenia trifoliata* and *Astrantia major*

Sidalcea 'Elsie Heugh' and *Persicaria amplexicaulis* 'Jo and Guido's Form' have pink flowers of differing tones and shapes

Gold-toned *Anemanthele lessoniana* complements the different flower shapes in this blue-themed border

Kniphofia 'Green Jade' enhances the blue of *Strobilanthes wallichii* and (far left) the lime-green blooms of *Euphorbia schillingii*

Yellow and purple flowers ,such as *Rudbeckia trifoliata* and *Aster novae-angliae* 'Mrs S. T. Wright', look stunning together

The paler pinks and whites of taller perennials create a beautiful backdrop for the rich-blue, wheel-like flowers of *Centaurea montana* in the foreground

Whether you are creating a border or just grouping a few new plants together, the foliage will be on show well before and after the flowers. Put plants with the same colour and similar shapes of leaf next to one another and the picture will have no definition, and may even be dull. But combine different leaf colours, shapes, and textures, and you will create a fabulous patchwork with shades of green, brown, silver, and yellow throughout the year.

COLOURED LEAVES

The main colour of leaves is, naturally, green, but look more closely and you will notice different tones varying from light to dark, as well as effects created by the leaf texture. Glossy leaves reflect light and define the three-dimensional quality of the plant, while hairs on leaves flatten the surface colour. Those leaves that invite you to touch them are often silver, for example furry *Stachys byzantina*. Silver foliage will also brighten up a dark spot, as does yellow, although it's best to avoid certain yellow-leaved plants, such as blue-flowered *Centaurea montana* 'Gold Bullion'. Its flowers and leaves clash badly and can look garish.

Very dark and-near black leaves are some of the most handsome. They are invaluable for adding contrast to a border, and they give definition to plants as well as flowers.

The rounded buds and striking red stems of *Paeonia* 'Lemon Chiffon' are emphasised by the contrasting grey leaves of *Achillea* 'Moonshine' and *Stachys byzantina*

The leaves of Hostas come in many shades

Aruncus dioicus foliage and red-tinged *Euphorbia amygdaloides* 'Purpurea'

Kniphofia and Siberian irises both have long, strappy leaves

Furry *Stachys*, divided *Sanguisorba* and fleshy *Sedum* leaves combine

The gold leaves of *Paeonia* 'Golden Frolic' turn yellow-green as they age

Geranium pratense 'Marshmallow' has eye-catching, reddish-brown leaves

VARIEGATED LEAVES

The presence of two colours on the leaves is invariably the result of a lack of chlorophyll. This weakens the surface of the leaf, so variegated plants may need to be grown in partial shade to prevent sun damage. The splashes and patches of white or pale cream are not to everyone's taste, but I use plants with variegated foliage to add extra colour and to knit certain colours together, such as green and purple.

The leaves of *Astrantia major* 'Sunningdale Variegated' turn plain green in summer

Iris × robusta 'Gerald Darby' and variegated *Brunnera macrophylla* 'Hadspen Cream'

LEAVES THAT CHANGE COLOUR

Unless they are evergreen, leaves don't stay the same all year: autumn hits most of them eventually. Some morph early in the season, such as the variegated leaves of *Astrantia major* 'Sunningdale Variegated', which turn plain green as the flowers open.

While autumn is the classic time for fiery colour in shrubs and trees, most perennials quickly disintegrate into a mass of brown leaves and stems when the temperature drops below 10°C. Some, like *Gillenia trifoliata*, remain handsome for a few weeks, but if you want year-round foliage colour, try bergenias. From autumn to spring, the leaves are burnished with red and purple.

Light green *Euphorbia palustris* foliage turns bright red for a short time in autumn

Autumn foliage and seed pods of *Amsonia tabernaemontana*

SCENTED LEAVES

Leaves of perennials can be scented, but it is often only apparent when the leaf is rubbed or crushed between the fingers or when brushed against. Roots can also be fragrant (peony roots have a very strong aroma, as do some irises) but you only discover this when dividing a plant. The following have scented foliage:

Agastache	*Nepeta*
Calamintha	*Origanum*
Geranium	*Salvia*
macrorrhizum	*Valeriana*
Monarda	

Origanum 'Rosenkuppel' has scented leaves and butterflies love the flowers

PERENNIALS WITH HANDSOME LEAVES

The perennials listed below are just some of the varieties with distinctive foliage.

Actaea D	*Heuchera* D
Ajuga E	*Hosta* V, Y
Anaphalis S	*Iris* - some D V
Astrantia - some E	*Lysimachia* D
Bergenia E	*Milium* Y
Brunnera types S, V	*Miscanthus* V
Calamagrostis V	*Ophiopogon* D
Campanula E	*Paeonia*
Dianthus S	*Pulmonaria* S
Epimedium E	*Sedum* D, Y
Eryngium V	*Stachys* S
Euphorbia E	*Thalictrum* Y
Geranium - some D E	*Valeriana* Y
Hakonechloa V	*Waldsteinia* D

Key D dark leaves, E evergreen, S silver, V variegated, Y yellow

Flowering is just one stage in the growing process of a plant. We grow perennials for their beautiful flowers, but they can also look fabulous from the first moment their young foliage pokes out of the ground to their final flourish in autumn. It pays to consider all stages in the plant's growth cycle when deciding which perennials to plant.

LEAF SHOOTS

The early shoots of some perennials are beautifully shaped, while others send up red-tinged new foliage. Both add to the delight of spring growth. Try these:

Dicentra
Euphorbia
Gillenia
Hosta
Lathyrus
Paeonia
Rhodiola
Sedum
Veronicastrum

Early shoots of *Veronicastrum*

The big, bright buds of *Paeonia* 'Paula Fay'

FLOWER BUDS

Buds, like flowers, can be distinctive and sculptural. The plants listed below have eye-catching buds, and those marked with an asterisk also have lovely stems.

Eryngium
Iris*
Kniphofia
Lysimachia
 clethroides*
Meconopsis
Oenothera*
Papaver
Paeonia*
Sanguisorba

Emerging red shoots of *Paeonia wittmaniana*

The flowers of *Oenothera* 'Summer Sun' open from red buds

FRAGRANT FLOWERS

Scent is an important attribute and one that many gardeners look for in a plant. Most perennial flowers have none or very little, but there are some exceptions. Certain varieties of *Phlox*, *Paeonia*, and *Dianthus*, for example, do emit a delicious scent. Even then, the fragrance is sometimes obvious only when the weather is warm or the flowers are cut and brought into a warm room. Check the plant descriptions for fragrance and also consider the following groups, which have scented varieties:

Actaea
Dianthus
Echinacea
Hemerocallis (yellow
varieties)
Iris
Paeonia
Phlox
Primula
Valeriana
Verbena

Fragrant *Valeriana officinalis* seeds freely about as does *Linaria purpurea*

Phlox paniculata 'Amethyst' is both a focal point and scented

SEEDHEADS

Once the flowers have gone to seed, the heads of many perennials create great structure and provide wildlife with winter food. These plants have lasting seedheads:

Achillea	*Iris*
Anemone	*Lunaria*
Astrantia	*Meconopsis*
Dictamnus	*Papaver*
Echinops	*Sedum*
Eryngium	*Selinum*

The seedheads of *Crocosmia* 'Emberglow' make a striking addition to indoor arrangements

Astrantia 'Buckland' seedheads look decorative against *Anemanthele lessoniana*

Lunaria rediviva has distinctive seed pods that turn transparent as they age

The bracts around the seedheads of *Eryngium alpinum* turn dry and papery

Dramatic, dark seed pods of *Paeonia* 'Garden Peace'

Leave *Phlomis russelliana* seedheads to catch falling snow

Before making the final selection of your perennials, it's important to consider when a plant will be in flower. A garden that flowers just for a month or two is a missed opportunity, but an easy trap to fall into. We are inclined to buy plants because we want colour when the garden is most used. Yet it is possible to have perennials in flower each month of the year. This might take a little planning, and you may need slightly more space, but it is not difficult to achieve. Sometimes it is easier to divide parts of the garden, or a big border, into the two main seasons: spring and summer. Planting small groups of perennials that flower at the same time of year together, rather than spreading them thinly, gives a sense of cohesion.

SPANNING THE SEASONS

One part of my garden is designed to be in full flower during July and August, a time when the majority of perennials bloom. It is also when the sun is at its highest, and the days are at their longest and warmest. This part of the garden is where we sit in the evenings, sipping a glass of wine, watching the sun go down. However, even when these borders are not in full bloom, they look interesting. In spring they are a tapestry of green, with leaves of all shapes, sizes, and colours merging, quickly covering the ground to prevent weeds. The first perennials start to bloom in May. These are mainly *Geum* and *Centaurea*. In June the bold flowers of irises and peonies catch the eye, and by high summer *Phlox*, *Achillea*, *Veronicastrum*, *Nepeta*, and *Persicaria* create a riot of colour. Some plants fade as the days shorten, but asters and anemones continue, sometimes as late as November and hellebore flowers add winter interest.

PLANTING FOR CONTINUOUS BLOOM

The same border, shot over three seasons. In May *Euphorbia palustris* and *Geum* create drifts of colour with peonies adding bolder accents. From June until September hardy geraniums, *Lychnis*, *Astrantia* and *Campanula* take centre stage with the foliage of *Sedum* 'Matrona' (front) adding texture. By August the *Sedum* has become a focal point while spires of *Veronicastrum* and blue *Echinops* add height. During October the *Sedum* heads have turned rusty brown and the gold stems of the moor grass, *Molinia*, catch the sun. The leaves of *Euphorbia palustris* are now red and asters add bright colour to the whole picture.

May

July

August

October

Spring is a joyous time. Perennials emerge from March onwards, but only a few are in flower before May. Most spring-flowering plants are woodlanders, which bloom before trees and shrubs have created a leafy canopy and taller perennials reach their full height. These plants are perfect for growing in shadier parts of the garden and next to later-blooming perennials because they don't mind being overshadowed. Later, the leaves of summer-flowering plants will add texture to a border. Spring perennials and their flowering times are given below:

FEBRUARY

Helleborus	Pulmonaria

MARCH

Bergenia	Lathyrus
Epimedium	Pulmonaria

APRIL

Brunnera	Lamprocapnos
Epimedium	Lunaria
Euphorbia	Primula

MAY

Aquilegia	Lamium
Astrantia - some	Lupinus
Centaurea	Papaver
Chaerophyllum	Paeonia
Dianthus	Polemonium
Digitalis	Polygonatum
Euphorbia	Symphytum
Geranium - some	Tellima
Geum	Thalictrum
Iris	Veronica

March: elegant *Helleborus* flowers, ranging from pure white to dark-speckled yellow

Lamprocapnos spectabilis and *Brunnera* bloom freely under a flowering cherry tree

April: Pink *Bergenia* 'Bressingham Bountiful' and frothy brown clumps of *Euphorbia dulcis* 'Chameleon' add colour to this predominantly green picture

Short perennials, such as these early hardy geraniums, provide soft colour in springtime

May: The bold colours of orange *Geum* 'Prinses Juliana' and *Paeonia* 'Honor' shine out against the grey leaves of *Stachys byzantina* and lime-green *Euphorbia*

With the arrival of warm, long days, summer is the time to enjoy the garden. Perennials are looking their best – July being the most generous month for flowers. There are so many summer-blooming perennials it is difficult to put a foot wrong when choosing plants for a garden filled with colour.

By midsummer tall, free-flowering perennials in a range of fabulous colours hold sway. Although spring-blooming plants have now retreated into the background, the foliage of some, such as *Pulmonaria*, remains attractive and will add structure and contrast to the border.

SUMMER-FLOWERING PERENNIALS

The following plants are the stars of the summer border and most of those listed will bloom for many months. Time and flowering period are given in the individual plant descriptions in the A–Z Plant Directory.

JUNE

Achillea	Knautia
Agastache	Lychnis
Alchemilla	Paeonia
Amsonia	Phlomis
Aruncus	Polemonium - some
Astrantia	Potentilla
Baptisia	Prunella
Campanula	Salvia
Catananche	Scabious
Centranthus	Senecio
Cirsium	Sisyrinchium
Delphinium	Stachys
Erigeron	Verbascum
Geranium - some	Verbena
Iris	

JULY

Acanthus	Ligularia
Anaphalis	Limonium
Anthemis	Lysimachia
Astilbe	Lythrum
Cephalaria	Monarda
Chelone	Morina
Crambe	Nepeta - some
Crocosmia - some	Oenothera
Echinacea	Origanum
Echinops	Persicaria
Eryngium	Phlox
Filipendula	Physostegia
Gaura	Rudbeckia - some
Gentiana	Sanguisorba
Gillenia	Selinum
Helenium	Sidalcea
Hemerocallis	Stokesia
Heuchera	Succisa
Hosta	Thalictrum
Inula	Tradescantia
Kniphofia	Trifolium
Leucanthemum	Valeriana
Liatris	Veronicastrum

AUGUST

Actaea	Crocosmia - some
Aconitum - some	Eupatorium
Ageratina	Helenium - some
Anemone	Kniphofia - some
Artemisia	Rudbeckia
Aster - some	Sedum
Calamintha	Solidago
Coreopsis	

June: Bright magenta flowers of *Geranium* 'Dragon Heart' seem to float among the silvery-blue spikes of *Eryngium* × *zabelii* 'Jos Eijking'

July: The tall flower spikes of *Digitalis* × *mertonensis* tower above *Centaurea* 'Blewitt', injecting structure and interest among other perennials yet to bloom

August: Brightly coloured *Crocosmia* draws the eye in the foreground with taller *Helenium*, *Persicaria*, *Phlox* and *Eupatorium* adding height further back

September: *Sedum* 'Mr Goodbud' and *S.* 'Herbstfreude' are in full flower as is stately *Eupatorium maculatum* 'Riesenschirm' and *Echinacea purpurea* 'White Swan'

October: Tall asters, *Persicaria affinis* 'Superba' (front) and *Verbena bonariensis* are still in bloom, while *Gillenia trifoliata* and *Euphorbia palustris* take on lovely autumn shades

November: Golds, rusty browns and yellows begin to dominate when perennials decline, but some, such as the lovely, see-through grass, *Molinia*, will stand tall until spring

September is usually a warm month and a few plants will be coming into their own, while others, such as *Rudbeckia*, that started to flower in July or August will continue to fill the border with colour until the end of the month. By October, as autumn progresses, most perennials are beginning to decline and November can signal the arrival of the first frosts. From this point, the lush growth of perennials will turn brown and collapse into heaps. Leave dead and dying foliage as winter protection for small creatures or, if you prefer a tidier look, cut it back and put it on the compost pile.

AUTUMN AND WINTER PLANTS

Autumn-blooming plants mingle happily with perennials that are the mainstays of the summer border. They are fewer in number so don't need a separate area. The range of perennials that flower in winter is limited, but plants with decorative seedheads or evergreen foliage add interest and hellebore flowers are always a welcome sight.

SEPTEMBER

Actaea   *Sedum*
Aster

OCTOBER

Chrysanthemum   *Tricyrtis*

NOVEMBER, DECEMBER, JANUARY

Helleborus

When it snows the skeletons of plants can be appreciated

Perennials are rarely grown in isolation. In the garden, they combine perfectly with annuals, bulbs, and, particularly, shrubs. Perennial plants will increase the richness and diversity of your garden, and add colour and form throughout the seasons.

Annuals

Growing and caring for annuals, which live for just one year, can be a labour intensive and expensive business. Yet they are useful for filling gaps while perennials mature or when they have gone over. I have grown swathes of white cosmos from seed to enliven a border where peonies were no longer in flower. Sweet peas are another favourite, not just for the scent but for adding a vertical dimension. I grow them up metal obelisks in the middle of my square borders to create height and structure. Biennials, such as *Lunaria* and foxgloves are good fillers and some seed about.

Bulbs

Most bulbs are perennial and can be planted in a border and left undisturbed. However, the majority lose their leaves after flowering and, if like me, you forget where you've planted them it's easy to dig them up when enthusiastically adding new perennials to a border. Don't worry, simply put them back in the ground. Alliums combine beautifully with other perennials. Tulips also work well but are best treated as annuals because they tend not to come back each year.

Allium 'Purple Sensation' can be dotted through a border

White tulips complement the white flowers of perennial *Lunaria rediviva*

Papaver 'Lauren's Grape' is an annual that seeds freely about

Biennial *Lunaria annua* 'Corfu Blue'

This white form of *Lilium martagon* loves shade as does the *Thalictrum* behind

Pot marigolds (*Calendula officinalis*) can be used to add a bright splash of colour

Shrubs

Apart from trees, there are no better plants than shrubs for year-round structure. Evergreen shrubs such as *Viburnum tinus* create a perfect backdrop for white-flowered perennials, such as anemone. Some of the best shrubs for growing with perennials are those with dark leaves – the rounded foliage of purple forms of *Cotinus* combines beautifully with iris blooms in shades of bronze or gold – while silver-leaved shrubs or shrubby *Potentilla* work really well nearer the front of a border.

The most obvious shrubs to grow with perennials are roses, but choose perennials that are softly coloured and have small blooms so they won't compete with the big, sophisticated flowers of many roses.

Phlomis fruticosa is an evergreen shrub that likes a sheltered spot. Here it grows happily in the raised beds with other perennials

Nepeta and *Geranium* combine perfectly with roses

Phlox paniculata 'Sweet Summer Surprise' with shrubby *Brachyglottis* 'Walberton's Silver Dormouse'

Hydrangea macrophylla and *Anemone* 'Wild Swan' thrive in a woodland setting or a partly shaded spot

Geranium 'Rozanne' will flower for months in most locations, as does sub-shrub *Perovskia* 'Blue Spire'

Now for the practical aspects of creating a perennial garden. This is where the hard work begins, although for me this is the fun part where all the ideas and dreams for the garden finally get underway. Let's start with the plants. There are various ways of acquiring plants. When friends and relatives are splitting plants, you can beg a piece, promising something in return later. Some perennials can be grown from seed, others from cuttings, but most gardeners have to buy the plants that really catch their eye.

WHERE TO BUY PLANTS

For many, the first port of call is probably a garden centre. Most of them display plants only when looking their best and in full flower, which means the number of varieties in stock can be limited. Nurseries, whether small, large, retail, or mail order, are the answer. If you are uncertain about a plant, nothing quite replaces seeing it in leaf and, ideally, flower. Yet mail-order, internet-based nurseries, such as ours, hope the quality of the stock and the details they provide will fulfil expectations. And they are often the only source for an unusual, treasured variety.

LARGE OR SMALL PLANTS?

When buying plants, size really doesn't matter. As long as a plant is well grown, preferably in a non-peat based compost, a small specimen in a 9cm-square pot can be just as successful as a bigger one in a 2-litre container, especially when planted in the spring. Some perennials are better bought bare-rooted, namely *Iris*, *Paeonia*, and *Phlox*. These all resent being confined in a pot of any size for more than a few months.

Once you've got your new treasures home, make sure they are kept watered, but not wet. Also, don't put them in a greenhouse, which will simply encourage soft top growth and increase the plants' susceptibility to fungal diseases. And there's no rush. I have a cluster of plants in pots outside waiting for a home. Depending on the time of year, they can be fine for a few months.

PREPARING THE SOIL

Whether you prepare the soil before or after you get the plants is up to you. The most important task, whether you are creating a small patch or a big border, is to ensure all perennial weeds are removed. Planting a lovely perennial only to find couch grass making its way through the pretty foliage is annoying. If you feel a need to test the soil for nutrients, now is the moment. It's also the time to add well-rotted manure or garden compost to feed and enrich the soil.

PLOTTING

Before I plant up a large area or border, I draw a plan on a piece of paper. This helps me to get an idea of the overall scheme and put the right plants together. But I am not a trained garden designer so my schemes are not what you would call precise. I don't mark the exact planting spots on the plan and I tend to estimate the number of plants required. What I always do first is to lay out the plants in their pots on the ground. Of course, you need to have some idea of how wide a plant will grow, but a basic rule of thumb is three perennials per square metre, and it seems to be a good guide. With big, tall plants, such as *Eupatorium*, I use just one or two plants per square metre. With smaller plants, such as *Senecio polyodon*, four plants will fit in the same space. The wider the plant, the fewer are needed.

Once all the plants are spaced out, I walk away then go back a day later to check I'm still happy with the arrangement. If all is well, the plants are put into the ground (usually by my husband). This system works best when there is some foliage or flower colour showing to aid the design.

PLANTING

Having dug the hole, put the plant in and back fill. I always water once plants are in the ground, even if it is raining. Then a label goes in, next to the plant, pushed far enough into the ground to stop it being blown away by the wind. It reminds me what the plant is, as well as where it is, especially if it dies back over winter.

IMMEDIATE AFTERCARE

It is important, particularly with newly planted borders, to keep weeds at bay. I love using my hoe, but in chunky clay soil like ours it can be hard work. Don't, however, neglect this chore; it will pay dividends later. Keep newly planted perennials watered for the first few days – longer if the weather is very dry. It will get the roots off to a good start and help them establish more quickly.

Make sure the new beds are cleared of weeds

Nurseries are often the best source of good-quality as well as unusual plants

Planting out after positioning pots

Once perennials have settled, in most cases there isn't much more to be done. Every three weeks or so, between May and October, I have a good look at everything, especially any new plantings.

STAKING

As perennials grow, those with large flowers, such as peonies, may need support to keep the flowers upright. This may not be necessary in the first year, but in later years when the flowers get bigger and heavier, you may need to stake the stems using hoops or canes. Put supports in early in the season as you will be less likely to damage the plant. The stems will also grow through and disguise their supports. Plants that topple over in high wind or heavy rain will also need support and short hoops are a great help.

DIVIDING

There are three reasons for dividing perennials: to increase the number of plants, to reduce the size of a plant, or to make it more vigorous. The method is the same, but the time to do this may vary. Most should, or can, be lifted and split every three years or so. Bear in mind that the growth of fast-growing perennials such as *Aster*, *Campanula*, *Geranium*, and *Nepeta* lessens as the plant gets older. Very tall plants, such as *Echinops* and *Eupatorium*, also use a lot of energy, but they can be reduced in size to keep them tidy. However, long-lived, slow-growing plants such as *Paeonia* are better left in situ for many years.

The time to divide a plant is once the foliage has died back in autumn. Cut off the old top growth, lift the plant out using a fork, then

The stems of *Paeonia* 'Coral Charm' are so tall they may need staking

The back garden in winter

Geranium 'Blue Cloud' trimmed back (with helper)

Geranium 'Blue Cloud' a few weeks after cutting back

knock as much soil off the roots as you can. Set the plant on a stable surface and use a large carving knife to cut through it. I have never done it, but you can use two border forks placed back to back to prise a mature, clumping perennial with large roots apart.

The divisions should not be too small, although this depends on the plant. After three years, the crown of some perennials can be up to 30cm across. Dividing these might yield 20 plants or more, but the sections would probably be very small. It's best to create larger divisions with lots of healthy shoots and strong roots. This should provide you with enough sections to replant with some over to give away. You can then discard the old, woody central section.

FERTILISING

I rarely feed my perennial plantings, not through any unwillingness but because it doesn't often cross my mind. Perennials' native habitats tend to be rough, wild areas so, in the main, they don't require much feeding. Overfeed them and many produce lots of top growth and no flowers. However, if your border hasn't been touched for some years, it may well benefit from a sprinkling of granular fertiliser in spring or autumn. Incorporating well-rotted farmyard manure or home-made garden compost into the soil is even more beneficial. Just don't overdo it: too much feeding will result in giants or heavy, floppy plants.

DEAD-HEADING AND CUTTING BACK

I do try and cut off dead flowers as they fade throughout the summer, concentrating my efforts on those plants that look really untidy. It's best to take off the flowering stem, not just the individual dead flowers. Removing flowering stems and cutting back the foliage to ground level also helps certain plants produce fresh growth and sometimes more flowers. These include *Achillea*, *Astrantia* (but not *A. maxima*), *Centaurea*, *Echinops*, and *Geranium*. Trimming back also keeps the plant tidy if it becomes unruly.

In late autumn, I begin to cut perennials back once the old leaves and stems have turned brown. Initially I choose only the tattiest plants; the neatest, most upright will provide interest and structure for many months until winter winds flatten them. Cutting back proper starts in spring, anytime between late February and March, just before new growth emerges. I also remove any weeds beneath the old stems to clean the ground for the summer to come.

Paeonia 'Lord Kitchener' produces lots of seeds, but it will only come true when divided

The best way to propagate *Papaver orientale* 'Forncett Summer' is to take root cuttings

Astrantia seeds are plentiful

Rather than buying perennials, which can be costly, you can propagate them yourself. Division from a mother plant or sowing seed are the easiest methods. Root and stem cuttings can be a matter of trial and error, but nothing ventured, nothing gained.

Divisions and runners

Almost all perennials can be divided and this will also keep them vigorous. The best time to divide a plant is during its dormant period, from autumn to spring. For advice on how to do this, *see* Dividing on p. 49. Some plants have roots that run, such as *Geranium macrorrhizum*, while others, like *Ajuga*, produce runners. To propagate both these plants, simply pull off pieces of the plant that have roots and pot them up.

Root cuttings

Some plants are best propagated from root cuttings. These include *Papaver*, *Echinops*, *Eryngium*, and *Phlox*. Lift the plant when dormant and, with a clean knife, cut a healthy piece of root into lengths of about 7cm. Cutting the bottom of the root at an angle will remind you to put this end in first. Then make a hole, using a pencil, in a deep pot of free-draining compost and sink the root, angled-end down, into it. If you have lots of roots, put them into a polythene bag with ample moist compost, and roll it up. Leave the pot or polythene bag in a shady place, sheltered from the rain, until green shoots appear in spring.

Seeds

I love collecting and sowing seeds. It is easy and very satisfying. Seeds form all summer, so keep your eyes open and as soon as a pod forms or the flower turns brown, cut the stem off. Do this on a dry day and store the whole stem upside down in a paper bag (don't use plastic: the seeds will sweat and then rot). The seeds should drop off easily; if they don't give them a good rattle. Seeds can be sown at any time, but I usually choose February – a month when little else happens. Sow them into a tray of peat-free, potting compost and cover them according to the size of the seed. Small seeds need very little covering; just enough compost to stop them drying out. Tiny seeds, such as *Digitalis*, can simply be watered in; large seeds, such as *Lupinus*, can be pushed in.

Keep the compost moist, but not wet and place outside or in a cool greenhouse. Germination depends on the plant, but it can be slow. Don't give up until you are absolutely sure nothing is left growing in the tray; you might miss that last gem.

PERENNIALS TO RAISE FROM SEED

Those listed below are usually grown from seed, but remember that named varieties will not come true from seed. Plants with a single asterisk are, in my experience, slow to germinate; those with two are also difficult.

Agastache	*Lathyrus*
Alchemilla	*Lupinus*
Astrantia*	*Lychnis*
Baptisia*	*Morina*
Campanula	*Phlomis**
Centaurea	*Pimpinella***
Delphinium*	*Primula**
Dictamnus**	*Rudbeckia*
Digitalis	*Sanguisorba**
Echinacea	*Selinum*
Echinops	*Senecio*
Eryngium*	*Stachys*
Eupatorium*	*Stokesia**
Euphorbia	*Succisa*
Geranium	*Thalictrum**
Geum	*Thermopsis**
Gillenia*	*Uvularia***
Helleborus**	*Valeriana*
Knautia	*Verbena*
Lamium orvala*	*Veronica**

Stem cuttings

I propagate *Anthemis* and *Dianthus* from stem cuttings; it is possible to use the same method with *Delphinium* and *Lupinus* but they are difficult. Take cuttings in March or April, when the plant is in full growth. The short off-shoots, found at the leaf junctions, are suitable for cutting. Carefully tear off those shoots that are quite large and preferably without flower buds. If there are buds, pinch them out. Then trim the base straight with a sharp, clean knife and poke it into a pot of moistened, but well-drained compost. Cover the pot with a polythene bag to prevent the cuttings from drying out and place on a windowsill or in a greenhouse – somewhere not too hot.

LONGEVITY

It is fairly safe to say that perennials which grow very easily from seed do not live for long. You only have to look at *Echinacea purpurea* to discover that it grows very easily from seed, which is why it is not long-lived. A plant that produces large quantities of seed uses up a lot of energy, but I've found that if you remove the seedheads, the plant can live for longer. By contrast, plants that are difficult to raise from seed, such as *Paeonia* and *Dictamnus*, naturally live for a long time. Growing these plants from seed is difficult and time consuming, therefore they are better raised from divisions.

Snails sometimes eat iris leaves

Silkies in the garden

Mullein moth caterpillars on *Verbascum*

INSECTS AND OTHER PESTS

The leaves and flowers of perennials are soft and lush, which makes them more prone to attack by insects and other garden pests than to disease. These are the main culprits:

Aphids

It is a fact of gardening that aphids – both green and black – will appear in great quantities to feast on certain plants. Lupins, for instance, are a favourite. Either spray them with an insecticide or squash them by hand to reduce numbers. Do nothing and the whole plant will be weakened.

Caterpillars

I find the only perennial that really suffers from caterpillars is *Verbascum*, which has its very own predator. The caterpillars of the mullein moth – creamy-white with yellow and black markings – graze on the emerging flower stems, stunting the growth. I leave them alone: not only are they attractive to look at, but once they have turned into chrysalises, the plant sends up more flower stems and recovers. If these pests really annoy you, remove them by hand or if you must, spray with an insecticide.

Slugs and snails

These voracious pests tend to home in on precious plants – particularly those growing in a shady, damp place. They also trawl their way up the leaves of irises. Slugs always seem to lurk in grass, while snails hide under vegetation. Pellets can be applied, but they get washed away in rain, and picking slugs off by hand is unpleasant. You can sink a pot of beer in the ground, and it does work for a while, but my own solution – and I realise it's not for everyone – is to keep hens. Small, decorative hens, such as bantams, love slugs and snails, and won't trash the garden. Also, encourage thrushes and hedgehogs – good slug and snail predators – into the garden.

Vine weevils

If you grow a plant in a pot for too long, especially a *Heuchera*, you are likely to encourage vine weevils. Evidence is easy to see: the adults nibble the edge of the leaves, while the larvae eat the roots. Once a plant has been attacked, it's best to discard it.

ANIMAL PESTS

While beneficial insects are welcome in the garden, some mammals are best kept out. Rabbits and deer are two that can cause considerable damage to certain perennials. Deer don't try to eat our garden plants but rabbits do. The only way to deter rabbits is to erect a physical barrier round your garden. Put up a fence and bury the wire netting below ground to stop rabbits tunnelling underneath. You can also avoid growing plants they like. Plants listed below are not foolproof – certain rabbits will eat anything – but worth a try.

RABBIT-PROOF PLANTS

Aconitum	*Iris*
Alchemilla	*Kniphofia*
Anemone	*Lamium*
Aquilegia	*Lysimachia*
Aster	*Miscanthus*
Astilbe	*Nepeta*
Bergenia	*Paeonia*
Campanula lactiflora	*Papaver*
Crocosmia	*Persicaria*
Digitalis	*Polygonatum*
Epimedium	*Pulmonaria*
Eupatorium	*Sedum*
Helenium	*Tellima*
Helianthus	*Tradescantia*
Helleborus × hybridus	*Trillium*

DISEASES

Most perennials are trouble free and suffer from very few diseases. These are the principal complaints:

Leaf spot

Dark spots on leaves on very hot summer days after early rain are usually the result of leaf scorch. Spots that appear during milder weather are likely to be symptoms of the fungal disease leaf spot. Hellebores and irises are prone, especially if the weather is warm and damp, or in autumn when the plants are beginning to die back. The best option is to remove and destroy affected leaves. Having said that, I've never had a perennial die because of leaf spot.

Mildew

Mildew can be a pain, especially later in summer when the weather is warm and wet. The first symptom is a fine silver-grey film on the leaves. *Monarda* and Michaelmas-daisy types of *Aster* often suffer from mildew, as do *Stachys byzantina*, *Pulmonaria*, some hardy geraniums, and *Aquilegia*. According to one theory, the disease is more prevalent in dry soils, yet it also affects plants that grow in our moist clay loam. The best solution is to cut the whole plant back to encourage new, stronger growth.

The Perennial Directory

The following pages are dedicated to the plants I love, and these are all plants I would not be without. The sections on *Iris* and *Paeonia* are unashamedly long because over the years I have grown hundreds of varieties. There are far too many to include all of them here so I've chosen the most reliable hybrids and my current favourites. In years to come these might alter.

The information given in each main entry appears as follows:

- **ACHILLEA** This is the family name of the plant.
- (Yarrow) The common name appears after the family in brackets.
- An overall description of the family follows.
- **Needs** The amount of sun and drainage plants in this family generally require.
- **Great for** The best place in the border to grow the plants.
- **Bees & Butterflies** Indicates whether the plants attract these beneficial insects.
- **For Cutting** Indicates which plants make good cut flowers.
- **Care** Advice and tips that will help you grow the plants successfully.
- **'Credo'** or *filpendulina* **'Gold Plate'** The name of the cultivar or variety is in bold after the family name.
- The flowering periods are given in months except for *Iris* and *Paeonia*, which are designated 'Early', 'Mid', and 'Late'.
- **H x S** tells you the height and spread of the plant.
- **AGM** Included at the end of certain plant entries, this stands for 'Award of Garden Merit'. It is given by the Royal Horticultural Society to plants grown in trials over some years that are judged to have fulfilled certain criteria, such as disease resistance. The trials can be limited, but they are a useful guide to performance, and an AGM can be taken to signify a good garden plant. No AGM awards have been included for irises or peonies because these plant groups are being re-assessed.

The back border at White Hopton Farm in late May.
Front to back - *Veronica* 'Ellen Mae', *Paeonia* 'First Arrival', *Aquilegia vulgaris* var. *stellata* 'Ruby Port'

Acanthus mollis

Acanthus spinosus

Achillea 'Credo'

Achillea filipendulina 'Gold Plate'

Achillea millefolium 'Lilac Beauty'

ACANTHUS

These stately plants add a touch of grandness to a border. Both varieties produce white flowers with two floppy lips that shelter under a shell-like purple hood. The flowers are carried up a sturdy stem to form a thick spike that rises elegantly from a broad, slowly spreading clump of leaves.

Needs Well-drained soil in sun or partial shade
Great for Middle or back of a border
Bees & Butterflies No
For Cutting Yes
Care Long-lived, resistant to drought. Can be difficult to eradicate once established

mollis (Bear's breeches) A vigorous plant with big, sculpted, dark green, shiny leaves. June to August. **H × S** 150cm × 90cm

spinosus (Armed bear's breeches) More deeply divided leaves than *A. mollis*; each leaf division is tipped with a little pin. June to August. **H × S** 120cm × 90cm

ACHILLEA (Yarrow)

Excellent for adding layers of horizontal colour to a border, achilleas perfectly complement clump-forming plants. Each broad head is made up of smaller flowers and carried on tall, stiff stems above long, deeply divided, often feathery and scented leaves. The flowers of some varieties change colour as they open. Most last well, creating a layered effect of two-tone colour.

Needs Well-drained soil in sun
Great for Front or middle of the border
Bees & Butterflies Yes
For Cutting Yes
Care Remove faded flowers to encourage more, leaving the last blooms to add strong shape to the border throughout winter. Achilleas can be short lived in soil that is not well-drained.

'Credo' A gentle plant with upright stems of soft-yellow flowers and mid-green, feathery leaves. June to September. **H × S** 90cm × 60cm. AGM

filipendulina **'Gold Plate'** Stiffly upright stems are topped with shallow-domed heads of bright-yellow flowers above neatly divided, grey-green leaves. 'Coronation Gold' is similar but flowers a little earlier and grows to 90cm. July to September. **H × S** 120cm × 90cm. AGM

millefolium **'Lilac Beauty'** A pretty, two-tone plant with soft lilac-pink flowers fading to almost white over time and carried above a mound of fluffy, lush green leaves. June to September. **H × S** 70cm × 45cm

Achillea millefolium 'Red Velvet'

Achillea 'Moonshine'

Achillea 'Paprika'

millefolium 'Red Velvet' Unlike many red varieties, its blooms do not fade as they age. The broad heads of rich-red flowers combine beautifully with soft grey-green leaves to create a neat mounding plant. June to September. **H × S** 75cm × 60cm. AGM

'Moonshine' Small heads of sulphur-yellow flowers are carried on well-branched, grey stems above evergreen, soft-grey leaves to from an open, domed mound. June to September. **H × S** 60cm × 45cm. AGM

'Paprika' A variety with flowers that open scarlet and fade to a paler red. The leaves are finely divided and grey-green. June to September. **H × S** 70cm × 60cm

ptarmica 'The Pearl' The sprays of small, button-like, pure white flowers are borne on slim but strong stems with slender, dark green leaves. This upright plant is inclined to spread freely when the soil suits it. The flowers are good for cutting. June to September. **H × S** 60cm × 45cm

'Terracotta' Ideal for hot borders, the heads of burnt-orange flowers turn rich yellow with age and are carried on stiffly upright stems with soft, grey-green leaves. June to September. **H × S** 75cm × 60cm

'Walther Funcke' Heads of red flowers, each with a yellow eye, fade to tangerine-orange. A good upright plant with feathery, grey-green foliage. June to September. **H × S** 60cm × 45cm

Achillea 'Terracotta'

Achillea ptarmica 'The Pearl'

Achillea 'Walther Funcke'

Aconitum 'Bressingham Spire'

ACONITUM (Monkshood)

These dignified, upright plants are a great alternative, if a little shorter in stature, to delphiniums in gardens where slugs are a problem. The flowers are really small and hidden under helmet-shaped hoods. Aconitums generally produce tall spikes with deeply divided, shiny, rather leathery, deep-green leaves at the base. They spread slowly into a substantial clump.

Needs Well-drained soil in sun or partial shade
Great for Middle or back of the border
Bees & Butterflies Bees
For Cutting Yes
Care All parts are poisonous so wear gloves when handling. After flowering, the entire plant dies back, leaving only the tuberous roots. Feed in spring to keep it vigorous

'Bressingham Spire' An elegant plant that produces slender columns of deep indigo-blue flowers. July to September. **H × S** 90cm × 50cm. AGM

× *cammarum* 'Bicolor' The white flowers are broadly stained along the edges with violet. Carried on short branches, they form a thick, upright spire. June to August. **H × S** 120cm × 60cm. AGM

***carmichaelii* 'Arendsii'** A late-flowering plant that produces dumpy spikes of rich-blue flowers. Perhaps the easiest variety to grow. August to October. **H × S** 120cm × 60cm. AGM

'Spark's Variety' A 'see-through' plant with deep violet-blue flowers carried on well-spaced, slender side branches above deeply divided, glossy, dark green leaves. June to August. **H × S** 150cm × 90cm. AGM

Aconitum × *cammarum* 'Bicolor'

Aconitum 'Spark's Variety'

Aconitum carmichaelii 'Arendsii'

ACTAEA (Bugbane)

Graceful, majestic, and eye-catching, the long, slender, bottle brush-like spikes of tiny, scented, white flowers turn fluffy as the stamens emerge. The seed pods are also decorative. Flower spikes are carried on slender stems above an elegant, open clump of deeply divided leaves that hold themselves proudly. Many dark-leaved varieties look similar.

Needs As long as soil remains moist, will grow in sun and partial or near-total shade
Great for Woodland and shady spots
Bees & Butterflies Bees
For Cutting Yes
Care Dark-leaved varieties may scorch in bright sunlight. Can be slow to establish

simplex **Atropurpurea Group** A plant with dark flower stems and dark purple leaves. August to October. **H × S** 150cm × 75cm

simplex **Atropurpurea Group 'Brunette'** The leaves are really dark maroon, almost black. August to October. **H × S** 150cm × 75cm. AGM

simplex **'Pink Spike'** The name of this fine plant is slightly confusing. The flower buds are pink, not the flowers, which are white. When fully open these form a long fluffy spike that rises from a clump of mahogany leaves. August to October. **H × S** 150cm × 75cm.

AGASTACHE (Giant hyssop)

Upright, bushy plants with long, fat spikes of small flowers that resemble those of mint and are loved by bees. These are carried on stiff stems with aromatic, light-green leaves that when crushed have a scent similar to that of liquorice.

Needs Well-drained soil in sun or partial shade
Great for Middle of a border
Bees & Butterflies Yes
For Cutting No
Care Trouble free but liable to seed about

'Blue Boa' The purple-blue flowers of this showy plant pop out of purple calyces over a very long period. June to September. **H × S** 80cm × 60cm

'Blue Fortune' Raised from seed, this variety has soft violet-blue flowers. July to September. **H × S** 90cm × 75cm. AGM

rugosa **f.** *albiflora* The white flowers poke out of green calyces, making them appear off-white in tone. July to September. **H × S** 90cm × 75cm

Actaea simplex Atropurpurea Group

Actaea simplex Atropurpurea Group 'Brunette'

Actaea simplex 'Pink Spike'

Agastache 'Blue Boa'

Agastache 'Blue Fortune'

Agastache rugosa f. *albiflora*

Ageratina altissima 'Braunlaub'

Ageratina altissima 'Chocolate'

Ajuga reptans 'Catlin's Giant'

Alchemilla conjuncta

Alchemilla mollis

AGERATINA

Formerly listed as *Eupatorium*, these bushy, upright plants start into growth late in spring and flower long after most perennials have gone over. The flowers form small balls with fluffy stamens and are held in shallow domed heads on well-branched stems with oval leaves.

Needs Moist soil in sun or partial shade
Great for Middle of a border
Bees & Butterflies Bees
For Cutting No
Care Trouble free in the right soil

altissima **'Braunlaub'** Fluffy white heads are carried just above a leafy, upright clump of oval, mid-green leaves. August to October. **H × S** 90cm × 75cm

altissima **'Chocolate'** The deep purple-brown leaves form a handsome bushy clump that is more useful and attractive in a border than the off-white flowers. August to October. **H × S** 90cm × 75cm

AJUGA (Bugle)

reptans **'Catlin's Giant'** A ground-hugging plant with broad, stumpy spikes of large, bright-blue flowers similar to those of mint. These are held above a dense carpet of big, leathery, evergreen, shiny, purple leaves. April to June. **H × S** 15cm × 45cm. AGM

Needs If the soil retains moisture, will tolerate sun right through to shade
Great for Edging borders
Bees & Butterflies No
For Cutting No
Care May suffer from mildew

ALCHEMILLA (Lady's mantle)

A discreet and undemanding plant that is invaluable for its ground-covering mounds of interesting, scalloped leaves and loose, airy heads of greenish-yellow flowers.

Needs Well-drained soil in sun or partial shade
Great for Edges of borders
Bees & Butterflies No
For Cutting Yes
Care Remove flowers before they set seed if you don't want an invasion of plants

conjuncta Clusters of lime-green flowers sprout from shiny, deep-green leaves that are silver below and edged with a fine, silver line. July to August. **H × S** 30cm × 30cm

mollis Lacy sprays of tiny, yellow-green flowers on long stems spill out from a mound of large, round, soft-green leaves. May to August. **H × S** 60cm × 75cm. AGM

AMSONIA (Blue star)

These North American natives produce sprays of small, starry blue flowers. The long, slender leaves are particularly lovely in autumn when they turn buttery shades.

Needs Well-drained soil in sun or partial shade
Great for Middle of a border
Bees & Butterflies No
For Cutting No
Care Slow to establish, but long-lived

hubrichtii A feathery plant with straight stems clothed all the way up with extremely slender leaves and topped with clusters of small, pale blue flowers. Once established, it copes in drier soils than *A. tabernaemontana*. June to August. **H × S** 90cm × 75cm

tabernaemontana An open, upright plant with stiff, slender, almost black stems. These carry sprays of small, starry, pale-blue flowers towards the top. The shiny, soft-green, willow-like leaves are handsome and turn yellow in autumn. June to August. **H × S** 75cm × 60cm

ANAPHALIS

This pretty plant harmonises easily with many other perennials. The white flowers are papery to the touch and last for ages.

Needs Well-drained soil that retains moisture in sun
Great for Front and middle of the border
Bees & Butterflies Yes
For Cutting Yes
Care Trouble free in the right soil

margaritacea (Everlasting pearl) A dome of lance-like silver leaves is covered with clusters of small, white flowers. July to September. **H × S** 45cm × 60cm.

triplinervis Long stems of soft, felted, grey leaves are topped with domed sprays of small, double white flowers. July to August. **H × S** 75cm × 60cm. AGM

ANCHUSA (Alkanet)

azurea **'Loddon Royalist'** Very few perennials offer such vivid blue flowers. Small and bright, they are carried in a spike on tall, hairy, reddish stems above a basal clump of long, hairy, mid-green leaves. May to July. **H × S** 90cm × 75cm

Needs Well-drained soil that remains moist, but not boggy, in sun or partial shade
Great for Back of the border
Bees & Butterflies No
For Cutting No
Care In wet soils the roots will rot. Remove old flower stems to encourage more blooms

Amsonia hubrichtii

Amsonia tabernaemontana

Anaphalis margaritacea

Anaphalis triplinervis

Anchusa azurea 'Loddon Royalist'

Anemanthele lessoniana

Anemone hupehensis 'Hadspen Abundance'

Anemone hupehensis var. *japonica* 'Bressingham Glow'

Anemone hupehensis var. *japonica* 'Pamina'

Anemone hupehensis var. *japonica* 'Prinz Heinrich'

ANEMANTHELE (Pheasant-tail grass)

lessoniana A tufting clump of very slender, mid-green leaves turns orange-bronze as autumn approaches. The autumnal colour remains through the winter. In late summer wispy stems of small, purple flowers are produced. Also known as *Stipa arundinacea*. August to September. **H × S** 50cm × 45cm

Needs Well-drained soil in sun
Great for Front of a border
Bees & Butterflies No
For Cutting No
Care Cut back in spring

ANEMONE (Japanese anemone)

A determined, long-lived plant with large, simple blooms carried elegantly on slender, branched stems. Forms colonies of dense mounds of vine-shaped, mid-green leaves. Left on the stem, the seedheads burst open to reveal fluffy seeds that provide food for small birds during the winter months.

Needs Well-drained soil that remains moist in sun or partial shade
Great for Back of the border
Bees & Butterflies Yes
For Cutting Yes
Care After taking a year or two to settle, the plants can be left untouched for years

***hupehensis* 'Hadspen Abundance'** Single, satiny, deep-pink flowers with pale-pink backs. August to October. **H × S** 90cm × 75cm. AGM

***hupehensis* var. *japonica* 'Bressingham Glow'** The large, semi-double flowers are a deep shade of rose pink. August to September. **H × S** 90cm × 80cm.

***hupehensis* var. *japonica* 'Pamina'** Deep-pink, semi-double flowers carried on a network of dark red, wiry stems. August to September. **H × S** 75cm × 60cm. AGM

***hupehensis* var. *japonica* 'Prinz Heinrich'** Ruffled, semi-double, dark pink flowers with slender petals. August to September. **H × S** 90cm × 75cm. AGM

***× hybrida* 'Honorine Jobert'** Single, white flowers. A classically elegant plant. August to September. **H × S** 90cm × 75cm. AGM

***× hybrida* 'Königin Charlotte'** Large, slim-petalled, soft-pink flowers. August to September. **H × S** 90cm × 75cm. AGM

***× hybrida* 'September Charm'** Soft-pink, single flowers, darker underneath, with three larger petals. August to September. **H × S** 90cm × 90cm. AGM

***× hybrida* 'Whirlwind'** Rosette-shaped, pure-white, semi-double flowers. August to September. **H × S** 90cm × 75cm

Anemone × hybrida 'Königin Charlotte'

Anemone × hybrida 'September Charm'

Anemone × hybrida 'Honorine Jobert'

'Wild Swan' Early to flower, the large, single white blooms have lilac backs to the petals and are carried on slender stems above a mound of vine-shaped, mid-green leaves. I have found it slow to get established and best in a woodland location. July to September. **H × S** 45cm × 30cm

ANTHEMIS (Chamomile)

These cheerful plants produce a mass of daisy-shaped flowers on slender stems that cover a mound of fragrant, finely cut leaves.

Needs Well-drained soil in sun
Great for *A. tinctoria* types will fill borders quickly. *A. punctata* subsp. *cupaniana* is good for softening the edges of borders, paths, and patios
Bees & Butterflies Yes
For Cutting Yes
Care Cut back in spring

punctata subsp. *cupaniana* Beneath a sea of white daisies lies a tumbling mass of deeply cut grey leaves. May to August. **H × S** 30cm × 75cm. AGM

tinctoria **'E. C. Buxton'** Masses of light-lemon flowers are carried on long stems with mid-green leaves. June to August. **H × S** 60cm × 60cm

Anemone × hybrida 'Whirlwind'

Anemone 'Wild Swan'

Anthemis punctata subsp. *cupaniana*

Anthemis tinctoria 'E. C. Buxton'

Aquilegia vulgaris var. *alba*

Aquilegia vulgaris var. *stellata* 'Nora Barlow'

Aquilegia vulgaris var. *stellata* 'Ruby Port'

Aquilegia vulgaris 'William Guiness'

Anthriscus sylvestris 'Ravenswing'

ANTHRISCUS

sylvestris **'Ravenswing'** (Cow parsley) Tall, almost black stems are topped with flat, lacy heads of tiny white flowers. The feathery leaves are deep purple-maroon. This will seed around, but some of the seedlings may have green leaves. Great for a wilder style of garden, although short-lived. May to June. **H × S** 90cm × 60cm

Needs Well-drained soil in sun or partial shade
Great for Back of the border, wild garden
Bees & Butterflies No
For Cutting No
Care Allow it to seed around

AQUILEGIA (Columbine, Granny's bonnet)

This classic cottage-garden plant bears its dangling flowers, which often have short spurs, on slender stems above a mound of lobed, mid-green leaves. When the differant varieties are planted near to one another they will hybridize with each other producing flowers of varying colours.

Needs Well-drained soil in sun or partial shade
Great for Middle of the border
Bees & Butterflies Bees
For Cutting Yes
Care Will seed freely around the garden

vulgaris **var.** *alba* Pure-white flowers with short spurs above pale-green leaves. May to July. **H × S** 75cm × 45cm

vulgaris **var.** *stellata* **'Nora Barlow'** A frilly, double, deep-pink variety with paler edges to the petals and no spurs. May to July. **H × S** 75cm × 45cm

vulgaris **var.** *stellata* **'Ruby Port'** A richly coloured plant with deep-red, spurless flowers. May to July. **H × S** 75cm × 45cm

vulgaris **'William Guiness'** Eye-catching black-purple, long-spurred flowers with white edges and centres. May to July. **H × S** 75cm × 45cm

Artemisia ludoviciana 'Valerie Finnis'

ARTEMISIA

***ludoviciana* 'Valerie Finnis'** Tall stems of soft-grey leaves with jagged tips form a bushy clump that is topped with insignificant yellow flowers. An excellent if unassuming companion to grow with softly coloured flowers. August to September. **H × S** 60cm × 60cm. AGM

Needs Well-drained soil in sun
Great for Middle of a border
Bees & Butterflies No
For Cutting No
Care Trouble free and ideal for dry soils

ARUNCUS (Goatsbeard)

Although not a colourful perennial, this makes a really impressive plant.

Needs Soil that remains moist in sun, partial shade or shade
Bees & Butterflies No
For Cutting No
Great for Front and back of the border
Care Trouble free, but slow to establish

dioicus A big plant to use as a focal point. Tiny cream flowers form fluffy spikes that rise from a mound of mid-green leaves. June to July. **H × S** 180cm × 150cm. AGM

***dioicus* 'Kneiffii'** From a mound of gauzy, mid-green leaves, sprays of tiny, cream flowers erupt like a firework on long, arching stems. June to August. **H × S** 60cm × 45cm

'Horatio' The spikes of tiny white flowers splay out like Bonfire Night sparklers. The flowers turn red with age and the leaves become rust coloured in autumn. June to July. **H × S** 90cm × 45cm

Aruncus dioicus with the orange blooms of *Pilosella aurantiaca*

Aruncus dioicus 'Kneiffii'

Aruncus 'Horatio'

Aster amellus 'Rosa Erfüllung'

Aster 'Coombe Fishacre'

Aster divaricatus

Aster ericoides 'Erlkönig'

Aster × frikartii 'Mönch'

Aster 'Kylie'

ASTER

I cannot overstate the usefulness of these late-flowering plants. The choice of asters is extensive although many have now been reclassified into two family groups: *Eurybia* and the unpronounceable *Symphyotrichum*. For the benefit of the majority of gardeners, I am using the old, familiar name. The new one is in brackets. In this varied group, some form tight, leafy mounds, some are stiffly upright, while others form open clumps. All produce sprays of daisy-like flowers that will brighten up the dullest of autumn days. The most colourful are the true Michaelmas daisies (*A. novi-belgii*), which some might consider a little too bright. Others are less showy and bloom only in shades of lilac.

Needs Well-drained soil that remains moist in sun
Great for All parts of the border
Bees & Butterflies Yes
For Cutting Yes
Care *A. novi-belgii* types can suffer from mildew in warm, damp years. Otherwise trouble free

amellus **'Rosa Erfüllung'** A stiffly upright plant with open sprays of smallish, pale-pink flowers and soft, mid-green leaves. August to October. **H × S** 60cm × 45cm. AGM

'Coombe Fishacre' A really nice plant with small, pale-mauve flowers covering a clump of little, deep-green leaves. September to October. **H × S** 90cm × 60cm. AGM

divaricatus (*Eurybia*) Sprays of small, starry, white flowers rise from an uneven mound of heart-shaped, deep-green leaves. September to October. **H × S** 60cm × 60cm

ericoides **'Erlkönig'** (*Symphyotrichum*) This very late-blooming plant forms an open, airy clump. The tiny, star-shaped, lilac flowers are carried all the way along arching stems with small, deep-green leaves. October to November. **H × S** 100cm × 90cm

× *frikartii* **'Mönch'** One of the earliest and longest flowering asters, it produces a continuous display of large, single, lilac daisies. The plant forms a neat dome with disease-free, mid-green leaves. August to September. **H × S** 60cm × 60cm. AGM

'Kylie' This cross between *Aster novae-angliae* and *A. ericoides* produces long sprays of small, soft pink-lilac flowers that fade with age. Stiff stems with mid-green leaves form a big bush that requires no staking. August to September. **H × S** 100cm × 90cm

lateriflorus **'Prince'** (*Symphyotrichum*)
A tight, bushy plant with tiny, dark green leaves and stiff branches coated with small, white, pink-centred flowers. October to November. **H × S** 90cm × 75cm

laeve **'Glow in the Dark'** (*Symphyotrichum*)
Asters with lilac flowers are many, but few have such distinctive flower stems. Slender, and near black, the leaves are also very dark. The lilac flowers seem almost to have been stuck on the plant. Although it may need staking, this plant remains eye-catching throughout the growing season. September to October. **H × S** 120cm × 60cm

'Little Carlow' (*Symphyotrichum*) A lovely aster with hefty sprays of bright, mid-blue flowers and mid-green leaves that blends effortlessly with other perennials. September to October. **H × S** 90cm × 75cm. AGM

Aster lateriflorus 'Prince'

Aster laeve 'Glow in the Dark'

Aster 'Little Carlow'

Aster novae-angliae
'Andenken an Alma Pötschke'

Aster novae-angliae 'Harrington's Pink'

Aster novae-angliae 'Herbstschnee'

Aster novae-angliae 'September Ruby'

Aster novae-angliae 'Violetta'

Aster novae-angliae (New England asters)
Now listed under Symphyotrichum, the plants in this group produce colourful clusters of flowers at the top of stiffly upright stems. These become bare at the base and need no staking as they are strong enough to support themselves. Their rough leaves do not suffer from mildew.

novae-angliae **'Andenken an Alma Pötschke'** Clusters of bright cerise-pink blooms adorn this tall variety. September to November. **H × S** 120cm × 75cm

novae-angliae **'Harrington's Pink'** A neat variety with soft-pink flowers. September to November. **H × S** 120cm × 75cm. AGM

novae-angliae **'Herbstschnee'** The single pure-white flowers are carried on stiffly upright stems. September to November. **H × S** 120cm × 75cm

novae-angliae **'September Ruby' ('Septemberrubin')** A vibrantly coloured plant, the purple-red daisies, which are borne in clusters towards the end of the long flower stems, almost glow. September to October. **H × S** 130cm × 90cm

novae-angliae **'Violetta'** The rich purple flowers make an eye-catching feature in an autumn border. September to November. **H × S** 150cm × 90cm

Aster novi-belgii (Michaelmas daisies)
Of all the asters, these bear the brightest, most colourful flowers on slim, stiff stems. The shiny, deep-green leaves can suffer from mildew. Now listed as Symphyotrichum

novi-belgii **'Fellowship'** The semi-double, soft-pink flowers are held in small clusters. September to October. **H × S** 90cm × 75cm. AGM

novi-belgii **'Lady In Blue'** A free-flowering, short plant with single, violet-blue flowers. September to October. **H × S** 30cm × 30cm

novi-belgii **'Marie Ballard'** A tall plant with double, soft lilac-blue flowers. September to October. **H × S** 90cm × 75cm

novi-belgii **'Neron'** Sprays of double, vibrant pink flowers. September to October. **H × S** 40cm × 35cm

novi-belgii **'Winston Churchill'** Shaggy bright cerise-red, semi-double flowers. September to October. **H × S** 80cm × 75cm

pyrenaeus **'Lutetia'** Large, single, lilac flowers tumble out in a mass of stars to form a low, spreading clump with slender, mid-green leaves. August to October. **H × S** 75cm × 70cm

'Vasterival' Open sprays of small, pink-lilac flowers borne on almost-black stems fade to palest pink. Forms an airy, upright clump. August to September. **H × S** 90cm × 80cm

Aster novi-belgii 'Fellowship'

Aster novi-belgii 'Lady In Blue'

Aster novi-belgii 'Marie Ballard'

Aster novi-belgii 'Neron'

Aster novi-belgii 'Winston Churchill'

Aster pyrenaeus 'Lutetia'

Aster 'Vasterival'

Astilbe 'Betsy Cuperus'

Astilbe chinensis 'Vision in Red'

Astilbe 'Erica'

Astilbe 'Europa'

Astilbe 'Fanal'

Astilbe 'Weisse Gloria'

ASTILBE

Tidy in their growing habit, astilbes carry fluffy spikes of tiny flowers on slender stems above a decorative mound of deeply divided leaves. They will grow in any soil that does not dry out, but are most useful in wet soils or around the edge of a pond. They look particularly good planted in groups.

Needs Soil that remains very moist: wet clay, boggy soils or beside a stream or pond
Great for Wet, shady areas
Bees & Butterflies Yes
For Cutting Yes
Care Trouble-free in the right soil

'Betsy Cuperus' *(thunbergii* hybrid*)* An elegant variety with frothy spikes of tiny pale-pink flowers on long stems rising above a mound of handsome, deep green divided foliage. One of the tallest in this group. June to August. **H × S** 120cm × 90cm

chinensis **'Vision in Red'** A free-flowering plant that bears slim, fluffy, purple-red blooms. These open from rich-red buds held well above the deep green leaves. July to August. **H × S** 45cm × 45cm

'Erica' (× *arendsii*) A tall variety with sprays of tiny soft-pink flowers borne on red stems above glossy, dark green foliage. July to August. **H × S** 120cm × 90cm

'Europa' (*japonica* hybrid) The tiny, soft-pink flowers form thick spires above glossy, mid-green leaves. June to July. **H × S** 50cm × 40cm

'Fanal' (× *arendsii*) Open plumes of bright-scarlet flowers on red stems rise above a neat mound of leaves. The foliage contrasts handsomely with the flowers. July to August. **H × S** 30cm × 30cm. AGM

'Weisse Gloria' (× *arendsii*) A free-flowering hybrid with candy-floss spikes of creamy-white flowers carried above a compact mound of mid-green leaves. July to August. **H × S** 75cm × 60cm

ASTRANTIA (Masterwort)

Among the loveliest border perennials, their distinctive, papery flowers look like small pin cushions. These are carried in upright sprays on wiry, branched stems above a mound of deeply cut leaves. When I started in the nursery trade there were just a few varieties, but astrantias readily cross pollinate so there are now many more to choose from. Some are very similar – so similar it is difficult to tell the difference.

Needs Given well-drained soil that remains moist, will grow in sun, partial shade, and even fairly shady spots
Great for Middle of a border
Bees & Butterflies Yes
For Cutting Yes
Care Cut back (except *A. maxima*) after flowering to stop the plant seeding around

'Buckland' One of the earliest- and longest- flowering varieties with soft, dusky-pink flowers and mid-green leaves. May to July. **H × S** 60cm × 50cm

'Hadspen Blood' Rich-red flowers are produced above deep-green foliage, and the leaves are also highlighted with red. June to August. **H × S** 60cm × 45cm

major Flower size varies, but the colour is white, often tinged with pink. The leaves are mid-green. May to July. **H × S** 90cm × 60cm

major **'Claret'** Not a vigorous variety, this has very dark red flowers on near-black stems and red-tinted, dark green leaves. May to July. **H × S** 60cm × 50cm

major **Gill Richardson Group** Raised from seed, the plants can be variable. Most have dark, wine-red flowers and flower stems and the leaves tend to be heavily brushed with purple. May to July. **H × S** 75 cm × 60cm

Astrantia 'Buckland'

Astrantia 'Hadspen Blood'

Astrantia major with *Veronicastrum virginicum* 'Pink Glow' in the light of early evening

Astrantia major 'Claret' with *Digitalis lutea* and *Geum* 'Prinses Juliana'

Astrantia major Gill Richardson Group

Astrantia 'Roma' in front of *Paeonia* 'Shirley Temple' in a border that gets sun for only part of the day

major subsp. *involucrata* **'Shaggy'** Large white flowers are surrounded by big bracts that are elegantly tipped with green. The leaves are mid-green. May to August. **H × S** 90cm × 50cm. AGM

major **'Rubra'** The easiest red-flowered variety to grow, it bears pure, deep-maroon flowers and has dark green leaves. May to July. **H × S** 60cm × 50cm

major **'Ruby Wedding'** Although slow to multiply, when fully established this variety produces handsome, dark ruby-red flowers on red stems with reddish, deep- green leaves. May to July. **H × S** 60cm × 45cm

major **'Sunningdale Variegated'** This plant is especially handsome in spring when the young foliage emerges. At first light green and heavily splashed with soft yellow, the leaves turn mid-green when the stems of white flowers appear. May to August. **H × S** 90cm × 50cm. AGM

maxima The last astrantia to bloom, this plant bears lovely, large, dusky-pink flowers. The mid-green leaves are not as divided as those of the *A. major* group. If not grown in soil that is reliably damp, however, it can be the slowest to multiply. May to July. **H × S** 60cm × 55cm. AGM

'Roma' An excellent variety with glowing, rich-pink flowers and mid-green leaves. Performs really well in a shady spot. May to September. **H × S** 75cm × 50cm. AGM

'Ruby Star' Pointed dark red bracts sit under a pincushion of tiny flowers to create star-like blooms that open in clusters. Dark green flower stems rise above deep green, red-tinted leaves. A short plant. May to July. **H × S** 45cm × 35cm. AGM

Astrantia major subsp. *involucrata* 'Shaggy'

Astrantia major 'Rubra'

Astrantia major 'Ruby Wedding'

Astrantia major 'Sunningdale Variegated'

Astrantia maxima

Astrantia 'Ruby Star'

Baptisia australis

Bergenia 'Baby Doll'

Bergenia 'Bressingham White'

Bergenia 'Claire Maxine'

Bergenia 'Eroica'

Bergenia 'Pink Dragonfly'

BAPTISIA (False indigo)

australis An elegant, upright plant with slender stems of well-spaced, small, indigo-blue, pea-like flowers reminiscent of lupins. Below the flowers round, soft-green leaves are arranged in alternating pairs to the very bottom of the stems. June to July. **H × S** 90cm × 60cm. AGM

Needs Well-drained soil in sun
Great for Middle of the border
Bees & Butterflies Yes
For Cutting No
Care Remove old flower stems for neatness. May take a little while to establish

BERGENIA (Elephant's ears)

Evergreen perennials are few in number, making these tough plants extra special. Invaluable for suppressing weeds, they form a thick, ground-covering clump of large, leathery, spatula- or spoon-shaped leaves. In spring, sturdy flower stems rise up, topped with fist-like buds that open into clusters of bell-shaped flowers. From autumn to spring the leaves of some varieties are heavily tinged with red or burnished with bronze.

Needs Well-drained soil in sun to shade
Great for Evergreen ground cover. Also good in a pot
Bees & Butterflies No
For Cutting Yes; flowers and leaves
Care Remove old leaves as they die and divide plants when woody growth appears in the centre to keep them neat

'Baby Doll' This short plant produces tight clusters of very pale-pink flowers just above a compact clump of round, serrated leaves. April to May. **H × S** 30cm × 30cm

'Bressingham White' One of the cleanest white varieties with bell-like flowers and long, broad, deep green leaves. March to April. **H × S** 40cm × 45cm. AGM

'Claire Maxine' The magenta-pink flowers bloom off and on from spring onwards and sit well above shiny, round leaves. These are flushed with red in the autumn. March to October. **H × S** 50cm × 60cm. AGM

'Eroica' Taller than most bergenias with sprays of rich magenta-pink bells. These are borne on red stems above upright, smooth, oval deep green leaves that turn rich red in autumn. Sometimes sold as 'Overture'. March to May. **H × S** 45cm × 30cm. AGM

'Pink Dragonfly' A free-flowering plant with open, pure-pink flowers cascading from red stems above small, oval, deep-green leaves. A particularly good variety for pots as well as the border. March to September. **H × S** 30cm × 30cm

BRUNNERA (Siberian bugloss)

The large, rough-textured, heart-shaped leaves grow into a dense mound that is covered for weeks with open sprays of little, forget-me-not blue flowers. The leaves remain in good shape well into autumn, covering the ground thickly enough to reduce weed growth.

Needs Well-drained soil in sun or partial shade. If grown in a sunny spot the soil needs to retain some moisture, but in shadier areas plants tolerate fairly dry soils
Great for Shady areas, especially in woodland
Bees & Butterflies Bees
For Cutting Yes, but short-lived
Care Trouble free in the right soil

macrophylla The original green-leaved species, it forms a large, mounding dome covered with sprays of simple, soft-blue flowers. April to June. **H × S** 60cm × 75cm

macrophylla **'Betty Bowring'** A lovely plant for brighten up a dark spot. The sprays of tiny, pure-white flowers sit above a thick clump of mid-green, heart-shaped leaves. April and May. **H × S** 60cm × 60cm

macrophylla **'Hadspen Cream'** A very handsome plant, especially when seen from a distance. The mid-green leaves are edged with cream; the flowers are blue. April to June. **H × S** 60cm × 75cm. AGM

macrophylla **'Jack Frost'** Perhaps the best of the silver-leaved varieties. With their heavy covering of silver, the handsome green-veined leaves make a lovely backdrop for the sprays of soft-blue flowers. April to June. **H × S** 60cm × 75cm. AGM

Brunnera macrophylla

Brunnera macrophylla 'Betty Bowring'

Brunnera macrophylla 'Jack Frost'

Brunnera macrophylla 'Hadspen Cream' with
Centaurea montana Purpurea and *Geum* 'Marmalade'

Calamagrostis x *acutiflora* 'Karl Foerster'

Calamagrostis x *acutiflora* 'Overdam'

Calamintha grandiflora

Calamintha nepeta

Calamintha nepeta subsp. *glandulosa* 'Blue Cloud'

Calamintha nepeta subsp. *glandulosa* 'White Cloud'

CALAMAGROSTIS (Reed grass)

These are some of the most beautiful of all grasses, with dense clumps of fine leaves that stay upright throughout the year. Late in summer tall, slender stems carry delicate plumes of small, tan-coloured flowers. They don't seed around the garden and are tolerant of many situations.

Needs Well-drained soil in sun or partial shade
Great for Back of the border
Bees & Butterflies No
For Cutting No
Care Trouble free. Cut back in spring

× *acutiflora* 'Karl Foerster' An upright clump of fine, mid-green leaves produces very tall stems topped with slender plumes of soft-brown flowers. The stems remain rigid over a long period. August to November. **H × S** 180cm × 90cm

× *acutiflora* 'Overdam' A light, airy plant with green leaves striped with white and sprays of pink-tinged flowers. Ideal for a darker spot in the garden. August to November. **H × S** 180cm × 90cm

CALAMINTHA

Similar to *Nepeta* (*see* p. 135) in both style and use, *Calamintha* blooms much later. Spikes of small, mint-like flowers rise from a bushy clump with very fragrant leaves.

Needs Well-drained soil in sun
Great for Front of the border
Bees & Butterflies Yes
For Cutting No
Care *C. nepeta* types are a little slow to get going and may take two years to fill out

grandiflora A bushy plant producing an abundance of lilac-pink flowers that open between small, pale-green leaves on upright stems. June to August. **H × S** 45cm × 45cm

nepeta A neat, broad mound of small, peppermint-scented leaves produces sprays of tiny, pale-pink flowers. A more upright plant than the blue or white varieties below. July to October. **H × S** 45cm × 60cm

***nepeta* subsp. *glandulosa* 'Blue Cloud'** A long-flowering plant that produces a hazy mound of soft-blue flowers and little, fragrant, shiny leaves. July to October. **H × S** 45cm × 60cm

***nepeta* subsp. *glandulosa* 'White Cloud'** The aromatic soft-green foliage is less dense than others in the group. Tiny, pure-white flowers open from cream bracts over a long period. July to October. **H × S** 45cm × 60cm

CALTHA (Marsh marigold, Kingcup)

palustris This delightful plant is ideal for lighting up the edge of a pond. The bright yellow flowers are carried on well-branched stems above a dense clump of large, round, glossy, fresh-green leaves. May to June. H × S 45cm × 45cm

Needs Wet soil in sun or partial shade
Great for Pond edges
Bees & Butterflies Yes
For Cutting No
Care Easy to grow in any wet or damp soils

CAMPANULA (Bellflower)

These charming, versatile plants, producing bell-shaped flowers in a variety of white, blue or pink shades, blend effortlessly with all garden perennials. The best varieties for borders are selected from just a few species and most are easy to grow.

Needs Well-drained soil in sun or partial shade
Great for All parts of the border
Bees & Butterflies Yes
For Cutting Some
Care Trouble free. Try removing old blooms to encourage a few more flowers. Remove any leaves that suffer from rust

alliariifolia A plant with little finesse, yet the display of cream bells dangling all the way up tall, slender stems, makes it ideal for the front of the border. The flower stems sprout from a tight mound of rough, soft-green, heart-shaped leaves that tip gently forward to form a wide, but open plant. June to August. H × S 60cm × 60cm

glomerata **var.** *alba* (Clustered bellflower) Bell-shaped white flowers form tight clusters and whorls of further flowers are carried down the stiff, leafy stems. These rise above a slowly creeping carpet of mid-green leaves. June and July. H × S 45cm × 60cm

glomerata **'Caroline'** Held in tight domes, the flowers of this lovely plant are particularly pretty. The lilac bells are edged with a darker tint, although this subtle colouring disappears as the flower opens. June and July. H × S 45cm × 60cm. AGM

glomerata **'Superba'** Richly coloured, deep blue-purple bells cluster together on this robust plant. June and July. H × S 45cm × 60cm. AGM

'Iridescent Bells' A free-flowering plant with long, soft lilac bells that drop from upright, leafy stems. It forms a bushy, tumbling mass that needs no staking. June to September. H × S 75cm × 45cm

Caltha palustris

Campanula alliariifolia

Campanula glomerata var. *alba*

Campanula glomerata 'Caroline'

Campanula glomerata 'Superba'

Campanula 'Iridescent Bells'

Campanula lactiflora

Campanula lactiflora 'Alba'

Campanula lactiflora 'Loddon Anna'

Campanula latiloba 'Hidcote Amethyst'

Campanula persicifolia

Campanula latiloba 'Highcliffe Variety'

lactiflora (Milk bellflower) A billowing, upright, bushy plant carrying clusters of lilac-blue flowers all the way up tall, leafy stems. 'Prichard's Variety' is a lovely dark blue form, but all too often the plant supplied has soft-blue flowers like the seed-grown species listed here. June to August. **H × S** 120cm × 90cm

lactiflora **'Alba'** Large heads of upright, pure-white bells are borne the length of long stems covered in light-green leaves. A big, frothy plant like the others in the *lactiflora* group. June to August. **H × S** 120cm × 90cm. AGM

lactiflora **'Loddon Anna'** On this tall, bushy variety, long stems with soft-green leaves bear foaming heads of pretty, lilac-pink flowers. June to August. **H × S** 120cm × 90cm. AGM *latiloba* **'Hidcote Amethyst'** (Broad-leaved bellflower) Short spires of large, pinkish-lilac flowers bloom on slender stems that rise from rosettes of shiny, bright-green leaves. June to August. **H** × **S** 90cm × 45cm

latiloba **'Highcliffe Variety'** (Broad-leaved bellflower) Tall stems bearing a few slender leaves are studded with large, open, violet-blue bells. An elegant, sturdy plant. June to August. **H** × **S** 75cm × 50cm. AGM

persicifolia (Peach-leaved bellflower) Generous quantities of large, mid-blue, cupped blooms are borne on short branches. The slender flower stems rise from a thick, slowly spreading carpet created by the rosettes of long, shiny, deep-green leaves. June to August. **H** × **S** 90cm × 60cm

persicifolia **var. *alba*** The cupped, white flowers are carried all the way up slender stems above the mound of deep-green leaves. June to August. **H** × **S** 90cm × 60cm

punctata **f. *rubriflora*** Long, puffy, purple-pink flowers cluster thickly along slender, dark red stems above a slowly creeping carpet of mid-green leaves. June to August. **H** × **S** 60cm × 90cm

'Sarastro' A bushy plant with elongated, tubular, violet-blue bells hanging from leafy, short stems above long, matt-green leaves. Forms a dense, upright clump. June to August. **H** × **S** 60cm × 60cm

takesimana **'Elizabeth'** Short and spreading, its slender stems of long, maroon bells have paler interiors, attractively spotted with soft maroon. June to August. **H** × **S** 45cm × 60cm

trachelium **'Bernice'** (Nettle-leaved bellflower) The papery, double, deep-violet pixie-hat flowers curl back prettily at the edges. They are carried on slender, upright stems with mid-green, saw-edged leaves. June to August. **H** × **S** 90cm × 60cm

CATANANCHE (Cupid's dart)

caerulea A quick-growing perennial that forms an open clump with wiry stems of flat, semi-double, lavender-blue flowers. The slender petals are fringed at the top and papery. At the base are thin, grass-like leaves. June to September. **H** × **S** 60cm × 45cm

Needs Well-drained soil in sun
Great for Front of a border
Bees & Butterflies Yes
For Cutting Yes
Care Can be short-lived, especially in soil that stays wet during winter

Campanula persicifolia var. *alba*

Campanula punctata f. *rubriflora*

Campanula 'Sarastro'

Campanula takesimana 'Elizabeth'

Campanula trachelium 'Bernice'

Catanache caerulea

Centaurea 'Caramia'

Centaurea 'John Coutts'

Centaurea 'Jordy'

Centaurea macrocephala

CENTAUREA (Knapweed)

These free-flowering, clump-forming plants can be divided into two groups: tall and upright with large, knob-like flowers or short and mounding with flat, wheel-like flowers. In my garden the shorter types form the backbone of the mid-spring border. All have flowers that emerge from a distinctive boss of scaly, papery bracts, and the foliage is also very handsome.

Needs Well-drained soil that does not dry out, in sun or partial shade
Great for Front or back of the border
Bees & Butterflies Yes
For Cutting Yes
Care Remove the old stems and leaves to encourage new flowers and discourage the plant from seeding

'Caramia' The feathery flowers bloom on stiff stems with mid-green leaves that resemble *Rudbeckia* foliage. June to September. **H × S** 60cm × 30cm

'John Coutts' A variety with large, soft-mauve flowers and deeply lobed, mid-green leaves, that are white beneath. It forms a broad, mounding clump. May to July. **H × S** 60cm × 60cm

'Jordy' The most gloriously coloured of all knapweeds with deep-burgundy flowers set off by grey-green leaves. It can get rather leggy, so cut back after flowering. May to August. **H × S** 60cm × 45cm

macrocephala A sturdy, upright plant with thick, leafy stems topped by large, deep-yellow, thistle-like flowers. The long, pointed, bright-green leaves in alternate pairs form a beautifully sculpted clump, even before the flowers open. June to September. **H × S** 90cm × 75cm

Centaurea montana

Centaurea montana 'Alba'

montana A tough, mound-forming plant with violet-blue flowers carried on short stems, and broad, long silvery leaves. May to September. **H × S** 45cm × 60cm

montana **'Alba'** Less vigorous than the blue form, this has pure-white flowers and silver leaves. Planted at the front of a border, it creates an attractive, wide clump. May to June. **H × S** 45cm × 60cm

montana **'Carnea'** With its soft-pink flowers and soft-green leaves, this plant harmonises with many other colours in the border. May to June. **H × S** 45cm × 60cm

montana **'Purple Heart'** Given the right conditions, this is a vigorous, spreading plant. It produces purple-centred, pure-white flowers and silver leaves. May to June. **H × S** 45cm × 75cm

CENTRANTHUS (Red valerian)

Often seen growing wild in southern counties of the UK, this familiar perennial bears tiny flowers in foamy clusters on short branches with long, waxy, mid- to grey-green leaves. The flowers, which are carried all the way down the flower stems, are followed by fluffy white seeds.

Needs Very well-drained soil, including poor, either clay or sandy, in sun
Great for Middle of a border
Bees & Butterflies Bees
For Cutting Yes
Care Cut back the flower stems as soon as the plant begins to set seed if you don't want it to colonise the garden

ruber Grown from seed, as is the white form (below), this makes an upright, bushy plant with pinkish-red flowers and mid- to grey-green leaves. June to September. **H × S** 75cm × 45cm

ruber **'Albus'** A neat, clean plant with fluffy heads of tiny white flowers and grey-green stems and leaves. June to September. **H × S** 75cm × 45cm

CEPHALARIA (Scabious)

gigantea As the name *gigantea* suggests, this impressive plant needs a good deal of room. It produces large, soft-yellow scabious-like flowers on tall, widely branched stems that rise from a large clump of mid-green leaves. A great choice for a see-through effect in a big border. June to September. **H × S** 180cm × 60cm

Needs Well-drained soil; sun or partial shade
Great for Back of the border
Bees & Butterflies Yes
For Cutting Yes
Care Trouble free

Centaurea montana 'Carnea'

Centaurea montana 'Purple Heart'

Centranthus ruber

Cephalaria gigantea

Centranthus ruber 'Albus'

Chaerophyllum hirsutum 'Roseum'

Chelone obliqua

Chrysanthemum 'Clara Curtis'

Chrysanthemum 'Duchess of Edinburgh'

Chrysanthemum 'Mary Stoker'

CHAEROPHYLLUM (Chervil)

***hirsutum* 'Roseum'** A delightful plant that looks rather like a pink version of our native cow parsley. The flat heads of tiny, soft-pink flowers are carried on thick stems above a lush, broad mound of lacy, soft-green leaves. May to June. **H × S** 90cm × 90cm

Needs Well-drained soil that remains moist in sun or partial shade
Great for Middle of the border
Bees & Butterflies Bees
For Cutting Yes
Care Wild rabbits love this plant so take precautions (*see* p. 51)

CHELONE (Turtlehead)

obliqua Forming a leafy, well behaved, and upright clump, this plant is named for its distinctive blooms, each shaped like the head of a turtle. Short spikes of flowers open towards the top of the rigid stems, clustered four to each side above oval, pointed, dark green leaves. July to September. **H × S** 90cm × 75cm

Needs Well-drained soil that remains moist in sun or partial shade
Great for Middle of the border
Bees & Butterflies Bees
For Cutting No
Care May take a while to establish, but otherwise trouble free

CHRYSANTHEMUM

Once very popular with cottage gardeners, especially for cutting , the late-flowering hardy chrysanthemums are an absolute delight on dull autumn days. More subtle than the exhibition varieties, these produce sprays of smaller, daisy flowers with slim petals carried on stiff stems with deeply cut leaves. They form soft, mounding clumps.

Needs Well-drained soil in sun
Great for Middle of borders
Bees & Butterflies Yes
For Cutting Yes
Care Trouble free

'Clara Curtis' This pretty plant produces sprays of single, yellow-centred, pure-pink flowers that cascade over a broad mound of leaves. September to November. **H × S** 75cm × 75cm

'Duchess of Edinburgh' Long stems bear shaggy, dark brick-red, flowers. September and October. **H × S** 75cm × 75cm

'Mary Stoker' Sprays of single, soft apricot-yellow blooms cover a dense mound of leaves. September to November. **H × S** 75cm × 75cm

CIRSIUM

The thistle-like flowers of these long-lived plants are borne in clusters on tall, stiff stems that branch towards the top. At the base is a bushy clump of long, mid-green, rather prickly leaves. Perfect for bringing upright, see-though structure into a border.

Needs Well-drained soil in sun or partial shade
Great for Middle of the border
Bees & Butterflies Yes
For Cutting No
Care Cut back when the flowers are spent

rivulare **'Atropurpureum'** Few perennials have the same intense burgundy colour as these flowers. June to September. **H × S** 120cm × 50cm. AGM

rivulare **'Trevor's Felley Find'** Also called 'Trevor's Blue Wonder', the flowers are a lovely deep heather-purple. June to September. **H × S** 120cm × 50cm

COREOPSIS (Tickseed)

The yellow forms of this ever-expanding group of plants are the most reliable and bear masses of starry flowers. The stems are wiry and the leaves slim, almost linear. Some varieties are more upright than others.

Needs Well-drained soil in sun
Great for Front of the border
Bees & Butterflies Yes
For Cutting Yes
Care Foliage doesn't emerge until late spring and plants take a while to establish

verticillata Bright-yellow flowers and slender, mid-green leaves adorn this upright form. June to September. **H × S** 45cm × 60cm

verticillata **'Moonbeam'** Soft-lemon flowers on wiry stems with bronze-tinted, green leaves form a misty dome. June to September. **H × S** 45cm × 60cm

verticillata **'Zagreb'** Ideal for smaller plots, this carries a mass of bright-yellow flowers. June to September. **H × S** 40cm × 45cm. AGM

CRAMBE

cordifolia When this handsome plant is in bloom it is not the immense size that first strikes you, but the scent. The large sprays of little white flowers exude a strong, honey fragrance. At the base is a mound of big, rough, dark green leaves. July to August. **H × S** 180cm × 150cm. AGM

Needs Well-drained soil in sun or partial shade
Great for Back of the border
Bees & Butterflies Bees
For Cutting No
Care Once established it is trouble free

Cirsium rivulare 'Atropurpureum'

Cirsium rivulare 'Trevor's Felley Find'

Coreopsis verticillata

Coreopsis verticillata 'Moonbeam'

Coreopsis verticillata 'Zagreb'

Crambe cordifolia

Crocosmia × crocosmiiflora 'Emily McKenzie'

Crocosmia × crocosmiiflora 'George Davison'

CROCOSMIA (Montbretia)

Indispensable for their warm, late-summer colours, crocosmias carry sprays of small, lily-like flowers on stems that arch over clumps of grassy, mid-green leaves. Red varieties tend to be hardier than yellow ones.

Needs Well-drained soil in sun
Great for Middle of the border
Bees & Butterflies No
For Cutting Yes
Care Trouble free. Yellow varieties can be less hardy in wet ground

× *crocosmiiflora* **'Emily McKenzie'** Adds a bold splash of rich orange to any border. July to September. **H × S** 60cm × 50cm

× *crocosmiiflora* **'George Davison'** A tough, bushy plant with sprays of small, soft apricot-yellow flowers and mid-green leaves. July to September. **H × S** 75cm × 60cm

× *crocosmiiflora* **'Harlequin'** A free-flowering plant with long sprays of small, trumpet-shaped, yellow flowers that open from vermilion-red buds. July to September. **H × S** 60cm × 60cm

'Emberglow' A neat plant with small red flowers and pleated, mid-green leaves. July to September. **H × S** 90cm × 75cm

'Lucifer' Adding drama to any border, the brilliant red flowers are upward-facing and its sword-like leaves are pleated. July to September. **H × S** 90cm × 75cm. AGM

'Okavango' Displaying a fruity mix of vibrant orange overlaid with pink, the flowers form neat 'V'-shaped sprays. July to September. **H × S** 75cm × 60cm

'Paul's Best Yellow' A good yellow variety with large, bright, outward-facing flowers. July to September. **H × S** 90cm × 60cm. AGM

Crocosmia × crocosmiiflora 'Harlequin'

Crocosmia 'Emberglow'

Crocosmia 'Lucifer'

Crocosmia 'Okavango'

Crocosmia 'Paul's Best Yellow'

Delphinium 'Black Knight'

Delphinium 'Blue Bird'

Delphinium 'Astolat'

Delphinium 'Galahad'

DELPHINIUM

These stalwarts of the grand herbaceous border offer structure and well-defined height. Although there are many named varieties, most are expensive and difficult to obtain. The varieties described here are raised from seed selected from the Pacific Hybrids Series of plants. They were raised decades ago in the USA, so colours may vary slightly. All bear flower spikes packed with disc-like blooms, which have buff or black centres known as 'bees' or 'eyes'. The spikes tower above a mounding clump of delicately fingered, mid-green leaves.

Needs Well-drained soil in sun
Great for Back of the border
Bees & Butterflies Bees
For Cutting Yes
Care Give plants rich, deep, well-dug soil and add manure to get the best results. Protect from slugs

'Astolat' A variety with spikes of semi-double, soft lilac-pink blooms with buff or black 'bees'. June to July. **H × S** 180cm × 90cm

'Black Knight' The single, dark blue flowers of this elegant plant have centres that are generally black, but sometimes white. June to July. **H × S** 180cm × 90cm

'Blue Bird' A good mixer that bears semi-double, mid-blue flowers with white centres. June to July. **H × S** 180cm × 90cm

'Galahad' A white-flowered, semi-double form with contrasting black centres. June to July. **H × S** 180cm × 90cm

'Summer Skies' Lovely soft-blue, semi-double flowers with white eyes. June to July. **H × S** 180cm × 90cm

Delphinium 'Summer Skies'

Dianthus carthusianorum with *Geranium* 'Rozanne'

Dicentra 'Aurora'

Dicentra formosa

Dicentra 'King of Hearts'

Dictamnus albus

DIANTHUS (Pink)

carthusianorum In the first edition of this book, I included a number of garden pinks. This time I have chosen just one: a delightful plant with tight clusters of single, rich-pink flowers carried on wiry stems above a tight clump of long, grey leaves. Will seed around if happy. May to July. **H × S** 50cm × 23cm

Needs Well-drained soil in sun
Great for Front of the border
Bees & Butterflies Bees
For Cutting Yes
Care Allow it to seed around

DICENTRA (Bleeding heart)

Although these small plants are truly delightful, they can be fussy about where they choose to grow. The three included here perform well in a border. The flowers look like puffy hearts and are carried on brittle stems just above a slowly spreading mound of lush, almost succulent-looking, lacy leaves. The foliage will die right back after flowering.

Needs Cool, humus-rich soil that remains moist in partial or full shade
Great for Shady areas such as woodland
Bees & Butterflies No
For Cutting No
Care Trouble free in the right spot

'Aurora' Charming clusters of slim, white hearts rise above deeply cut, grey-green leaves. May to July. **H × S** 45cm × 40cm

formosa The small sprays of slender, locket-shaped, soft-pink flowers arch above deeply divided, fresh-green leaves. May to June. **H × S** 45cm × 45cm

'King of Hearts' This is an incredibly long-flowering plant with small clusters of perfect heart-shaped, rich-pink flowers on slender stems above a spreading mound of handsome, lacy, grey-green leaves. May to October. **H × S** 30cm × 45cm

DICTAMNUS (Burning bush)

albus The delicate white flowers, which resemble butterflies, have maroon-veined, widely spaced petals and long, curling stamens. They are carried in open spires up sticky, red-tinged stems with thick, shiny, mid-green leaves. Most plants are raised from seed, so may be variable in colour. July to August. **H × S** 90cm × 75cm. AGM

Needs Well-drained soil in sun or partial shade
Great for Middle of the border
Bees & Butterflies No
For Cutting No
Care Trouble free but slow to establish

Dierama pulcherrimum

Digitalis ferruginea

Digitalis grandiflora

DIERAMA (Angel's fishing rod)

pulcherrimum In warmer spots this handsome plant can reach its full potential. The large, bell-shaped, rich-pink flowers dangle two or three at a time from long, wiry stems causing the flower stem to elegantly, but gently curve forward. At the base is a thick clump of grass-like leaves. July to August. **H × S** 120cm × 60cm

Needs Well-drained or dry soil in sun
Great for Hot, dry gardens
Bees & Butterflies No
For Cutting No
Care Will need protection in cold winters

DIGITALIS (Foxglove)

Elegant and very upright, these glorious plants add gracefulness to a border with their spires of long, tubular flowers arising from an evergreen rosette of leaves. Many are biennial and die after flowering; those listed here are perennial, but short-lived.

Needs Well-drained soil in sun or shade
Great for Middle of a border
Bees & Butterflies Bees
For Cutting Yes
Care Can be short-lived, so allow the plants to seed

ferruginea The small, honey-coloured flowers, veined inside with brown, are subtle and stylish. They are borne above a rosette of evergreen, shiny, dark green leaves. June to September. **H × S** 90cm × 30cm. AGM

grandiflora The large, pale-yellow flowers and soft-green leaves create a pretty effect. June to July. **H × S** 75cm × 30cm. AGM

Digitalis lutea

lutea Slender spikes of small, pale-lemon flowers are displayed above long, shiny deep-green leaves. June to September. **H × S** 90cm × 30cm. AGM

× *mertonensis* Stumpy spikes covered with dusky-pink flowers adorn this variety, which can be temperamental. July to August. **H × S** 75cm × 30cm. AGM

Digitalis × *mertonensis*

Echinacea 'Green Envy'

Echinacea 'Orange Passion'

Echinacea purpurea 'Green Jewel'

Echincea purpurea 'Magnus'

Echincea purpurea 'Virgin'

Echincea purpurea 'White Swan'

ECHINACEA (Coneflower)

The spiky centres of these striking daisies start out flat then, as the flower ages, they increase in size to form a tall, often pointed, cone. Carried on stiff, upright stems, in some varieties they are scented, and all are held above oval, pointed, mid-green leaves. In North America, where they grow wild, flower colours tend to be pinks or yellows. In recent years, however, there has been an eruption of new varieties, extending the colour range to include orange and green. Some do not thrive in our wet climate.

Needs Well-drained soil in sun
Great for Middle of the border
Bees & Butterflies Yes
For Cutting Yes
Care Coneflowers are gaining a reputation for being short-lived and they can be tricky to keep going. I cut off the seedheads as soon as possible

'Green Envy' An unusual colour for flowers, the green of this variety is heavily stained with magenta. There are big gaps between the petals and the central disc is brown. July to September. **H × S** 90cm × 50cm

'Orange Passion' When the petals first appear they are coral pink and change to bright orange as they unfurl. The large flat cone in the centre is ginger. Stick your nose in the flower and enjoy the lovely aroma. July to September. **H × S** 75cm × 50cm

purpurea **'Green Jewel'** A variety with frilly, lime-green flowers and a prominent green centre. July to September. **H × S** 75cm × 50cm

purpurea **'Magnus'** An award-winner with large, fragrant, reddish-pink flowers. Usually raised from seed so may be variable. July to September. **H × S** 90cm × 60cm. AGM

purpurea **'Virgin'** Pure white flowers with large, spiky centres open lime green and turn ginger over time. I have found this to be more reliably long-lived in heavier soils than some coneflowers. July to September. **H × S** 60cm × 50cm

purpurea **'White Swan'** Surrounded by white petals, the large, greenish cones of this variety turn bronze. Usually seed-raised. July to September. **H × S** 90cm × 60cm

'Sunrise' The glossy, rich-yellow flowers of this fragrant variety have pink undersides and their green centres turn copper with age. July to September. **H × S** 90cm × 50cm

Echinacea 'Sunrise'

ECHINOPS (Globe thistle)

Loved by butterflies and bees, the flowers of these long-lived, sculptural plants are intriguing. The small florets are packed so closely together they form a tight, perfectly round ball that is spiky when in bud. As the flowers open into little stars, the ball softens into a fuzzy sphere. They are carried on tall, rigid, usually silver stems, above a clump of long, mid-green, deeply divided leaves with silver undersides. Drought tolerant, they will grow in a wide range of soils.

Needs Well-drained soil in sun or partial shade
Great for Middle or back of the border
Bees & Butterflies Bees
For Cutting Yes
Care Trouble free

bannaticus **'Taplow Blue'** Pale-blue flowers are carried on mid-green stems above a handsome clump of mid-green leaves with silver undersides. An easy variety to grow. July to September. **H × S** 120cm × 90cm

ritro A robust plant that should be given a bit of space. The silver-blue flowers are carried on stiff, mid-green stems with rough, mid-green leaves. July to September. **H × S** 90cm × 60cm. AGM

ritro **'Veitch's Blue'** The rich-blue spheres, which are smaller than other *Echinops*, are borne on silver stems above silver leaves. July to September. **H × S** 90cm × 50cm

Echinops bannaticus 'Taplow Blue'

Echinops ritro

Echinops ritro 'Veitch's Blue'

Epimedium 'Amber Queen' with *Lamprocapnos spectabilis* 'Alba'

Epimedium grandiflorum 'Lilafee'

Epimedium 'Pink Elf'

Epimedium 'Domino'

EPIMEDIUM (Barrenwort)

Demure yet very hardy, these shade-loving spring flowering plants are covered with sprays of small (sometimes tiny), cupped flowers that usually are topped off with long spurs. The flowers are held daintily on wiry stems and dance above a mound of often papery, sometimes leathery, heart-shaped leaves. Many are evergreen and some turn gorgeous colours in autumn.

Needs Well-drained soil with leaf mould, in partial shade or full shade. *E.* × *versicolor* varieties cope with dry soils
Great for Shade near or beneath shrubs and trees
Bees & Butterflies Bees
For Cutting No
Care Most will take a little time to establish, otherwise trouble free

'Amber Queen' Long, airy sprays of small, copper-yellow flowers with long, curved spurs are borne on such fine stems that the flowers seem to be suspended in the air. The deep-green, serrated leaves are evergreen. April to June, and often in September. **H × S** 45cm × 60cm

'Domino' A cloud of pale-pink flowers with dark pink centres is carried on dark red stems above a mound of handsome, oval leaves with long points. The bronze-green foliage looks rather like camouflage material. April to May. **H × S** 60cm × 100cm

grandiflorum **'Lilafee'** The deep rose-pink flowers are carried in small sprays above a delicate mound of bright green leaves that are purple tinged when young. April to May. **H × S** 23cm × 60cm

'Pink Elf' A small plant that is transformed when the loose sprays of tiny, pale-pink flowers with dark centres suddenly emerge above the dense mound of bright green leaves. April to May. **H × S** 30cm × 45cm

pubigerum A demure plant with long, frothy sprays of tiny, cupped, pale-pink flowers. These are borne the length of the well-balanced slender stems. April to May. **H × S** 45cm × 60cm

× *rubrum* The large, yet delicate, bright-red flowers displaying white centres. The thick leaves are richly tinted with red in spring. April to May. **H × S** 30cm × 45cm. AGM

× *versicolor* **'Cupreum'** Soft pink-red flowers with pale-yellow centres are carried in dense sprays above evergreen, lime-green leaves that turn orange-red in autumn. April to June. **H × S** 45cm × 60cm

× *versicolor* **'Sulphureum'** Sprays of pale-yellow and white flowers. These are carried just above evergreen, deep-green leaves handsomely burnished with red from autumn to spring. April to May. **H × S** 45cm × 75cm. AGM

× *warleyense* **'Orangekönigin'** Produces open sprays of delicate, peach-orange flowers with tight, yellow centres. They seem to flutter above the evergreen leaves, which are heavily tinged with red in winter. April to June. **H × S** 45cm × 60cm

× *youngianum* **'Niveum'** A charming plant with small, white flowers carried on reddish stems above a neat mound of leaves. These are coppery at first. April to May. **H × S** 30cm × 45cm. AGM

Epimedium pubigerum   *Epimedium* × *rubrum*

Epimedium × *versicolor* 'Cupreum'

Epimedium × *versicolor* 'Sulphureum'   *Epimedium* × *warleyense* 'Orangekönigin'   *Epimedium* × *youngianum* 'Niveum'

Erigeron 'Dunkelste Aller'

Erigeron karvinskianus

Erigeron 'Schneewittchen'

Erodium manescavii

Eryngium agavifolium

Eryngium alpinum

ERIGERON (Fleabane)

Simple and delightful, these small, slim-petalled daisies sit well next to most perennials. The flowers are produced in great quantities above a low, spreading clump of mid-green leaves.

Needs Well-drained soil in sun or partial shade
Great for Front of the border
Bees & Butterflies Yes
For Cutting Yes
Care Rabbits love them, especially the larger types, otherwise trouble free

'Dunkelste Aller' A free-flowering plant with semi-double, violet flowers carried on short stems above mid-green leaves. June to August. **H × S** 45cm × 60cm

karvinskianus This prostrate plant is littered with little daisies for months. Each bloom opens pink, slowly turning to white and creating a two-tone effect. Good in pots and in walls, it will seed around when happy. June to August. **H × S** 15cm × 60cm. AGM

'Schneewittchen' Charming white, semi-double flowers become tinged with palest pink as they age. On a raised edge, it will create a waterfall of pure white over time. June to August. **H × S** 45cm × 60cm. AGM

ERODIUM (Heron's bill)

manescavii This plant resembles a hardy geranium and in many ways behaves like one. The open pink flowers are carried on straight stems that shoot like sparklers from a crown of deeply divided, mid-green leaves. The seedheads are spear-like. June to September. **H × S** 45cm × 45cm. AGM

Needs Well-drained soil in sun
Great for Front of the border
Bees & Butterflies Yes
For Cutting No
Care Trouble free

ERYNGIUM (Sea holly)

The flowers of these architectural plants bring an abstract quality to a border. Cone-shaped and surrounded by spiky collars, they are borne on stiff stems above a clump or rosette of evergreen leaves.

Needs Well-drained soil, including very dry and clay soils, in sun
Great for Front or middle of the border
Bees & Butterflies Yes
For Cutting Yes
Care Dislikes waterlogged soils; perfect for coastal and gravel gardens

Eryngium bourgatii

Eryngium variifolium

agavifolium Large, flat whorls of mid-green leaves with shark's teeth edging, send up strong, upright stems with a candelabra of small, oval, moss-green flowers. Evergreen and rather exotic. July to September. **H × S** 150cm × 60cm

alpinum An extremely beautiful plant with towering soft-green cones that turn steely- blue. These are encased within a lacy upturned ruff with short, spiky edges. The shiny leaves are bright green. July to August. **H × S** 102cm × 45cm

bourgatii Stiffly upright, the blue, well-branched stems are topped by small, mid-blue flowers with prickly, blue collars. The leaves are dark green. July to September. **H × S** 60cm × 45cm

planum A network of slender blue stems carries little, light-blue flowers above a rosette of spatula-shaped, deep-green leaves. Usually seed grown, so variable. July to August. **H × S** 90cm × 45cm

variifolium Small white flowers, arranged up stout, soft-maroon stems, turn blue with age. The spiky, green leaves display white marbling and form a flat rosette. July to August. **H × S** 45cm × 30cm

yuccifolium (Button eryngo) Tiny, round, and faintly prickly, the flowers open soft green and turn white. They bloom at the top of stiff, branched stems above a rosette of long, slightly spiky leaves. July to September. **H × S** 120cm × 90cm

× zabelii 'Big Blue' The strikingly shaped flowers with large, ink-blue, starry collars are attractive to bees. They are carried on well-branched stems above divided, mid-green leaves. July to August. **H × S** 60cm × 30cm. AGM

Eryngium planum

Eryngium yuccifolium

Eryngium × zabelii 'Big Blue'

Eupatorium dubium 'Little Joe'

Eupatorium maculatum 'Riesenschirm'

Eupatorium purpureum

Euphorbia amygdaloides 'Purpurea'

Euphorbia amygdaloides var. *robbiae*

EUPATORIUM (Joe Pye weed)

Initially unremarkable, by midsummer and right through to late autumn, this large plant evolves into a truly handsome upright clump. The stems are usually dark red with whorls of long, deep-green, pointed leaves carried right to the top. Broad, domed heads of little flowers pale in colour as they age and become fluffy. They make a wonderful larder for all insects.

Needs Well-drained soil that remains moist in sun or partial shade.
Great for Back of the border
Bees & Butterflies Yes
For Cutting Yes
Care Trouble free in heavy soils and those that don't dry out. Usually needs no staking

dubium **'Little Joe'** Most eupatoriums are large. This shorter variety has rosy-purple flowers on purple stems with deep-green, oval leaves. August to September.
H × S 105cm × 75cm

maculatum **'Riesenschirm'** A majestic plant. Large, domed, dusky-pink heads are carried on dark maroon stems. August to September. **H × S** 180cm × 90cm. AGM

purpureum Loosely domed heads of purple-pink flowers on upright red stems with whorls of pointed, mid-green leaves. August to September. **H × S** 180cm × 90cm

EUPHORBIA (Spurge)

Perfect for creating year-round structure, most euphorbias have evergreen leaves, which make whorls around the stiff stems, and grow into neat, leafy mounds. In spring these are topped with clusters or spires of small flowers that are almost hidden by large, colourful bracts.

Needs Well-drained soil in sun or partial shade; some varieties prefer shade
Great for Front or middle of the border
Bees & Butterflies No
For Cutting No
Care Wear gloves when handling – some people are allergic to the milky sap that seeps out of broken stems

amygdaloides **'Purpurea'** (Wood spurge) Broad, towering spikes of lime-green flowers are carried above a dense mound of evergreen, dark green leaves heavily tinged with maroon. Ideal for a semi-shady spot. April to June. **H × S** 60cm × 60cm

amygdaloides **var. robbiae** Whorls of leathery, dark green leaves produce short stems topped with tall spikes of yellow-green flowers. Great for a dry, shady spot, where it will spread slowly. April to June. **H × S** 60cm × 90cm. AGM

griffithii 'Fireglow' A upright plant that slowly creeps. Long, red- tinged, mid-green leaves are carried up red stems that are topped with flat clusters of red-orange flowers. In autumn the leaves turn fiery-red for a short time before they fall. May to July. **H × S** 90cm × 75cm

myrsinites The distinctive grey leaves of this evergreen remind me of dinosaur scales. They form whorls around long, prostrate stems that end in flat clusters of lime-green flowers. A short plant for well-drained soils, including poor and dry ones. April to June. **H × S** 15cm × 60cm. AGM

palustris (Marsh spurge) A spectacular, erect plant with tall stems of light green leaves topped with flat clusters of sulphur-yellow flowers. In autumn the whole plant turns red. May to July. **H × S** 90cm × 75cm. AGM

polychroma (*epithymoides*) The heads of bright yellow-green flowers are carried on upright stems. These spring from a central crown to form a neat mound. April to May. **H × S** 60cm × 45cm

schillingii Loose, flat heads of lime-green blooms are borne on thick, straight stems of long, grass-green leaves. Grows into an upright, well-behaved clump. July to September. **H × S** 100cm × 60cm. AGM

seguieriana **subsp.** **niciciana** A bushy plant with long slender stems of narrow, grey-green leaves and clusters of sulphur-yellow flowers that last for ages. Ideal for edging a border. July to October. **H × S** 30cm × 30cm

Euphorbia griffithii 'Fireglow'

Euphorbia myrsinites

Euphorbia palustris

Euphorbia polychroma

Euphorbia schillingii

Euphorbia seguieriana subsp. *niciciana*

Geranium 'Blue Cloud' (foreground) with *Astrantia* 'Roma' and *Salvia nemorosa* 'Caradonna'

GALIUM (Sweet woodruff)

odoratum In spring, the flowers of this charming perennial resemble clusters of tiny, white stars. Faintly scented, they are carried on slender stems ringed by narrow, bright green leaves. These create a short, lush, slowly spreading carpet – the perfect ground-cover for shady areas. April to May. **H × S** 30cm × 60cm

Needs Well-drained soil in partial shade
Great for Shade, especially among shrubs and trees
Bees & Butterflies No
For Cutting No
Care Trouble free

GERANIUM (Hardy geranium)

Perhaps the most versatile perennials, hardy geraniums blend effortlessly into a border and, with hundreds of varieties to choose from, there is a plant for every style of garden. The flowers are produced in great quantities and most are carried on long stems just above the lush, deeply divided leaves, which enhance the garden's green tapestry.

Needs Well-drained soil in sun to light shade
Great for Front and middle of the border; a few varieties are fine for the back
Bees & Butterflies Bees
For Cutting No
Care Trouble free. To keep soft-pink flowered varieties in check, dead-head before the seeds are scattered around. Shorter varieties are slower to establish. Cut spent top growth right back to soil level after flowering to encourage further flowers

'Ann Folkard' A low, spreading plant, the black-eyed, deep magenta flowers are carried on long, sprawling stems. The mid-green leaves are yellow when young. May to September. **H × S** 30cm × 75cm. AGM

'Anne Thomson' Although a spreader, this is a neat plant. The leaves are initially yellow-green but turn mid-green as the magenta flowers emerge. June to September. **H × S** 45cm × 90cm. AGM

'Azure Rush' A sport of *G.* 'Rozanne', the flat, soft-blue flowers with white eyes are saucer-shaped. They are carried above a carpet of mid-green, deeply divided leaves. June to October. **H × S** 30cm × 60cm

'Blue Cloud' Impressive for the misty waterfall of shallowly cupped, soft lilac-blue flowers on short, branching stems above deeply divided leaves. May to August. **H × S** 60cm × 75cm. AGM

Galium odoratum

Geranium 'Ann Folkard'

Geranium 'Azure Rush'

Geranium 'Anne Thomson'

Geranium 'Brookside'

Geranium clarkei 'Kashmir White'

Geranium 'Dilys'

Geranium 'Dreamland'

Geranium 'Dragon Heart'

'Brookside' Violet-blue flowers, each with a tiny, white centre, smother a broad clump of divided, mid-green leaves over a long period. June to September. **H × S** 45cm × 60cm. AGM

clarkei **'Kashmir White'** White geraniums are few. This one has sprays of large, mauve-veined flowers and deeply divided leaves. May to June. **H × S** 45cm × 60cm

'Dilys' A short, sprawling plant with pretty mid-green leaves. Scattered above the foliage are saucer-shaped, lilac-pink flowers that bloom for months. June to October. **H × S** 23cm × 60cm. AGM

'Dragon Heart' Magenta, black-centred flowers, larger than most, are borne on slender stems with deeply cut leaves. A plant that sprawls and weaves its way around others. June to September. **H × S** 45cm × 60cm

'Dreamland' A pretty spreading plant with smooth, soft-pink flowers and soft-green leaves that are not dissimilar to those of *G.* 'Mavis Simpson. May to August. **H × S** 40cm × 60cm

'Elke' A neat carpeting plant, perfect for the front of a border, covered with small, deep-pink flowers. Their paler edges and white centres make them stand out. May to August. **H × S** 23cm × 30cm

himalayense **'Derrick Cook'** A great plant for edging a border. It spreads to form a tumbling mound of mid-green leaves covered with masses of large, white, maroon-veined flowers. June to August. **H × S** 45cm × 60cm

himalayense **'Gravetye'** At one time a very popular blue variety, this has largely been superseded by longer-flowering plants. Still worth growing for its spreading foliage that takes on beautiful red tones in autumn. June to August. **H × S** 45cm × 60cm

'Johnson's Blue' A classic variety with saucer-shaped, indigo-blue flowers borne above a compact mound of delicate-looking, deeply divided, dark green leaves. May to August. **H × S** 60cm × 60cm

'J. S. Matu Vu' A small, very compact form of *Geranium psilostemon* with large, black-eyed, carmine-pink flowers covering deeply divided, mid-green leaves. May to September. **H × S** 35cm × 35cm

macrorrhizum An excellent hardy geranium for ground-cover in shady, dry spots. The clusters of flat, cerise-pink flowers on longish stems rise above a thick carpet of leaves. These are round, hairy, unusually scented, and semi-evergreen. May to June. **H × S** 45cm × 60cm

Geranium 'Elke'

Geranium himalayense 'Derrick Cook'

Geranium himalayense 'Gravetye'

Geranium 'Johnson's Blue'

Geraranium 'J. S. Matu Vu'

Geranium macrorrhizum

Geranium macrorrhizum
'Ingwersen's Variety'

Geranium macrorrhizum 'White-Ness'

Geranium maculatum 'Espresso'

Gerararanium × magnificum

Geranium 'Mavis Simpson'

Geranium 'Nimbus'

macrorrhizum **'Ingwersen's Variety'** Similar to the species, but with flowers of a softer lilac-pink. May to June. **H × S** 45cm × 60cm. AGM

macrorrhizum **'White-Ness'** A dwarf plant that spreads over time to form a ground-covering mat. The clusters of pure white flowers are carried just above small, round, bright-green leaves. May to June. **H × S** 30cm × 45cm. AGM

maculatum **'Espresso'** The open, flat, lilac-pink flowers are carried above a mound of deeply divided, coffee-coloured leaves. This neat little plant is best grown in a shady place where the leaves won't get scorched. May to June. **H × S** 45cm × 45cm

× *magnificum* Large, flat, rich-blue flowers with purple veins are carried above a vigorous mound of mid-green leaves. For a short time in autumn these turn pure red. June to August. **H × S** 60cm × 60cm. AGM

'Mavis Simpson' A prostrate carpet of small, round, grey-green leaves is covered with neat, open, silvery-pink flowers. Best grown in a very well-drained soil. June to September. **H × S** 23cm × 45cm. AGM

'Nimbus' Incredibly free flowering, this variety sends out sprays of mid-sized, lilac-blue flowers, each with a tiny white centre. They are carried above a pretty mound of finely divided, mid-green leaves. June to September. **H × S** 45cm × 45cm. AGM

nodosum The little, lilac-pink, trumpet-shaped flowers are scattered across a dense hummock of divided, glossy foliage. Often grown from seed, the flowers can vary from soft pink to deep lilac. Good for shady areas, even where the soil is fairly dry. June to August. **H × S** 30cm × 60cm

nodosum **'Silverwood'** As the name suggests, the flowers of this variety are pure white and combine beautifully with the hummock of divided, glossy foliage. Not widely available but well worth seeking out. June to August. **H × S** 30cm × 60cm

'Orion' A very free-flowering variety that forms a loose, spreading plant. The large, glowing, deep-blue flowers with white centres are carried well above the mound of deeply divided, mid-green leaves. June to September. **H × S** 75cm × 60cm. AGM

'Patricia' Abundant sprays of open, cerise-pink flowers rise above a spreading mound of mid-green leaves. The foliage is deeply cut into three sections. June to September. **H × S** 75cm × 90cm. AGM

Geranium nodosum

Geranium nodosum 'Silverwood'

Geranium 'Orion'

Geranium 'Patricia'

Geranium phaeum 'Album'

Geranium phaeum 'Lily Lovell'

phaeum **'Album'** Excellent for brightening up shady areas, this variety bears almost translucent white flowers in loose sprays. The upright stems have mid-green leaves. May to June. **H × S** 75cm × 45cm

phaeum **'Lily Lovell'** The rich-purple flowers are borne in loose clusters above a dense clump of mid-green leaves. May to June. **H × S** 75cm × 45cm

phaeum **'Raven'** Named for its flat, darkest-purple flowers borne on tall stems above a mound of divided, bright-green leaves. May to June. **H × S** 75cm × 45cm

phaeum **var.** *phaeum* **'Samobor'** The flowers are dark burgundy, like those of *G. phaeum*, but the mid-green leaves are decorated with a broad ring of maroon. May to June. **H × S** 90cm × 60cm

Geranium phaeum 'Raven'

Geranium phaeum var. *phaeum* 'Samobor'

Geranium 'Philippe Vapelle'

Geranium pratense 'Marshmallow'

Geranium 'Prelude' with *Stachys byzantina* 'Big Ears'

Geranium psilostemon

Geranium psilostemon 'Catherine Deneuve'

Geranium renardii

Geranium × *riversleaianum* 'Russell Prichard'

'Philippe Vapelle' Not the longest-flowering variety but when the large, pale-violet flowers fade, the tight mound of velvety, grey-green leaves remains very attractive. June to July. **H × S** 30cm × 30cm

pratense **'Marshmallow'** The large, pale-pink, saucer-like flowers are carried in open sprays on pink-red stems with pink-red leaves. May to June. **H × S** 75cm × 60cm

'Prelude' A froth of pretty little, lilac flowers hides a dome of divided, mid-green leaves. May to July. **H × S** 50cm × 60cm

psilostemon The tallest hardy geranium with masses of black-eyed, vivid magenta flowers. These are held in sprays on slender stems well above a mound of deeply divided, mid-green leaves. Best grown towards the back of the border. June to August. **H × S** 105cm × 90cm. AGM

psilostemon **'Catherine Deneuve'** The colouring of one of its parents – *Geranium psilostemon* – is apparent in the rich cerise-pink of the flowers but they are small and look like stars. The blooms are scattered above a lush, low mound of mid-green leaves. May to July. **H × S** 105cm × 90cm

renardii A lovely plant with a soft mound of round, notched, velvety, sage-green leaves. Clusters of open, purple-veined, white flowers are held just above the foliage. May to June. **H × S** 30cm × 30cm. AGM

× *riversleaianum* **'Russell Prichard'** This prostrate, slowly spreading plant has deep cerise-pink flowers and silver-grey leaves. More reliable grown in very free-draining soil. June to July. **H × S** 23cm × 45cm. AGM

'Rozanne' A much applauded, free-flowering plant with large, blue, white-centred flowers carried for many months just above a spreading clump of deeply divided leaves. May to September. **H × S** 60cm × 75cm. AGM

sanguineum **'Album'** (Bloody cranesbill) Ideal for the front of the border where it can be appreciated, the white flowers cover a low dome of small, mid-green leaves. June to July. **H × S** 23cm × 60cm. AGM

sanguineum **'Apfelblute'** A tight mound of divided, mid-green leaves is covered with large, saucer-shaped, soft-pink flowers. June to September. **H × S** 23cm × 30cm

sanguineum **'Max Frei'** A carpeting plant with divided, mid-green leaves. The large flowers are a vivid shade of magenta. June to July. **H × S** 23cm × 45cm

'Sirak' Blooming over a long period, the clusters of large, lilac flowers rise above a neat mound of soft grey-green leaves. June to August. **H × S** 45cm × 45cm

Geranium 'Rozanne' with *Persicaria amplexicaulis* 'Jo and Guido's Form'

Geranium sanguineum 'Max Frei'

Geranium sanguineum 'Album'

Geranium sanguineum 'Apfelblute'

Geranium 'Sirak'

Geranium sylvaticum 'Album'

Geranium sylvaticum 'Mayflower'

Geranium sylvaticum f. roseum 'Baker's Pink'

Geranium versicolor

sylvaticum 'Album' (Wood cranesbill) Bright-white flowers are carried in sprays on tall, branched stems above deeply divided, bright-green leaves. Great for shadier spots. May to June. **H × S** 75cm × 45cm. AGM

sylvaticum 'Mayflower' Sprays of glowing, violet-blue flowers on upright, branched stems sit above divided, bright green leaves. May to June. **H × S** 75cm × 45cm. AGM

sylvaticum f. roseum 'Baker's Pink' A delightful plant with open sprays of shiny, pale-pink flowers and light green leaves. May to June. **H × S** 78m × 45cm

versicolor The small, trumpet-shaped, soft-pink flowers are prettily netted with maroon veins. These appear just above a thick mound of mid-green leaves. Will tolerate drier conditions than some hardy geraniums. May to July. **H × S** 45cm × 60cm

wallichianum 'Crystal Lake' An impressive sprawling, free-flowering plant. Medium-sized, soft lilac-blue flowers with dark purple veins are carried in ones and twos above deeply divided, mid-green leaves. June to September. **H × S** 45cm × 60cm

wallichianum 'Rosetta' Large, lilac-pink flowers are carried above the deeply divided mid-green leaves. The stems are long and wandering, making this plant perfect for the front of a border. Allow it to tumble over walls or scramble through other perennials. June to September. **H × S** 30cm × 75cm

wlassovianum The last of the geraniums to bloom. Small, open, dark violet flowers on arching stems emerge from a mound of dark green leaves that turn briefly red in autumn. July to September. **H × S** 60cm × 75cm

Geranium wallichianum 'Crystal Lake'

Geranium wallichianum 'Rosetta'

Geranium wlassovianum

Geum 'Alabama Slammer' (Cocktail Series)

Geum 'Bell Bank'

Geum 'Borisii'

Geum 'Cosmopolitan' (Cocktail Series)

Geum 'Flames of Passion'

GEUM (Avens)

This group of eye-catching plants includes spring-flowering varieties and others that bloom from early summer right through to mid-autumn. The flowers are often brightly coloured and single or semi-double; some open flat, while others are bell shaped. They are carried on branched stems above a carpet or mound of hairy leaves.

Needs Well-drained soil that remains moist in sun or partial shade
Great for Front of a border, but can be grown in containers
Bees & Butterflies Bees
For Cutting Yes, but only the tall varieties
Care If the short varieties dry out they are easily revived with water

'Alabama Slammer' (Cocktail Series) One of the 'Cocktail Series' of geums with semi-double, bright yellow, rosette-shaped flowers. The edges are picked out in soft orange. April to June. **H × S** 30cm × 45cm

'Bell Bank' Slender stems of nodding, semi-double, reddish-pink flowers bloom for many weeks above a dense, spreading clump of mid-green leaves. May to July. **H × S** 45cm × 45cm

'Borisii' The upward-facing, single, deep-orange flowers are held individually above a low, neat mound of mid-green leaves. The first flush is followed by occasional blooms through until autumn. May to September. **H × S** 30cm × 30cm

'Cosmopolitan' (Cocktail Series) Another geum from the 'Cocktail' series originating from Illinois, USA. This produces great quantities of semi-double flowers that are a blend of soft peach and palest yellow with darker edges. The yellow fades as the flowers age. May to July. **H × S** 45cm × 45cm

'Flames of Passion' Handsome and free-flowering, the semi-double flowers of this variety open red and fade with age to tones of orange. The blooms dangle from tall stems above a dense mound of leaves. May to July. **H × S** 45cm × 45cm

Geum 'Lady Stratheden'

Geum 'Lemon Drops'

Geum 'Mai Tai' (Cocktail Series)

Geum 'Mrs J. Bradshaw'

Geum 'Prinses Juliana' (front) with *G.* 'Georgenberg' (centre left) and *G.* 'Lisanne' (back)

Geum 'Totally Tangerine'

'Georgenberg' A carpeting plant with a slowly spreading mound of mid-green leaves. The short stems of upward-facing, single flowers are a bright yet deep yellow. May to July. **H × S** 30cm × 30cm

'Lady Stratheden' Well-known and popular, this blooms for many weeks and the cut flowers last well in water. Tall stems of semi-double, rich-yellow flowers are held high above a clump of mid-green leaves. Comes true when raised from seed. May to September. **H × S** 60cm × 50cm. AGM

'Lemon Drops' A delightful plant with many small, bell-shaped, lemon flowers on branched bronzed stems just above a broad, spreading mound of leaves. May to June. **H × S** 30cm × 45cm

'Lisanne' This free-flowering plant produces lots of cheerful lemon, open flowers. May to July. **H × S** 30cm × 45cm

'Mai Tai' (Cocktail Series) The large, frilly, semi-double, apricot-peach flowers sit above a wide mound of mid-green leaves, softening in colour as they age. May to July. **H × S** 45cm × 45cm

'Mrs J. Bradshaw' The large, semi-double, scarlet flowers are carried on tall, upright, branched stems above a clump of mid-green leaves. Reliably raised from seed. May to September. **H × S** 60cm × 30cm. AGM

'Prinses Juliana' A very free-flowering plant with lots of tall stems carrying semi-double, orange flowers above a clump of upright, mid-green leaves. May to August. **H × S** 50cm x 60cm

'Totally Tangerine' Tall, well-branched stems of soft-orange flowers, faintly tinged red, are carried on upright stems above a dense clump of mid-green leaves. Said to be the most free-flowering *Geum*, I find it no more floriferous than *G*. 'Prinses Juliana'. May to September. **H × S** 60cm × 60cm

GILLENIA (Bowman's root)

trifoliata An all-round excellent perennial that grows into a glorious, upright, bushy plant with frothy sprays of small, fluttering, white flowers borne on slender, branched, red stems. The oval, pointed, mid-green leaves turn a beautiful glowing orange in autumn. June to August. **H × S** 90cm × 75cm. AGM

Needs Well-drained soil in sun to partial shade
Great for Middle of a border
Bees & Butterflies Bees
For Cutting No
Care Trouble free and long-lived

Gillenia trifoliata

GYPSOPHILA (Baby's breath)

paniculata **'Bristol Fairy'** A flower arranger's dream, this airy plant features a light mound of slim, grey foliage at the base and open sprays of tiny, double, white flowers. These are scattered over a network of slender, much-divided stems and form misty clouds. Planted in the border, it is very useful for concealing the faded blooms of spring-flowering plants. June to July **H × S** 105cm × 90cm

Needs Well-drained soil in sun
Great for Middle and front of a border
Bees & Butterflies No
For Cutting Yes
Care Slow to establish, otherwise easy and long-lived.

Gypsophila paniculata 'Bristol Fairy'

Hakonechloa macra 'Aureola'

Helenium 'Goldrausch'

Helenium 'Mardi Gras'

Helenium 'Moerheim Beauty'

Helenium 'Pipsqueak'

Helenium 'Rubinzwerg'

HAKONECHLOA

macra **'Aureola'** A lovely, fluffy, tufted grass with yellow-lined, soft-green leaves. Slender stems of tiny, soft-brown flowers are almost hidden among the foliage. In autumn the leaves turn red. August to September. **H × S** 45cm × 45cm. AGM

Needs Very well-drained soil that remains moist in sun or partial shade
Great for Containers or edging
Bees & Butterflies No
For Cutting No
Care Cut back in spring

HELENIUM (Sneezeweed)

Nothing can compare to a swathe of heleniums for late-summer colour. The daisy flowers have frilly petals that often change from one bright shade to another with age. The centres, too, begin as a flat disc then grow into a pouffe-like dome, ringed by yellow stamens. The flowers are held on rigid, branched stems above a slowly expanding clump of long, mid-green leaves that rarely needs extra support.

Needs Well-drained soil that remains moist in sun
Great for Back of the border
Bees & Butterflies Yes
For Cutting Yes
Care Be restrained when dividing clumps. Otherwise trouble free

'Goldrausch' The bright-yellow flowers are flecked and flushed with red-brown and carried in clusters on top of sturdy stems. July to September. **H × S** 120cm × 75cm

'Mardi Gras' The large yellow daisies, which turn orange as they age, are carried on stiff stems with mid-green leaves. Forms a neat, well-behaved mound. July to September. **H × S** 75cm × 60cm

'Moerheim Beauty' A deservedly popular plant with warm, reddish-brown flowers fading to burnt orange. July to September. **H × S** 90cm × 75cm. AGM

'Pipsqueak' The yellow flowers on this short plant have petals that frill outwards, like the edges of a skirt. July to September. **H × S** 60cm × 45cm

'Rubinzwerg' A variety with brick-red flowers that turn orange over time. July to September. **H × S** 75cm × 60cm. AGM

'Sahin's Early Flowerer' This has yellow flowers flecked with red, that turn red. July to September. **H × S** 90cm × 75cm. AGM

'Waltraut' From a distance the yellow flowers, which deepen to soft red, appear bronze. July to September. **H × S** 90cm × 75cm. AGM

Helenium 'Sahin's Early Flowerer'

Helenium 'Waltraut'

Helenium 'Wyndley'

'Wyndley' The relaxed, yellow flowers are marked with the occasional fleck of red. July to September. **H × S** 90cm × 75cm

HELIANTHUS (Perennial sunflower)

'Lemon Queen' This big, vigorous plant carries bright-lemon daisies on stiff, upright stems with dark green leaves. In time, it will form an imposing upright clump. August to September. **H × S** 180cm × 105cm. AGM

Needs Well-drained soil in sun
Great for Very back of the border
Bees & Butterflies Yes
For Cutting No
Care Trouble free and, despite being tall, it needs no staking

Helianthus 'Lemon Queen'

Helleborus argutifolius

Helleborus foetidus

Helleborus × hybridus

Helleborus × hybridus dark form

Helleborus niger

HELLEBORUS

Invaluable for late-winter and early-spring colour and form, hellebores add a touch of classic beauty to the barrenness of a winter garden. Elegant, simply shaped flowers emerge from clumps of handsome, evergreen leaves. Perfect for shadier spots and some adapt well to containers.

Needs Well-drained soil that remains moist in full or partial shade
Great for A shady or woodland garden
Bees & Butterflies No
For Cutting Yes
Care All varieties are slow to establish but are generally disease-free, although *H. niger* and × *hybridus* sometimes suffer from leaf spot. Removing the old leaves in early spring not only tidies up a plant, it helps to reduce the risk of blotches

argutifolius Clusters of large, cupped, soft-green flowers are carried on thick stems above a dome of evergreen, leathery, deep-green leaves, serrated along the edges. March to April. **H × S** 75cm × 60cm. AGM

foetidus (Stinking hellebore) Our native hellebore (rarely seen growing wild) has big sprays of small, ball-shaped, soft-green buds carried on thick, upright stems. These open into cupped flowers above finger-like, deep-green leaves, that smell like roast beef when bruised. February to April. **H × S** 80cm × 60cm. AGM

× *hybridus* (Lenten rose) A variable, seed-raised plant. The large, open flowers in shades through maroon to white, many of them freckled inside, emerge just above divided, dark green leaves. There are also named varieties, including doubles and yellow forms, but these can be tricky to grow. February to March. **H × S** 60cm × 60cm

× *hybridus* double forms (Lenten rose) This group of doubles seems to be increasing year on year. Many have lovely names like 'Double Ellen'. To select the best, choose a variety when you see it in flower. February to March. **H × S** 60cm × 60cm

niger (Christmas rose) Once the most popular hellebore, the open, pure-white flowers are carried on short stems. The leaves, which form an open clump, are not reliably evergreen. February to March. **H × S** 45cm × 45cm

HEMEROCALLIS (Daylily)

Reliable, easy to grow and difficult to kill, these tough plants are ideal for those who want a perennial they can forget about. The flowers of daylilies are produced in great abundance, each stem loaded with flower buds that open one a day over many weeks. The flowers are trumpet shaped or flat and range in size from 5cm to 15cm in diameter. They are carried on strong stems that emerge from a thick clump of long, slender, mid-green leaves. From over 3,000 listed by the Royal Horticultural Society, I have tried to select plants that are easily obtained and represent the enormous variety on offer.

Needs Any soil, except boggy, in sun, partial shade, or shade
Great for All areas of the garden and border
Bees & Butterflies No
For Cutting No
Care In some parts of the UK, the grubs of a tiny fly that is attracted to daylilies, the gall midge, can hatch inside the flower buds. These subsequently become deformed and fail to open. We had one instance at the nursery so I swiftly removed the buds and burnt them. The later flowers opened successfully without any deformities.

'Barbara Mitchell' A smooth, soft cream-pink flower with gently crimped edges to the petals, which are brushed with apricot. July to August. **H × S** 45cm × 45cm

'Black Arrowhead' The long, dusky-red petals of the starry flowers are marked with darker red. These are carried a few at a time on tall, slender stems high above mid-green leaves. July to August. **H × S** 90cm × 75cm

'Burning Daylight' The bright, rich-yellow flowers are scented and so lightly brushed with red that they can, in certain lights, appear orange. July to August. **H × S** 75cm × 75cm. AGM

'Catherine Woodbery' One of the first pink varieties I grew – at that time very popular for its large, open flowers. Three of the petals are lilac pink, three are pale pink. July to August. **H × S** 75cm × 75cm

'Cherry Cheeks' Large, red-pink flowers with wide petals open into a broad trumpet shape and reveal an orange centre. The flowers are carried on stiffly upright stems. July to August. **H × S** 60cm × 60cm. AGM

'Cherry Eyed Pumpkin' The wide, rich-orange flowers, which open in clusters, have a distinctive ring of pale maroon around the centre and little ruffles along the petal edges. July to August. **H × S** 75cm × 60cm. AGM

Hemerocallis 'Barbara Mitchell'

Hemerocallis 'Black Arrowhead'

Hemerocallis 'Burning Daylight'

Hemerocallis 'Catherine Woodbery'

Hemerocallis 'Cherry Cheeks'

Hemerocallis 'Cherry Eyed Pumpkin'

Hemerocallis 'Crimson Pirate'

Hemerocallis 'Custard Candy'

Hemerocallis 'Ed Murray' with *Lysimachia punctata* 'Alexander'

Hemerocallis 'El Desperado'

Hemerocallis 'Frank Smith'

Hemerocallis 'Frosted Vintage Ruffles'

'Crimson Pirate' The small, starry, trumpet-shaped, bright-red flowers have yellow centres. They are produced in succession on slender stems high above the leaves. July to August. **H × S** 75cm × 75cm

'Custard Candy' An extremely floriferous plant. The small, round, soft-yellow flowers have a maroon circle round the throat. They cover a neatly domed clump of leaves. July to August. **H × S** 60cm × 60cm. AGM

'Ed Murray' Good enough to eat, its velvety flowers are darkest red and not over-large. They are carried in clusters of two or three on slender stems high above the leaves. July to August. **H × S** 75cm × 75cm

'El Desperado' A charming plant that produces clusters of the large, soft-yellow flowers just above the leaves. Each flower has deep-maroon flares, a lime-green centre, and lightly laced edges to the petals. July to August. **H × S** 70cm × 70cm

'Frank Smith' A distinctive, bright-orange flower that opens flat to reveal a darker red that extends up over the petals. July to August. **H × S** 60cm × 60cm

'Frosted Vintage Ruffles' Fragrant and soft pink, the broad flowers are flushed with lime-yellow and the petals have frilly edges. July to August. **H × S** 60cm × 60cm

fulva **'Flore Pleno'** This old variety has large, trumpet-shaped, deep-orange flowers that feature an inner set of petals, making this a double form. Each of the petals is brushed with red. June to August. **H × S** 105cm × 75cm

'Gentle Shepherd' One of the first large, near-white flowers that I grew, although in reality the colour is nearer cream than white. The crêpe petals surround a lime-green throat. July to August. **H × S** 75cm × 75cm

'Grape Velvet' A small-flowered plant with muted-purple, trumpet-shaped blooms with paler mid-ribs and lime-green centres. The velvety-textured flowers sit just above the leaves. July to August. **H × S** 75cm × 75cm

'James Marsh' A handsome plant with large, trumpet-shaped, true-red flowers carried just above a clump of deep-green leaves. July to August. **H × S** 70cm × 60cm

'Joan Senior' The creamy, open blooms fade to almost white with time. The flowers are held just above the leaves. July to August. **H × S** 65cm × 60cm

'Lemon Bells' For the best scent, choose the yellow varieties of daylily. This one produces lots of heavily lemon-scented, small, bright-yellow, trumpet-shaped flowers on slender stems. June to August. **H × S** 75cm × 75cm

Hemerocallis fulva 'Flore Pleno'

Hemerocallis 'Gentle Shepherd'

Hemerocallis 'Grape Velvet'

Hemerocallis 'James Marsh'

Hemerocallis 'Joan Senior'

Hemerocallis 'Lemon Bells'

Hemerocallis 'Mary Todd'

Hemerocallis 'Mauna Loa'

'Mary Todd' Broad, rich-yellow flowers with slightly frilled edges to the petals open just above a short clump of mid-green leaves. July to August. **H × S** 60cm × 60cm

'Mauna Loa' Carried on strong stems, the vibrant-orange flowers seem to glow in the border. They rise from a broad clump of mid-green leaves. July to August. **H × S** 60cm × 60cm

'Night Embers' The round, dark red flowers have a further swirl of petals in the centre. The edges are very gently ruffled and outlined in yellow. July to August. **H × S** 70cm × 60cm

'Pardon Me' One of the best of the small-flowered, rich reds. Blooms are produced one at a time over weeks on upright, slender stems above a short clump of leaves. July to August. **H × S** 45cm × 45cm

'Pink Damask' This classic variety bears smooth, trumpet-shaped, rich salmon-pink flowers. These are produced in great abundance even in a shady spot. July to August. **H × S** 80cm × 75cm. AGM

'Strawberry Candy' One of the free-flowering 'Candy' series. Its neat, rounded, apricot flowers with frilled edges are marked with a red inner ring. They are carried just above a broad clump of leaves. July to August. **H × S** 60cm × 60cm. AGM

'Summer Wine' A compact plant with lots of mid-sized, neat, trumpet-shaped flowers borne above the leaves. The soft pink-purple hue literally glows. July to August. **H × S** 60cm × 60cm

Hemerocallis 'Night Embers'

Hemerocallis 'Pardon Me'

Hemerocallis 'Pink Damask'

Hemerocallis 'Strawberry Candy'

Hemerocallis 'Summer Wine'

HESPERANTHA

***coccinea* 'Major'** Once listed as *Schizostylis*, this needs a warm spot where its large, silky, crimson flowers inject a welcome burst of colour. They sit at the top of graceful stems, above a clump of grassy, mid-green leaves that are just about evergreen. October to November. **H × S** 75cm × 45cm. AGM

Needs Soil that retains moisture in sun
Great for Front of border
Bees & Butterflies Yes
For Cutting Yes
Care Given a sunny, sheltered position in soil that does not dry out, the clump will slowly get bigger and better

HEUCHERA (Coralbells)

There are hundreds of heucheras, some with evergreen foliage in greens, reds, and even orange. Some are so similar it is difficult to tell them apart, others are not very hardy, and some are hard to combine with other perennials. All produce spikes of tiny, funnel-shaped flowers on very slender stems above a dense mound of vine-shaped leaves.

Needs Well-drained soil in sun or partial shade
Great for Front of the border and pots
Bees & Butterflies No
For Cutting Yes
Care May be attacked by vine weevil. Some varieties dislike wet soils

'Caramel' Copper leaves tinted with pink and yellow reveal red undersides. They form a flat mound that is attractive throughout the growing season. Tiny creamy-white flowers are borne on fine, upright stems. Great for containers. July to August. **H × S** 30cm × 40cm

'Obsidian' A really dark plant sending out smooth, almost black leaves that form a neat dome. Wispy spikes of tiny, cream flowers are carried on slender stems. July to September. **H × S** 60cm × 30cm

'Strawberry Swirl' Flowery in comparison with other varieties, sending up frothy stems of delicate-pink blooms. These sit above a loose mound of jagged, rich-green leaves. June to August. **H × S** 60cm × 30cm

***villosa* 'Palace Purple'** From loose mounds of large, mahogany-red leaves with bronze tints, airy spikes of white flowers emerge. July to August. **H × S** 60cm × 45cm

Hesperantha coccinea 'Major'

Heuchera 'Caramel'

Heuchera 'Obsidian'

Heuchera 'Strawberry Swirl'
with *Geranium* 'Elke'

Heuchera villosa 'Palace Purple'

Hosta 'Barbara Ann'

Hosta 'Halcyon' (Tardiana Group)

Hosta 'Krossa Regal'

Hosta 'Honeybells' with
Persicaria amplexicaulis 'Taurus'

Hosta 'Patriot'

HOSTA

The main reason to grow these striking plants is for the big handsome leaves, although the flowers are also ornamental and are often scented. They are a must if you garden in shady, damp spots. Sadly, they seem to be one of the go-to plants for slugs, but there are steps you can take.

Needs Best in soil that remains moist, but will grow in any soil, except very dry
Great for Shady borders and containers
Bees & Butterflies bees
For Cutting Yes
Care If your garden is regularly visited by slugs and snails, grow hostas in pots and stand them on slabs or gravel. Also choose varieties with thicker leaves, which tend to be more resistant to slugs

'Barbara Ann' Large, grey-green leaves are broadly edged with white and deeply veined and puckered. They form a neat clump that produces white flowers. July to August. **H × S** 90cm × 80cm. AGM

'Halcyon' (Tardiana Group) Rising from a compact mound of heart-shaped, blue-grey leaves, the short stems are packed with big, trumpet-shaped, lilac flowers. July to August. **H × S** 45cm × 60cm. AGM

'Honeybells' This classic hosta produces a dense mound of long, soft-green, deeply ridged leaves and stems of scented, soft-lilac bells. July to August. **H × S** 90cm × 80cm

'Krossa Regal' This elegantly shaped plant has deeply veined, grey-green leaves that arch upwards then splay out. Lilac, bell-shaped flowers are carried on long stems. July to August. **H × S** 120cm × 60cm. AGM

'Patriot' This forms a low clump of eye-catching, oval, grass-green leaves, broadly edged with white. The bell-like flowers are a light lavender shade. July to August. **H × S** 75cm × 75cm. AGM

siebold iana var. *elegans* A sizeable plant when mature with round, deeply veined and puckered, blue-green leaves. The thick spikes of lilac flowers are outward facing. July to August. **H × S** 90cm × 80cm. AGM

'Sum and Substance' Magnificent in a pot as well as the border, this hosta bears very large, deeply ridged, yellow leaves and lilac flowers. July to August. **H × S** 105cm × 90cm. AGM

Hosta sieboldiana var. elegans

Hosta 'Sum and Substance'

Inula magnifica

INULA (Fleabane)

A small group of bright yellow, daisy-flowered plants with fine rays surrounding the centre. The leaves are big and hairy.

Needs Well-drained soil that does not dry out, including clay soils
Great for Front and back of the border
Bees & Butterflies Yes
For Cutting Yes
Care Trouble free but can spread rapidly

hookeri Ideal for cool moist soils. The flowers are carried proudly above a broad, mounding clump of leaves. July to August. **H × S** 75cm × 70cm

magnifica A majestic plant with large, golden flowers on tall, leafy stems that often need no staking to stay upright. July to August. **H × S** 200cm × 90cm

Inula hookeri

Iris

Irises have the most colourful and flamboyant flowers of all perennials. Ranging from white to almost black, every possible tone is available except red – a colour that does not exist in the iris family. The flowers are three dimensional in structure with large, thick petals that are smooth or outrageously ruffled, and when planted in the garden, they always inject that 'wow' factor. Given the right conditions, they are easy to grow and there is a variety for every possible garden site and situation. And that's not all: with just a few plants, you can have irises in flower every month of the year. The iris world is a large one with more than 200 species found throughout the Northern Hemisphere. The plants are classified according to how they grow below ground (rhizomes or bulbs), then, for gardening purposes, into two further groups – bearded or beardless. Beardless irises are the most numerous in terms of species, with varieties for every situation in the garden, but there is a much greater choice of flower colour and height when it comes to Bearded irises.

THE FLOWERS

The flowers of all irises are proportionally large when compared to the rest of the plant. They have six petals: three upper ones known as standards, and three lower petals called the falls. Bearded irises have what looks like a hairy caterpillar crawling out of the throat of the falls, and they take their name from this distinctive feature. The beards are replaced by a yellow flash, called a signal, on the flowers of beardless irises. These colourful devices – beards and signals – attract pollinating insects.

THE LEAVES

All irises produce long, pointed leaves. Those of bearded irises are sword-like and matt grey-green in colour. The leaves of beardless types are often shiny and mid- or soft green. In some, such as Pacific Coast irises, the leaves arch over, while Siberian iris leaves are ramrod straight and almost grass-like. All produce handsome clumps and are useful – I would even say essential – for complementing perennials with bigger, broader leaves.

THE ROOTS

Irises are tough, tolerant plants because they grow from either bulbs or rhizomes. These storage systems help the plant to survive in extreme conditions, including very dry and waterlogged soil.

The irises in this book all grow from rhizomes (*see* right). Found at the base of the leaves and flower stems, they are generally long and ridged. The rhizomes, from which the roots grow, are an underground extension of the flower stems.

WHERE TO GROW

Bearded irises require a very well-drained soil that is not acid, in a sunny situation. The beardless irises – a group that contains the most species – will grow in soils ranging from dry to wet, and situations that are either sunny or shady.

A border of bearded irises, June

The beard on a bearded iris

The signal on a beardless iris

The rhizome of a bearded iris

IRIS TERMS USED

FALLS The three lower petals

STANDARDS Three upper petals

BEARDS A 'caterpillar' of hairs on the falls of bearded irises

SIGNAL The blaze of yellow on the falls of beardless irises

REMONTANT Flowering twice; first in late spring or early summer, and again from late summer onwards

PLANTING TIME

Traditionally, irises are planted six weeks after flowering time, from July onwards. We don't start moving irises on the nursery until late August, after the hottest and driest days of the summer have passed. By then the rhizomes are fully matured and the ground, although it might be damper, is still warm. It is not wise to plant between late October and March because the dormant rhizome will sit in cold, wet soil and may rot. Irises can be planted in spring, but they are unlikely to flower the same summer.

MAINTAINING

As for maintenance, beardless irises are the easiest to grow because they need very little attention. Bearded irises should be divided every three years or so to maintain vigour and keep the clump flowering.

Irises do not need fertilising, although if you really feel this is necessary a granular fertiliser that is very low in nitrogen can be applied sparingly in spring or autumn.

DIVIDING BEARDED IRISES

Irises that grow from rhizomes multiply by simply sending out new rhizomes. These spread outwards as they go, creating a fan shape, while leaving a gap in the middle. Eventually there are so many old rhizomes the plant will stop flowering.

To divide an old clump, dig it up and shake off the soil. Snap off any rhizome with a green top. Discard the rhizome from which the new ones are sprouting; it won't flower again. Trim the roots of each remaining rhizome to make it easier to plant, and cut the leaves down to approximately the length of your hand. This will prevent the rhizome being loosened in windy weather. It doesn't matter whether the top of the leaves is cut straight or at an angle.

Irises add drama to a border but deciding where to position them in the border can be tricky. If bearded irises are planted near to plants that bush out as the season progresses, the foliage may cover the rhizomes and the iris may fail to flower or even grow. I favour placing them either along the border – they are ideal for edging paths – or if you want to grow them amongst other plants, make sure their neighbours are well-behaved. Neat mounding plants make perfect companions.

Irises without beards tolerate a wider range of growing conditions than bearded types. They are also better adapted to growing in the border because their rhizomes are smaller and generally sit lower in the ground. Siberian irises are perhaps the best type to combine with other border plants, and although the blooms are smaller than those of bearded irises, there are many of them. The finely shaped, linear leaves blend well with large-leaved perennials.

I have found the following perennials work well with bearded irises:

Achillea (small ones)	Penstemon
Aquilegia	Physostegia
Centaurea	Pulmonaria
Digitalis	Salvia
Geranium (compact varieties)	Sedum
	Stachys officinalis
Geum (upright ones)	Verbascum
Heuchera	Verbena
Papaver	

Iris 'Change of Pace' with Heuchera 'Obsidian'

Iris 'Bumblebee Deelite'
with Geum 'Prinses Juliana'

Iris 'Wild Wings' with Centaurea montana 'Carnea' and Paeonia 'Picotee'

Iris 'Caliente' with Achillea 'Moonshine'

WHERE TO FIND IRIS TYPES

TALL BEARDED IRISES

The most flamboyant of all bearded irises, these carry their blooms on thick, upright stems high above the clump of leaves. Most varieties flower during June; the earliest can produce flowers from late May.

'Aggressively Forward' A heavily scented variety. The standards are corn-yellow and the falls a softer yellow edged with maroon, with spots of colour on the falls. The beards are gold. **H** 90cm

'Annabel Jane' Raised in windy Britain, this lovely plant has robust stems. The lilac flowers are heavily ruffled and spicy scented. **H** 91cm

'Badlands' The large, ruffled, perfectly proportioned black flowers have silky black-purple standards, velvety, purple-black falls and purple beards. This plant blooms for a long time. **H** 97cm

'Benton Nigel' An old English variety, the gently ruffled flowers have deep-violet standards and velvety, dark purple falls that pale to purple around the edges. **H** 90cm

'Best Bet' A nice twice-blooming plant with ruffled pale-blue standards flushed at the base with purple, royal-blue falls, and short, blue beards. **H** 90cm

'Better Together' This produces large flowers with velvety, near-black falls, soft-blue standards that fade to palest blue, and ginger-tipped black beards. The side branches on the flower stems are widely spaced, allowing each individual bloom to stand out clearly. **H** 100cm

'Beverly Sills' The pale coral-pink flowers, with tangerine beards are sweetly scented and the thick petals have pretty frilled edges**. H** 91cm

Iris 'Aggressively Forward'

Iris 'Annabel Jane'

Iris 'Badlands'

Iris 'Benton Nigel'

Iris 'Best Bet'

Iris 'Better Together'

Iris 'Beverly Sills'

Iris 'Blue Rhythm'

Iris 'Blue Shimmer'

Iris 'Braithwaite'

Iris 'Caliente'

'Blue Rhythm' A classically beautiful iris that has lemon-scented, cornflower-blue flowers with broad, lightly ruffled petals. The falls are slightly darker blue and the white beards are tipped with deep yellow. **H** 110cm

'Blue Shimmer' This old, heavily scented variety blooms early in the season. The slender-petalled, ivory-white flowers are neatly speckled with soft blue. **H** 91cm

'Braithwaite' A tried-and- tested plant with long, velvety-purple falls, paler around the edges, and lilac-white, upright standards that touch at the top. The beards are short and yellow. **H** 84cm

'Caliente' There are no red-bearded irises, but this one comes quite close. The gently ruffled, scented, rich red-brown flowers have flaring, rounded falls with short, burnt-orange beards. **H** 97cm

'Carnaby' A distinctly feminine plant with frilly, lightly scented flowers. The peach-pink standards are flushed with lilac and the rose-purple falls are banded with soft peach. It has soft orange beards. **H** 89cm

'Celebration Song' Ruffled, scented flowers with pale lilac falls contrast with soft peach-pink standards and orange beards. The flowers tend to be a darker shade when they first open. Blooms over a long period. **H** 94cm

'Chasing Rainbows' Ruffled and strongly scented. The soft-violet falls have paler centres and a wash of buff-peach along the edges. The standards are also buff-peach, stained with lilac from the base, and the beards are orange. **H** 81cm

Iris 'Carnaby'

Iris 'Celebration Song'

Iris 'Chasing Rainbows'

Iris 'Class Ring'

Iris 'Coalignition'

Iris 'Cordoba'

Iris 'Crowned Heads'

Iris 'Country Charm'

'Class Ring' The moderate-sized flowers have burgundy-red standards and very ruffled white falls broadly banded with burgundy. The slender beards are bronze-gold. **H** 91cm

'Coalignition' A luxurious, spicy-scented flower with velvety, black-grape falls, silky wine-red standards, and eye-catching, mustard-coloured beards. Early to bloom in June. Blooms again from late August onwards. **H** 91cm

'Cordoba' Not acknowledged as a remontant iris, but we find it reliably so. The delightful orange flowers are also orange-scented with short, bright-orange beards. A long flowering plant that may produce more blooms from late August onwards. **H** 91cm

'Crowned Heads' Irises bred with darker standards than falls are fairly new. This excellent, scented variety has violet-blue standards and pale-blue falls; both are veined with blue. The beards are soft blue. **H** 97cm

'Country Charm' A late-blooming plant with well-branched stems bearing lightly ruffled flowers. These have frilly lemon standards and rose-purple falls with broad white patches where the white beards sit. **H** 97cm

'Dusky Challenger' The very large flowers are nicely ruffled and both standards and falls are a shiny, dark navy-blue. The scent is heavy, sharp, and reminiscent of hot chocolate. A long-flowering plant. **H** 99cm

Iris 'Dusky Challenger'

Iris 'English Cottage'

Iris 'Florentina'

Iris 'Florentine Silk'

Iris 'Fogbound'

Iris 'Happenstance'

Iris 'Haunted Heart'

'English Cottage' This most reliably remontant iris is also almost the first to bloom. White, heavily scented flowers are lightly speckled with soft violet and the white beards are tipped with yellow towards the back. **H** 98cm

'Florentina' The rhizomes of this plant were traditionally ground to a sweet-scented powder, which is sometimes added to pot pourri. The white blooms are lightly tinged with blue and have white beards. **H** 75cm

'Florentine Silk' A striking combination of soft-peach standards and violet falls that pale to peach around the edges. The violet beards are orange at the back. **H** 102cm

'Fogbound' A ruffled, scented flower with pale-purple standards stained darker at the base. The falls are paler lilac and have short, white beards touched with orange at the back. **H** 107cm

'Happenstance' Pink varieties are not always hardy but this is tougher than most. The distinctively scented, lightly ruffled, soft-pink flowers have laced petal edges and fat, coral-coloured beards. **H** 95cm

'Haunted Heart'. A well-deserved award winner with falls of delicate pale lilac washed and lined with lilac. The violet beards are just touched with pink. **H** 91cm

'Here Comes the Night' The shiny, virtually black flowers have ruffled edges and distinctive violet beards that are yellow at the back. **H** 90cm

'Here Comes the Sun' Glowing yellow, the flowers have bright orange beards and thick, smooth, lightly ruffled petals. **H** 90cm

'Ink Patterns' This exquisite white iris displays blue-purple stippling and fine etching around the petal edges. The beards are a soft blue. **H** 91cm

'Jane Phillips' Justly celebrated, this pale-blue, scented variety has petals like crêpe paper and white beards. The grey-green leaves are disease resistant. Over the years it has been the parent of many good irises. **H** 91cm

'Lady Friend' Very early to bloom with large ruffled flowers that are the colour of garnets and burnt-orange beards. **H** 97cm

'Lovely Again' Guaranteed to re-bloom, this iris has delicate-textured, smoothly shaped, scented, lavender flowers that soften in colour as the plant ages. The beards are yellow. **H** 76cm

'Lovely Senorita' Lightly ruffled and attractive, the large flowers have deep-orange standards and burnt-orange falls. These are flushed with violet in front of the short, bushy, tangerine beards. **H** 104cm

Iris 'Here Comes The Night'

Iris 'Here Comes The Sun'

Iris 'Ink Patterns'

Iris 'Lady Friend'

Iris 'Jane Phillips'

Iris 'Lovely Again'

Iris 'Lovely Senorita'

Iris 'Midnight Treat'

Iris 'Millennium Sunrise'

Iris 'New Leaf'

Iris pallida

Iris 'Parisian Dawn'

Iris 'Queen's Circle'

'Midnight Treat' The gently ruffled flowers have large, silky, rich-purple standards that flare out, and velvety, purple-black falls. The beards are dark purple. **H** 90cm

'Millennium Sunrise' Still one of the best orange varieties we grow, it has large, ruffled petals and rich-orange beards. **H** 99cm

'New Leaf' This handsome ruffled flower has flaring, velvety maroon falls that pale to near white at the edges and tangerine beards. The peach standards are stained with violet. **H** 81cm

pallida Widespread in gardens throughout Western Europe, this has scented, pale violet-blue flowers with white beards. The flowers withstand bad weather and the handsome grey-green leaves are disease resistant. **H** 110cm

'Parisian Dawn' Glamorous and flouncy, the soft-peach flowers are broadly washed with a delicate grey-lilac along the edges of the falls. The thick beards are orange. **H** 91cm

'Queen's Circle' Broad-petalled and late-blooming, the flowers have pure-white falls that are lightly ruffled and heavily stained around the edges with ink-blue. The white beards are tipped with orange. **H** 81cm

'Recurring Delight' A neatly ruffled, sweetly scented flower with rich violet falls, taupe standards, and yellow beards. Although not usually described as remontant, this blooms for us in mid-June, then again from late August. **H** 89cm

'Red Revival' Despite its name, this has bronze standards, brown falls heavily veined with yellow, and deep-orange beards. The colour of this remontant iris is much richer in autumn. **H** 76cm

'Rumor Has It' I value this plant for its deep purple buds that open into white, very ruffled flowers broadly edged in purple and etched with fine lines. The blooms appear late in the iris flowering season. **H** 91cm

'Sharp Dressed Man' This neatly shaped, tightly ruffled, sweetly scented flower has rose-purple standards and velvety dark purple falls that show off the bright-orange beards. **H** 91cm

'Shurton Inn' This English variety was named after a pub the breeder visited. It has flaring, soft-brown falls, white standards flushed with ochre, and dark yellow beards. **H** 86cm

Iris 'Recurring Delight'

Iris 'Red Revival'

Iris 'Rumor Has It'

Iris 'Sharp Dressed Man'

Iris 'Shurton Inn'

Iris 'Silverado'

'Silverado' Beautifully shaped, large, and slightly scented, the soft-blue flowers display delicate touches of purple. **H** 97cm

'Snowy Owl' The toughest white variety I have grown. Its ruffled flowers are pure white and the white beards are very gently brushed with yellow. **H** 97cm

'Spring Madness' Delicious is the only word for this daffodil-scented flower with thick petals that withstand bad weather. It has white standards and white-rimmed, yellow falls finely etched with lines of brown-purple. **H** 89cm

Iris 'Snowy Owl'

Iris 'Spring Madness'

Iris 'Stairway to Heaven'

Iris 'Stellar Lights'

Iris 'Superstition'

Iris 'Supreme Sultan'

Iris 'Susan Bliss'

Iris 'Sweet Musette'

Iris 'Undercurrent'

'Stairway to Heaven' A variety with lots of large flowers carried right to the bottom of the strong stems. Creamy-white standards rise above lavender-blue falls and yellow-tipped, white beards. **H** 102cm

'Stellar Lights' Re-flowering reliably, this plant has ruffled, shiny, dark violet flowers. The falls have central, white patches in front of the white beards. **H** 97cm

'Superstition' This reliable and free-flowering variety produces lots of lightly ruffled, purple-black flowers with a lovely silky sheen. **H** 91cm

'Supreme Sultan' Even though this variety has large flowers, the stems don't usually topple over. Flaring, red-brown falls display beards of deep gold and the ruffled standards are golden yellow. **H** 102cm

'Susan Bliss' The soft lilac-blue flowers of this old variety are small in comparison to those of modern irises. Gently scented, they are borne on stiff stems that rise from a clump of clean, greyish leaves. **H** 75cm

'Sweet Musette' As laced and frilled as a Victorian lady's underwear, this feminine flower has soft-peach standards, serrated along the edges. The pink-lavender falls are flushed with lavender and the beards are coral-red. **H** 94cm

'Undercurrent' This heavily scented, flouncy flower has soft-peach standards and rounded, soft-purple falls. These fade to delicate peach around the bushy, bright-orange beards. **H** 107cm

MEDIAN BEARDED IRISES

These are shorter than tall bearded irises and all flower freely, but at different times. The varieties listed are among the most useful for all areas of the garden. I don't usually recommend growing bearded irises in pots, except for standard dwarf bearded types. These will survive happily in containers for a few years.

The different types of median bearded iris (with abbreviations used for each type) and their flowering periods are as follows:

Border Bearded (BB)
Flowering Early to mid-June

Miniature Tall Bearded (MTB)
Flowering Early to mid-June

Intermediate Bearded (IB)
Flowering Late May to mid-June

Standard Dwarf Bearded (SDB)
Flowering Mid-April to early May

'Agatha Christie' A free-flowering variety. The white standards are speckled with violet and the white falls are broadly edged with purple. **H** 61cm (IB)

'Apricot Drops' A prolific award-winning variety. The small, perfectly shaped, soft-orange flowers have orange beards. **H** 46cm (MTB)

'Az Ap' Neat, sky-blue flowers, lightly flecked with purple and with bushy, bright-blue beards, bloom over a long period. **H** 56cm (IB)

'Blackcurrant' An excellent grower with scented, deep plum flowers that can appear darker in different lights. **H** 60cm (IB)

'Blue Splash' This vigorous plant with pale blue flowers has neatly ruffled petals. The falls flare out showing off soft-blue beards. **H** 64cm (IB)

'Bold Print' A free-flowering plant with white flowers. Neatly stitched with purple, they have short, violet beards. **H** 60cm (IB)

'Bumblebee Deelite' *(overleaf)* These dinky flowers with flaring, yellow-rimmed, black-maroon falls and short, yellow standards are a real delight. The blooms are carried on slender stems above bright green leaves. **H** 46cm (MTB)

'Chanted' *(overleaf)* Used extensively to raise plants with pink-toned flowers, this Australian iris has strongly scented, dusky apricot-pink flowers with pale-blue beards. **H** 34cm (SDB)

'Chubby Cheeks' *(overleaf)* Small and scented, the violet-speckled, white flowers have rather crumpled, rounded petals and bronze-tipped, soft-violet beards. **H** 30cm (SDB)

Iris 'Agatha Christie'

Iris 'Apricot Drops'

Iris 'Az Ap'

Iris 'Blackcurrant'

Iris 'Blue Splash'

Iris 'Bold Print'

Iris 'Bumblebee Deelite'

Iris 'Chanted'

Iris 'Chubby Cheeks'

Iris 'Dazzling'

Iris 'Fanciful Whimsy'

Dazzling' The eye-catching flowers have pure white standards and dark blue-purple falls that pale around the edges. The ruffled rims of the petals curl inwards to reveal the white undersides. **H** 60cm (IB)

'Fanciful Whimsy' Unusual blooms with buff-pink standards, rosy-purple falls, and white, yellow-tipped beards. **H** 64cm (IB)

'Fathom' I love this flower simply because its rich sky-blue petals are so thick and smooth. The beards are a matching blue. **H** 58cm (IB)

'Forever Blue' This never fails to bloom again in August with soft grey-blue flowers. There are green patches on the falls and bright-blue, V-shaped beards. **H** 30cm (SDB)

'Lady of the Night' The large, velvety, deep purple flowers with wavy edges have fat, bright-yellow beards. **H** 69cm (BB)

Iris 'Fathom'

Iris 'Forever Blue'

Iris 'Lady Of The Night'

Iris 'Lilli-white'

Iris 'Orinoco Flow'

Iris 'Pause'

'Lilli-white' The first white standard dwarf bearded iris to be bred, and still a good variety. It has pure-white flowers with white beards. **H** 30cm (SDB)

'Orinoco Flow' A long flowering plant with very ruffled, heavily scented, white flowers that are beautifully edged with bands of violet-blue 'stitching'. The beards are blue. **H** 64cm (BB)

'Pause' The unusual, sweetly scented flowers have delicate, soft-pink standards, violet falls, and tangerine-tipped, violet beards. **H** 30cm (SDB)

'Peebee and Jay' The flowers may be small, but the colour is vibrant. Rounded, caramel standards touch at the top, and the flaring, rose-violet falls are also rimmed with caramel. The beards are yellow. **H** 26cm (MTB)

'Pop Culture' All that can be said about the big extravagantly ruffled flowers is 'Wow'! They are best described as rich rose-violet. The falls have a pronounced dark maroon spot and soft-orange beards. **H** 69cm (IB)

'Princess Bride' A reliably vigorous plant that carries pretty, ruffled, creamy-white flowers on strong stems. The blooms have bushy, deep orange-yellow beards and big, thick petals. **H** 64cm (BB)

'Riveting' Strongly scented, pure-white flowers have open standards and flaring falls that are partly covered by a large, ink-blue spot. The beards are white. **H** 38cm (SDB)

Iris 'Peebee and Jay'

Iris 'Pop Culture'

Iris 'Princess Bride'

Iris 'Riveting'

Iris 'Blueberry Fair'

Iris 'Dreaming Late'

Iris 'Fond Kiss'

Iris 'Golden Edge'

Iris 'Here Be Dragons'

Iris 'Hohe Warte'

SIBIRICA IRISES

These are supremely graceful plants. The flowers are carried towards the top of tall, slender stems above upright clumps of slim, grassy foliage. Siberian irises are tolerant of many conditions: partial shade to full sun; dry spots – although they take longer to establish – to really wet and even quite acid soils. Some are a little more fussy; their preferences are given in the description.

Flowering These bloom from early to late June, the same time as tall bearded irises.

'Blueberry Fair' Basically violet-blue, the neatly ruffled petals flare outwards. A patch of white adds an extra dimension. **H** 81cm

'Dreaming Late' The ruffled, white flowers, with wide, flaring falls and round standards open just above the leaves. A long, free-flowering plant. **H** 89cm

'Fond Kiss' Short and delightful, the flowers are very pale lilac, a colour that shows as the flowers open and fades as they age. **H** 84cm

'Golden Edge' The petals of the navy blue flowers are very finely edged with yellow and have gold veins radiating from the top of the lightly ruffled falls. **H** 85cm

'Here Be Dragons' The corn-yellow falls are stencilled with maroon veins and washed with ink blue. As they age the blue stain fades. Not the easiest to grow, but very beautiful. **H** 90cm

'Hohe Warte' A delicate looking white flower, washed lightly with violet and gold at the back of the falls. The blooms are carried on very tall, slender stems. **H** 150cm

'Lavender Landscape' Soft-lilac flowers with flaring, show-off falls that are slightly deeper in colour are carried on slender stems high above the leaves. **H** 90cm

'Ruffles and Flourishes' An award-winning variety with broad, rosy-purple petals. The rounded, ruffled falls are edged in white, which also extends out from the golden flare. A lovely big flower this sits well above the leaves. **H** 90cm

'Salamander Crossing' Delicate and rather dignified, the flowers have rounded, soft-yellow falls, finely spotted and veined with lilac. Speckles of the same colour cover the white standards. **H** 107cm

'Shaker's Prayer' This elegant plant carries the small, neatly shaped violet flowers on slender stems. The white falls are marked with violet. **H** 91cm

Iris 'Lavender Landscape'

Iris 'Ruffles and Flourishes'

Iris 'Salamander Crossing'

Iris 'Shaker's Prayer'

Iris 'Silver Edge'

Iris 'Soft Blue'

'Silver Edge' The petals of the smoothly shaped, mid-blue flowers are finely rimmed with white and gently ruffled. **H** 80cm

'Soft Blue' The name says it all. The rounded falls and slender standards are soft blue. The colour pales towards the tips of the petals. **H** 76cm

'Summer Sky' This is one of the most softly coloured Siberian irises I have come across. The flowers are delicate blue, paling to white with age, and are carried on slender stems with fine leaves. **H** 60cm

'White Swirl' A pretty pure-white flower with gently ruffled, flaring petals. This important introduction was the first Siberian iris with falls that flared outwards. The base of the petals is golden-yellow. **H** 102cm

Iris 'Summer Sky'

Iris 'White Swirl'

Iris 'Ally Oops'

Iris 'Berlin Tiger'

Iris 'Chance Beauty'

Iris ensata

Iris ensata 'Crystal Halo'

Iris ensata 'Rose Queen'

While irises with beards are the most glamorous, irises without beards are the most versatile in terms of where they will grow in the garden. In this section you will find irises for growing in water (Iris ensata), for shade (I. foetidissima), for acid or dry soil and for everything in between.

'Ally Oops' This tall, elegant iris carries its exquisite flowers in twos or threes high above a wide clump of mid-green leaves. The tiny standards are lilac and the large, rounded, soft-lemon falls are traced with lilac veins. Thought to be a cross between a Siberian iris and *I. pseudacorus*. June. **H × S** 75cm × 75cm

'Berlin Tiger' A dramatic plant. Bronze flowers, heavily veined with maroon, bloom on branched stems just above a dense clump of long, slender leaves that needs space to spread. June. **H × S** 90cm × 100cm

'Chance Beauty' The tall, branched stems of this upright plant are topped with flat, bright-yellow flowers. The falls are finely stencilled with chocolate-brown veins. A cross between *Iris pseudacorus* and *I. ensata*, this robust plant thrives in soils that retain moisture. June. **H × S** 115cm × 80cm

ensata (Japanese iris) This is a big group, but the choice of garden-worthy varieties is limited. Usually grown from seed, it blooms in shades from soft lilac and white to dark purple –all with yellow flashes on the falls. This iris won't grow in water for long and prefers the margins of ponds or very moist soil. Late June to July. **H × S** 90cm × 75cm

***ensata* 'Crystal Halo'** This variety has distinctive, deep red-purple flowers. The petals are painted with broad, bright-yellow signals, and the edges of both the petals and the inner flower segments are bleached white. Late June to July. **H × S** 122cm × 75cm

***ensata* 'Rose Queen'** Soft lavender-pink flowers with round falls and tiny standards balance on slender stems above a dense clump of slender, upright, mid-green leaves. Late June to July. **H × S** 90cm × 75cm

***ensata* 'White Ladies'** A late-flowering iris with large white flowers. The petals sit flat on the strong, upright stems above a clump of tall, slender, sword-like leaves. Late June to July. **H × S** 90cm × 75cm

foetidissima Valued for its leaves and berries, rather than the flowers, this robust iris will grow in any soil in sun or shade. The upright clump of deep-green leaves is evergreen and short stems of yellowish-brown flowers turn into bright orange-red seeds in autumn. Late June to July. **H × S** 45cm × 90cm

Iris ensata 'White Ladies'

Iris foetidissima

Iris fulva

fulva The blackberry-purple flowers have long, slim petals with tiny yellow flares on the falls. These are held on straight stems rising from long, slender leaves. A plant for a warm, damp spot. June. **H** × **S** 90cm × 75cm

'Holden's Child' Great for a wet soil, and even a spot with little light. The flowers have very short, lilac standards and the purple falls, which have gold and white signals, look like dog's ears. A vigorous plant, its broad, mid-green leaves form a thick, bushy clump. June. **H** × **S** 90cm × 90cm

Iris **Pacific Coast Hybrid** These low-growing irises need to be grown in acid soil. Resenting disturbance, they are usually grown from seed, which is not difficult. The delicious flowers have flat, broad petals ranging in colour from white to dark red, yellow, and blue. They are borne in sprays on long stems that spring up from a broad, low mound of slender, deep-green, evergreen leaves. June. **H** × **S** 30cm × 60cm

pseudacorus (Yellow flag) Rising from a dense clump of mid-green leaves, tall, well-branched stems carry bright-yellow flowers. The falls usually, but not always, have dark brown markings and the standards are spoon-shaped. Useful for growing in bogs or large pools, it will tolerate most conditions, even well-drained, sandy soil. June **H** × **S** 120cm × 90cm

'Regal Surprise' A cross between *Iris pseudacorus* and *I. versicolor*, this variety has royal-purple flowers with large yellow patches lined with purple on the falls. The white inner segments of the flowers make this a distinctive plant. Perfect for moist soils. June. **H** × **S** 76cm × 90cm

Iris 'Holden's Child'

Iris Pacific Coast Hybrid

Iris pseudacorus

Iris 'Regal Surprise'

Iris × robusta 'Gerald Darby' with *Eryngium alpinum* (behind) and *Astrantia maxima*

Iris 'Roy's Repeater'

Iris setosa

× *robusta* 'Gerald Darby' I would grow this just for the long, purple-tinted stems that emerge from a vigorous, broad clump of wide, deep-green leaves. Later, violet-blue flowers appear in clusters over a long period. June. **H × S** 76cm × 90cm

'Roy's Repeater' A vigorous plant for moist soil. White flowers borne on slender stems have distinct yellow patches and pretty purple veining. The dark green leaves form a dense clump. June. **H × S** 105cm × 90cm

setosa In the wild, this is the most widely distributed iris, adapting to wet and dry soils alike. The soft-blue flowers have flaring, short standards; the falls are rounded and marked with yellowish-white and purple. The broad, arching leaves grow into a thick clump. Largely grown from seed, so colours and heights may vary. June. **H × S** 45–75cm × 60–90cm

unguicularis Evergreen and winter-flowering, this iris has scented, rich-lavender flowers that sit deep within a broad clump of deep green, narrow foliage. It prefers a dry soil in sun and can be slow to establish. December to February. **H × S** 60cm × 45cm

versicolor An iris for all types of soil, this produces up to nine elegant, blue-purple flowers on long, arching, slender, well-branched stems. The broad, grey-green foliage is stained at the base with purple and grows into broad, gracefully arching clumps. July. **H × S** 80cm × 80cm

Iris unguicularis

Iris versicolor

Iris 'Archie Owen'

Iris 'Betty Cooper'

Iris 'Lucky Devil'

SPURIA IRISES

The flowers of these stiffly upright, very hardy irises are similar to those of bulbous Dutch irises are carried up stiff stems above a dense clump of tall, deep-green leaves. They are the last of the summer-flowering irises to bloom, the flowers are great for cutting, and also loved by bees. Spuria irises thrive anywhere, but establish faster in moist soils. Flowering time is late June to early July.

'Archie Owen' Bright-yellow flowers with slender petals have ruffled standards and softer-yellow falls. **H** 90cm

'Betty Cooper' This iris has frilly, soft-lilac flowers with a large, yellow-orange spot on the falls. **H** 123cm

'Lucky Devil' The broad, deep-purple flowers are washed with magenta and the falls are stained with yellow. **H** 91cm

'Mahogany Lord' Elegant purple flowers are produced in ones and twos. The falls look almost brown because of the large, spreading yellow flare that runs down the petals. **H** 112cm

'Media Luz' A pretty shade of soft lavender, the falls are tinged with cream and have yellow signals. **H** 101cm

'Missouri Autumn' The burnt-orange flowers darken to a coppery-brown at the edges. **H** 102cm

orientalis This species form of Spuria iris can be raised from seed. The white flowers have a large patch of yellow on the falls and the same colour stains the standards. **H** 102cm

Iris 'Mahogany Lord'

Iris 'Media Luz'

Iris 'Missouri Autumn'

Iris orientalis

Kalimeris incisa 'Blue Star'

Kirengeshoma palmata

Knautia arvensis

Knautia macedonica

Knautia macedonica 'Mars Midget'

KALIMERIS

incisa **'Blue Star'** An airy, free-flowering aster-like plant with small, daisy-shaped, soft-blue flowers carried above a stiff bush of small, bright green leaves. July to September. **H × S** 50cm × 30cm

Needs Well-drained soil in sun or partial shade
Great for The front of a border
Bees & Butterflies Yes
 For Cutting No
Care Make bushier by pinching out the tops

KIRENGESHOMA

palmata This lovely, unusual, woodland plant sends up sprays of waxy, shuttlecock-like, soft-yellow flowers on long stems. Its maple-like, soft-green leaves form an open clump. August to September. **H × S** 120cm × 75cm

Needs Well-drained, humus-rich soil that remains moist in partial shade
Great for Woodlands and damp soils
Bees & Butterflies No
For Cutting No
Care Slow to establish. Protect from slugs

KNAUTIA

A must for the wildlife garden. The blooms of these somewhat unruly, free-flowering plants serve as landing pads for butterflies, bees and all types of flying insects. Allow them to seed around and they will soon add a natural rhythm to any planting.

Needs Well-drained soil in sun or partial shade
Great for Front or middle of the border
Bees & Butterflies Yes
For Cutting Yes
Care Easy to grow. Seeds freely about

arvensis (Field scabious) This tall, native wildflower of pasturelands is perfect for those wanting a wild yet pretty plant. Slender, rather elegant, well-branched stems carry flat, slightly domed, lilac flowers above a small clump of soft-green leaves. June to September. **H × S** 120cm × 45cm

macedonica Masses of scabious-like, blue-crimson flowers top a spindly network of well-branched stems with soft-green leaves. June to August. **H × S** 80cm × 60cm

macedonica **'Mars Midget'** Although very similar to *Knautia macedonica*, this variety is much shorter and mound forming, which makes it perfect for smaller borders. June to August. **H × S** 45cm × 45cm

Kniphofia 'Alcazar'

Kniphofia 'Bee's Lemon'

Kniphofia 'Green Jade'
with *Strobilanthes wallichii*

KNIPHOFIA (Red-hot poker)

Upright and stately, these bold plants carry fat spikes of long, tubular flowers. They are held on cylindrical stems high above a rosette of rush-like, evergreen usually mid-green leaves. Opening from the base of the spike first, the buds frequently vary in colour from the open blooms.

Needs Really well-drained soil in sun
Great for Vertical structure in the border
Bees & Butterflies Bees
For Cutting Yes
Care Will not thrive in soils that stay wet during winter

'Alcazar' An easily established, free-flowering variety with flaming-red spikes opening from bright-yellow buds. June to September. **H × S** 105cm × 60cm

'Bee's Lemon' Late to flower, its yellow pokers open from lime-green buds on bronze-tinted stems with slender leaves. August to October. **H × S** 75cm × 60cm

'Green Jade' The spears of long, tubular, soft-yellow flowers open from green buds on bronze flower stems. August to October. **H × S** 90cm × 60cm

'Ice Queen' The pale cream, green-tinged flowers turn white as they age. June to September. **H × S** 120cm × 80cm

'Tawny King' Loose spikes of soft-orange flowers open from cream buds. July to October. **H × S** 105cm × 60cm. AGM

'Timothy' Salmon-coloured flowers in thick spikes bloom on contrasting bronze stems. July to August. **H × S** 80cm × 60cm. AGM

'Toffee Nosed' Loose spikes of soft-orange flowers carried on bronze stems open from cream buds. July to October. **H × S** 105cm × 60cm. AGM

Kniphofia 'Ice Queen'

Kniphofia 'Tawny King'

Kniphofia 'Timothy'

Kniphofia 'Toffee Nosed'

Lamium galeobdolon 'Florentinum'

Lamium maculatum 'White Nancy'

Lamium orvala

Lamprocapnos spectabilis 'Alba'

Lamprocapnos spectabilis

LAMIUM (Deadnettle)

Most deadnettles make ideal ground-cover and all have leafy stems with whorls of small, hooded flowers and heart-shaped, jagged-edged, often decorative leaves. *Lamium orvala* forms an upright mound.

Needs Well-drained soil in sun, partial shade, or full shade
Great for Front of the border and woodland
Bees & Butterflies Bees
For Cutting No
Care Most are easy to grow, although *L. orvala* may take a while to establish

galeobdolon **'Florentinum'** (Yellow archangel) A vigorous plant and ideal for ground-cover in damp shade. Produces long, creeping stems of silver-splashed, heart-shaped leaves and yellow flowers. May to June. **H × S** 45cm × 75cm

maculatum **'White Nancy'** A low, carpeting plant with pure-white flowers rising from mid-green leaves that are coated almost entirely with silver. May to June. **H × S** 15cm × 30cm

orvala (Great deadnettle) Unlike the others in the group, this grows into a handsome, upright plant. Stiff stems of large, velvety, soft-purple flowers emerge between big, mid-green leaves. May to June. **H × S** 45cm × 45cm

LAMPROCAPNOS (Bleeding heart)

Still found under their old name *Dicentra*, these most graceful spring plants have large, locket-shaped flowers, each with a drooping, white teardrop. They dangle in a row from long, arching stems that emerge from a dense, upright clump of succulent, but soft, deeply divided leaves.

Needs Well-drained soil that remains moist in partial or full shade
Great for Wooded and shady spots
Bees & Butterflies No
For Cutting No
Care They die back entirely by midsummer

spectabilis Pure-pink flowers hang from thick, upright, red-tinted stems with lush, deeply divided, mid-green leaves. April to June. **H × S** 60cm × 50cm. AGM

spectabilis **'Alba'** Beautiful when fully established, this variety has pure-white flowers and fresh-green leaves. April to June. **H × S** 60cm × 50cm. AGM

spectabilis **'Valentine'** A wonderful, fairly recent addition to the clan. The vermilion-red flowers dangle along purple-tinged stems above deeply divided, green leaves tinted with maroon. April to June. **H × S** 60cm × 50cm. AGM

LATHYRUS (Everlasting pea)

vernus One of the very first perennials to bloom, this flowers before the leaves appear but does not climb, despite its name. Masses of slender stems unfurl into sprays of small, vibrant-purple flowers that have no scent. The long, pointed, deep-green leaves eventually form a neat clump. Colours can vary: the pink-flowered form is known as *L. vernus* 'Alboroseus'. March to May. **H × S** 30cm × 30cm. AGM

Needs Well-drained soil in sun or partial shade
Great for Front of the border
Bees & Butterflies No
For Cutting No
Care Remove seedheads if you don't want seedlings around the garden

LEUCANTHEMELLA

serotina A very late-flowering daisy with sprays of large, pure-white blooms on leafy branches towards the top of the tall stems. These are the only daisy-shaped perennials to turn their heads to face the sun, like sunflowers. September to October. **H × S** 150cm × 90cm. AGM

Needs Well-drained soil that retains its moisture, in sun or partial shade
Great for Very back of the border
Bees & Butterflies Yes
For Cutting Yes
Care Trouble free and needs no staking

LEUCANTHEMUM (Shasta daisy)

Once listed as *Chrysanthemum superbum*, only white forms of this perennial were available. Now yellow varieties have been bred. The large, daisy flowers are carried on stiff stems with no branches above a thick clump of semi-evergreen, long, mid-green leaves. They form broad clumps.

Needs Well-drained soil in full sun
Great for Front and middle of the border
Bees & Butterflies Yes
For Cutting Yes
Care Trouble free

× *superbum* 'Aglaia' Large, white blooms with shorter, central petals give this double 'frilly' form a distinctly shaggy look. June to August. **H × S** 90cm × 60cm

× *superbum* 'Becky' A clean plant with single, sometimes semi-double, white flowers that form a neat, round clump. June to August. **H × S** 90cm × 60cm

Lamprocapnos spectabilis 'Valentine'

Lathyrus vernus

Leucanthemella serotina

Leucanthemum × superbum 'Aglaia'

Leucanthemum × superbum 'Becky'

Leucanthemum × superbum 'Phyllis Smith'

Leucanthemum × superbum 'Snowcap'

× superbum 'Phyllis Smith' Carries very frilly, single, white flowers on stiff, stems that support themselves well. June to August. **H × S** 90cm × 75cm

× superbum 'Snowcap' This shorter variety is ideal for containers as well as borders. The large, single, pure-white flowers are borne on sturdy stems to form a neat mound. June to August. **H × S** 45cm × 45cm

× superbum 'T. E. Killin' An old variety with smooth, white outer petals and a further ring of shorter inner ones encircling a golden centre. June to August. **H × S** 90cm × 75cm. AGM

× superbum 'Wirral Supreme' White flowers with a flat, yellow disc are edged with rows of short petals. These extend over almost the whole centre of this double form. June to August. **H × S** 90cm × 60cm. AGM

LIATRIS (Gayfeather)

spicata More often seen in flower arrangements than in gardens, this plant is very easy to grow. Slender spikes of small, fluffy, rich-lilac flowers open from the top first. They are carried on strong stems that rise from a tuft of slim leaves. August to September. **H × S** 75cm × 45cm

Needs Well-drained soil, including very light soil that retains moisture in summer
Great for Middle of the border
Bees & Butterflies Yes
For Cutting Yes
Care Dig up and split the clumps every few years to keep the plant vigorous

LIBERTIA

grandiflora A striking, stately plant. The clusters of small, flat, white flowers carried on slender, almost wiry stems shine bright above a thicket of evergreen, dark green, grass-like leaves. Suitable for more exposed locations. May to July. **H × S** 95cm × 75cm

Needs Well-drained to moist soil in sun
Great for Middle of the border
Bees & Butterflies Yes
For Cutting No
Care Remove dead leaves or cut back in spring. Can seed about.

Leucanthemum × superbum 'T. E. Killin'

Leucanthemum × superbum 'Wirral Supreme'

Liatris spicata

Libertia grandiflora

LIGULARIA

These bold plants are ideal for gardens with damp soil. All produce yellow daisies in clusters or elegant spires, but the foliage is what makes the plants stand out. The leaves are big, some are round, and the most decorative are deeply divided into fingers.

Needs Soil that remains damp in sun, partial shade, or shade
Great for Very damp or wet ground
Bees & Butterflies Yes
For Cutting Yes
Care Does not thrive in dry or light soils

dentata **'Othello'** Sprays of big yellow daisies on branched stems sit high above rounded, deep purple-green leaves that are the colour of red wine underneath. July to August. **H × S** 90cm × 75cm

'The Rocket' Tall and handsome, this plant carries tapering spikes of small, star-like, golden flowers on black stems above a mound of large, deeply divided, mid-green leaves. July to August. **H × S** 180cm × 75cm. AGM

LIMONIUM (Sea lavender)

platyphyllum A haze of tiny, papery, lavender flowers hovers over slender, well-branched, almost woody stems. These spring from a rosette of long, leathery, mid-green leaves. August to September. **H × S** 45cm × 45cm

Needs Well-drained soil, including dry, in sun
Great for Front of the border
Bees & Butterflies Yes
For Cutting Yes
Care Good for seaside gardens

LINARIA (Toadflax)

These elegant and generous plants bear slender spikes of tiny flowers, shaped like miniature snapdragons. The upright stems with slim leaves need no support. Self-seeds freely around the garden.

Needs Well-drained soil in sun or partial shade
Great for Anywhere in the border
Bees & Butterflies Bees
For Cutting Yes
Care Deadhead promptly if you don't want lots of seedlings

purpurea This variety has tiny, rich-purple flowers and mid-green leaves. July to October. **H × S** 90cm × 45cm

purpurea **'Canon Went'** Spikes of small, pink flowers are carried above the grey leaves. July to October. **H × S** 90cm × 45cm

Ligularia dentata 'Othello'

Limonium platyphyllum

Linaria purpurea

Ligularia 'The Rocket'

Linaria purpurea 'Canon Went'

Liriope muscari

Lobelia cardinalis 'Queen Victoria'

Lobelia siphilitica

Lobelia × *speciosa* 'Hadspen Purple'

Lunaria rediviva

LIRIOPE (Lily turf)

muscari An evergreen plant with grass-like, mid-green leaves that forms arching tufts. These creep along the ground and send up dark maroon stems with tight spikes of bud-like, bright-violet flowers. July to October. **H × S** 45cm × 45cm. AGM

Needs Well-drained soil in sun to dappled shade
Great for Front of the border
Bees & Butterflies Bees
For Cutting No
Care Best in a shady spot as the flower colour can fade in strong sunlight

LOBELIA

All lobelias love moist soil and are easily grown from seed, but they can be tricky to keep going from year to year, especially in dry soils or after cold winters. Treat them as short-lived perennials and make sure you have new seedlings coming along.

Needs Soil that does not dry out
Great for Bog gardens and around ponds, in sun or partial shade
Bees & Butterflies Yes
For Cutting No
Care Lobelias can be rather short-lived

cardinalis **'Queen Victoria'** This handsome plant carries spires of large lipped, rich-red flowers on very deep-red stems with dark red leaves. July to September. **H × S** 90cm × 45cm. AGM

siphilitica The flowers are a deep shade of sky-blue and the lush, mid-green leaves grow into a handsome clump. July to September. **H × S** 90cm × 45cm

× *speciosa* **'Hadspen Purple'** The vibrant purple flowers are borne up purple-tinged stems with mid-green leaves. This variety won't come true from seed. July to September. **H × S** 60cm × 45cm

LUNARIA (Honesty)

rediviva This rather demure but desirable perennial form of honesty is not always easy to grow. An upright plant, it produces clusters of small, scented, palest-lilac flowers over a long period. Translucent, oval seed pods follow. Deep-green, heart-shaped leaves are carried right up the stiff stems. May to July. **H × S** 90cm × 45cm. AGM

Needs Well-drained soil in sun or partial shade; best in a rich soil
Great for Middle of the border
Bees & Butterflies Yes
For Cutting Yes
Care Slow to get established, otherwise trouble free

LUPINUS (Lupin)

These big, colourful plants send up their stately spires just as many spring flowers are fading. Tightly packed with large, pea-shaped flowers, they are carried above a shapely mound of deeply fingered, mid-green leaves.

Needs Well-drained soil in sun
Great for Middle to back of the border
Bees & Butterflies No
For Cutting Yes, but they have hollow stems and can wilt quickly.
Care Remove flowers before they go to seed to maintain vigour. Slugs can be a problem

'Chandelier' The flower colour of this seed-raised variety can range from soft- to mid-yellow. May to June. **H × S** 90cm × 80cm

'Masterpiece' This lovely plant carries its rich-purple flowers, which open from burgundy buds, in tight spires. May to June. **H × S** 75cm × 80cm

'Noble Maiden' A seed-raised plant with flowers in shades from pure white to palest cream. May to June. **H × S** 90cm × 80cm

'Persian Slipper' One of a new breed of short lupins with tight spikes of purple-blue flowers. Usually raised from stock plants rather than seed, so will not vary in colour. May to June. **H × S** 60cm × 50cm

'The Chatelaine' Flowers are usually salmon-pink with white lower petals, although the spikes are sometimes entirely pink. May to June. **H × S** 90cm × 80cm

'The Governor' On this variable, seed-raised plant, the flowers are usually deep-blue and white, but the lower petals can be lilac. May to June. **H × S** 90cm × 80cm

Lupinus 'Chandelier'

Lupinus 'Masterpiece'

Lupinus 'Noble Maiden'

Lupinus 'Persian Slipper' with *Sanguisorba menziesii*

Lupinus 'The Chatelaine'

Lupinus 'The Governor'

Lychnis chalcedonica with
Campanula lactiflora behind

Lychnis chalcedonica var. albiflora

Lychnis chalcedonica 'Carnea'

Lychnis coronaria

Lychnis coronaria 'Alba'

LYCHNIS (Campion)

Cheerful and prolific, these quick-growing plants have flat, open flowers on upright, well-branched stems.

Needs Well-drained soil in sun or partial shade
Great for Middle and back of the border
Bees & Butterflies Yes
For Cutting Yes (*L. chalcedonica*)
Care Trouble free but short-lived

chalcedonica (Maltese cross) Small, vivid-scarlet flowers sit in clusters on upright, bright-green stems that can be weak in the first year, but strengthen in the second. June to August. **H × S** 90cm × 60cm. AGM

***chalcedonica* var. albiflora** (Maltese cross) An upright clump of soft-green foliage and flower stems produces tight, flat-topped clusters of pure-white flowers. June to August. **H × S** 90cm × 60cm

***chalcedonica* 'Carnea'** (Maltese cross) Coming true from seed the flowers are an unusual shade of salmon pink. June to August. **H × S** 90cm × 60cm

coronaria (Dusty miller) A network of stiff, grey stems is topped with flat, strikingly coloured flowers in deep cerise. The woolly, grey leaves form a tight, upright clump. June to August. **H × S** 75cm × 60cm. AGM

***coronaria* 'Alba'** This cool, white form of dusty miller has soft, silvery foliage. The flowers bloom over a long period. June to August. **H × S** 75cm × 60cm. AGM

LYSIMACHIA (Loosestrife)

In early spring the newly emerging stems of these attractive perennials add interest to the garden. As the season progresses, they form an upright, broad clump with spires of starry flowers.

Needs Soil that remains moist in sun or partial shade
Great for Middle of the border
Bees & Butterflies Yes
For Cutting Yes
Care Vigorous, so more suited to bigger gardens

ciliata **'Firecracker'** This eye-catching plant has stems of long, pointed, mahogany leaves. Loose clusters of small, yellow flowers spring from each leaf joint. June to August. **H × S** 90cm × 90cm. AGM

clethroides A bushy plant with red stems bearing spikes of tiny, white flowers that arch gracefully forward. June to August. **H × S** 90cm × 90cm. AGM

ephemerum This elegant, rigidly upright plant has slender spikes of tiny, starry, white flowers. The stems and leaves are waxy and grey-green stems. June to August. **H × S** 90cm × 75cm. AGM

punctata A vigorous, spreading plant that will easily romp, filling a border quickly with tall stems of cupped, starry, yellow flowers opening between bright-green leaves. June to August. **H × S** 90cm × 90cm

punctata **'Alexander'** Like the one above, but much more decorative with slightly ruffled, cream-edged, soft-green leaves and spikes of yellow, cupped flowers. Not quite as vigorous. June to August. **H × S** 90cm × 90cm

Lysimachia ciliata 'Firecracker'

Lysimachia clethroides

Lysimachia ephemerum

Lysimachia punctata

Lysimachia punctata 'Alexander'

Lythrum salicaria 'Blush'

Lythrum salicaria 'Robert'

Lythrum salicaria 'Zigeunerblut'

LYTHRUM (Purple loosestrife)

These are garden hybrids of our native plant, which is found along streams. The flowers have rather unruly petals and form slender, tapering spikes above a strong, upright clump of slim, mid-green leaves.

Needs Soil that remains moist in sun or partial shade
Great for Middle of the border
Bees & Butterflies Yes
For Cutting Yes
Care Damp soils

salicaria **'Blush'** A pretty plant with long, tapering spikes of soft-pink flowers. Mid-green leaves colour in autumn. June to August. **H × S** 90cm × 75cm. AGM

salicaria **'Robert'** A short plant with spikes of rich-pink flowers and mid-green leaves. June to August. **H × S** 60cm × 45cm

salicaria **'Zigeunerblut'** A tall variety with elegant spires of rich carmine-pink flowers. The stiff flowering stems are gently tinted with red and bear deep-green leaves. July to August. **H × S** 120cm × 60cm

virgatum **'Dropmore Purple'** This variation of our native wildflower bears slender, spikes of purplish-pink flowers on stiff stems with dark green leaves. A neat, very upright plant. July to August. **H × S** 102cm × 60cm

Lythrum virgatum 'Dropmore Purple' with *Veronicastrum virginicum* 'Fascination'

MACLEAYA (Plume poppy)

microcarpa **'Kelway's Coral Plume'** This lofty plant produces tall, slender stems that end in wispy, feathery plumes of tiny, buff-pink flowers. Handsome, fig-shaped, blue-green leaves stand out horizontally towards the bottom of the stems and at the base. July to August. **H × S** 180cm × 105cm. AGM

Needs Well-drained soil in sun or partial shade
Great for Back of a big border
Bees & Butterflies Bees
For Cutting No
Care Can become invasive If it likes the spot

MELITTIS (Bastard balm)

melissophyllum I first saw this growing wild in a woodland in Devon. An upright plant with large, white, magenta-lipped flowers that spring from the stem above each pair of leaves. June to August. **H × S** 60cm × 50cm

Needs Soil that remains moist in partial shade
Great for Shady areas including woodland
Bees & Butterflies Yes
For Cutting Yes
Care May take a little while to establish, but trouble free

MERTENSIA (Virginia cowslip)

virginica On this pretty, slowly spreading plant loose clusters of trumpet-shaped, sky-blue flowers are held on waxy stems with oval, blue-green leaves. April to May. **H × S** 45cm × 45cm. AGM

Needs Reliably moist soil in partial shade
Great for Dappled shade
Bees & Butterflies No
For Cutting No
Care Tricky to grow and can attract slugs

MILIUM

effusum **'Aureum'** (Bowles's golden grass) A useful semi-evergreen grass. In spring, the new leaves are yellow, deepening to soft green by summer. The slender flower spikes are yellow. July. **H × S** 45cm × 50cm. AGM

Needs Soil that does not dry out in sun or partial shade
Great for Front of the border
Bees & Butterflies No
For Cutting No
Care Liable to seed around

Melittis melissophyllum

Macleaya microcarpa 'Kelway's Coral Plume'

Mertensia virginica

Milium effusum 'Aureum'

Miscanthus sinensis 'Flamingo'

Miscanthus sinensis 'Morning Light'

Miscanthus sinensis 'Silberfeder'

Miscanthus sinensis 'Variegatus'

Molinia caerulea subsp. *caerulea*
'Strahlenquelle'

MISCANTHUS (Silver grass)

Handsome and clump-forming, these upright grasses have slim, straight leaves and tall stems topped with plumes of very small, silky flowers in strands, like fly whisks. They are very hardy, long-lived, and ideal tall grasses for a border.

Needs Well-drained soil in sun or partial shade
Great for Back of the border
Bees & Butterflies No
For Cutting No
Care Cut the old leaves back in spring

sinensis **'Flamingo'** Arching plumes of tan-pink flowers rise from mid-green leaves with good autumn colour. August to September. **H × S** 120cm × 75cm. AGM

sinensis **'Morning Light'** A plant to lighten up a border, with silver-edged leaves and fluffy flowers that fade to silver. August to September. **H × S** 120cm × 75cm. AGM

sinensis **'Silberfeder'** Plumes of silver-pink flowers are reliably produced from a thick clump of mid-green leaves. August to September. **H × S** 180cm × 75cm. AGM

sinensis **'Variegatus'** The mid-green leaves, distinctively striped with cream, produce soft brown plumes. October to November. **H × S** 150cm × 75cm

MOLINIA (Moor grass)

caerulea subsp. *caerulea* **'Strahlenquelle'** This lovely 'see-through' grass produces a broad tuft of slender, mid-green leaves that turn gold in autumn. In late summer sprays of soft-purple flowers erupt turning soft brown as they age. August to September. **H × S** 90cm × 60cm

Needs Soil that remains moist in sun or partial shade
Great for Anywhere in the border where light can shine through
Bees & Butterflies No
For Cutting No
Care Not invasive and trouble free

Monarda 'Beauty of Cobham'

Monarda 'Cambridge Scarlet'

Monarda 'Prärienacht'

Monarda 'Schneewittchen'

Monarda 'Scorpion'

Morina longifolia

MONARDA (Bergamot)

Noted for their bright colours, bergamot flowers also attract bees. The stiff stems are crowned by long-lipped, tubular flowers on top of coloured bracts, and the plant forms a handsome, upright clump that needs no staking. When crushed, the mid-green leaves exude a distinctive, pleasant scent.

Needs Well-drained soil that remains moist in sun or partial shade
Great for Middle of the border
Bees & Butterflies Bees
For Cutting Yes
Care Can be prone to mildew, especially if the soil dries out

'Beauty of Cobham' A pretty, clump-forming plant with soft-pink flowers sitting on rosy-purple bracts. June to August. H × S 90cm × 60cm. AGM

'Cambridge Scarlet' On this showy variety, dark red bracts are topped with bright-scarlet flowers. June to August. H × S 90cm × 60cm

'Prärienacht' A free-flowering plant. The whorls of rosy-purple blooms sit on green bracts. June to August. H × S 90cm × 60cm

'Schneewittchen' Named after fairytale heroine Snow White, this variety has pure-white flowers with green bracts. June to August. H × S 90cm × 60cm

'Scorpion' Flowering a little later than the others, this variety has rosy-purple flowers and purple bracts. June to August. H × S 90cm × 60cm

MORINA

longifolia An intriguing and curious plant that may appear a bit too thistle-like for some. The long, drooping, white flowers emerge from a spiky, cup-like collar and are carried in whorls up the strong stems. As the flowers age, they are touched with pink. At the base of the plant the long, spiky, leathery, fresh-green leaves form an evergreen rosette. July to August. H × S 60cm × 30cm.

Needs Well-drained soil in sun
Great for Edge of the border alongside ground-covering plants
Bees & Butterflies Bees
For Cutting No
Care May take a year or two to develop

Nepeta 'Six Hills Giant' with *Gillenia trifoliata* (centre), *Geranium* 'Brookside' and *Geum* 'Prinses Juliana' (rear)

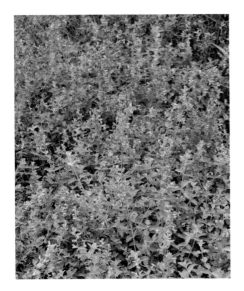

Nepeta × faassenii

Nepeta × faassenii 'Kit Cat'

NEPETA (Catmint)

Invaluable for mixing with other perennials, catmints are also useful for filling a border quickly. Many produce frothy stems of small, large-lipped flowers above a bushy clump of soft-green leaves, which are aromatic when crushed. More upright varieties are ideal for the back of a border.

Needs Well-drained soil in sun or partial shade
Great for Edges and the middle of a border
Bees & Butterflies Bees
For Cutting Yes
Care Cut back after the first flush to get more flowers

× *faassenii* A neat, bushy, mounding plant with soft-grey leaves, this variety has short, leafy spikes of tiny, pale-lavender flowers. May to September. **H** × **S** 45cm × 45cm. AGM

× *faassenii* 'Kit Cat' Shorter, more compact than the previous plant, it has soft-blue flowers and grey leaves. May to September. **H** × **S** 30cm × 30cm

govaniana This graceful, late-flowering, plant bears long, pale-yellow flowers at well-spaced intervals up slender, branched stems. The leaves are soft green. May suffer in cool, damp soils. August to September. **H** × **S** 90cm × 45cm

***grandiflora* 'Dawn to Dusk'** Only a few nepetas have pink flowers. This variety produces dense spikes of pale-pink flowers that sit in mauve calyces. June to September. **H** × **S** 90cm × 75cm

***grandiflora* 'Wild Cat'** Free-flowering and upright, this bushy nepeta produces attractive heads of soft violet-blue flowers. June to September. **H** × **S** 90cm × 75cm

Nepeta govaniana

Nepeta grandiflora 'Dawn to Dusk'

Nepeta grandiflora 'Wild Cat'

Nepeta racemosa 'Snowflake'

Nepeta racemosa 'Walker's Low'

Oenothera macrocarpa

Nepeta subsessilis

racemosa **'Snowflake'** A low, spreading plant with soft grey-green leaves and spikes of tiny, blue-tinted, white flowers. May to September. **H × S** 45cm × 45cm

racemosa **'Walker's Low'** The spikes of violet-blue flowers form a neat mound with grey leaves. May to September. **H × S** 60cm × 60cm. AGM

'Six Hills Giant' This excellent, floriferous plant creates a big, blue mound of long stems with small, mid-green leaves that terminate in whorls of little, true-blue flowers. June to September. **H × S** 120cm × 90cm (photo on p 150)

subsessilis Open spikes of large blue flowers bloom up strong stems with deeply toothed, soft green leaves. A gently spreading plant. July to September. **H × S** 90cm × 60cm

OENOTHERA (Evening primrose)

Masses of flower buds on leafy stems open into large, cup-shaped blooms, each lasting for just a day. Oil is extracted from the seeds.

Needs Well-drained soil in sun
Great for Front of the border
Bees & Butterflies Yes
For Cutting No
Care Trouble free

macrocarpa A prostrate plant with long stems of large, cupped, canary-yellow flowers and long, mid-green leaves. July to September. **H × S** 23cm × 60cm. AGM

'Summer Sun' An upright plant, that tends to tumble forward. Clusters of saucer-shaped, yellow flowers open from red buds on red-tinged stems with deep-green leaves. July to August. **H × S** 60cm × 60cm

Oenothera 'Summer Sun'

OMPHALODES (Navelwort)

verna Early to bloom with pretty sprays of soft-blue flowers held just above a slowly spreading mound of heart-shaped leaves. March to May. **H × S** 25cm × 45cm

Needs Well-drained soil in shade or partial shade
Great for Front of the border
Bees & Butterflies No
For Cutting No
Care Trouble free

OPHIOPOGON (Mondo grass)

planiscapus **'Nigrescens'** Black foliage is unusual in plants. This spreading perennial has grassy tufts of long, matt-black, evergreen leaves and short stems topped with tight spikes of small, lilac-pink flowers. July to August. **H × S** 23cm × 45cm. AGM

Needs Well-drained soil in sun or partial shade
Great for Front of the border and pots
Bees & Butterflies No
For Cutting No
Care Can be slow to establish

ORIGANUM (Marjoram)

A valuable yet small group of plants that are magnets for bees, butterflies and other pollinating insects. When the tiny flowers pop out of colourful bracts the plant really catches the eye. All marjorams are short and perfect for the front of a border.

Needs Well-drained soil in sun
Great for Front of the border
Bees & Butterflies Yes
For Cutting Yes
Care Trouble free. Sometimes seeds around

laevigatum **'Herrenhausen'** A gently creeping, bushy plant with tiny, mauve-pink flowers. These are carried in small, tight clusters up slender, dark red stems with rounded, dark green, mildly aromatic leaves. July to September. **H × S** 45cm × 60cm. AGM

'Pilgrim' Tiny pink flowers emerge from scale-like bracts that are tightly clustered along stems with small, scented leaves. The tops then gently droop over to create a unique and attractive mound that becomes looser over time but still looks good. June to September. **H × S** 30cm × 45cm

'Rosenkuppel' Gently domed heads of tiny purple-pink flowers surrounded by pinkish-purple bracts are held on stiff stems. Creates a neat clump. June to September. **H × S** 45cm × 45cm. AGM

Omphalodes verna

Ophiopogon planiscapus 'Nigrescens'

Origanum laevigatum 'Herrenhausen'

Origanum 'Pilgrim'

Origanum 'Rosenkuppel'

Paeonia 'Shirley Temple' in a semi-shaded border at White Hopton Farm with *Astrantia* 'Roma' and *Iris* 'Chance Beauty' in June

Paeonia

(Peony) The large, often blowsy flowers of peonies are among the most beautiful of all perennials and have been grown in gardens for centuries. Originating in China, peonies were cultivated in medieval Europe by Benedictine monks, who used the seeds and roots medicinally. Today peonies are classic border plants, but although dramatic, the flowering period can be short. To compensate, they produce a handsome clump of deeply divided foliage that is attractive from the moment the succulent shoots appear in spring until the autumn-tinted leaves die down. Once established, peonies are easy to grow, need little attention, and are the longest-lived of all perennials. Many of these glamorous plants also produce scented blooms and they look fabulous arranged in a simple glass vase.

HERBACEOUS PEONIES

In this book all the peonies are herbaceous. These are unlike woody tree peonies – which are usually listed as shrubs – in that the top growth dies right back in autumn. New shoots begin to break through the ground as early as February when the days start to lengthen. By mid-May (in our part of the country) the buds have filled out and, depending on the variety, they open from late May until late June.

INTERSECTIONAL PEONIES

A quiet revolution has been occurring in the peony world. The first crosses between tree and herbaceous peonies, were made in the 1960s but the resulting plants weren't available to gardeners until the 1990s. These fabulous plants, known as intersectional peonies, include the best of both types. The flowers, which can be up to 25cm across, are carried on short woody stems above handsome, leathery, deeply cut leaves that often take on lovely autumn colour before cleanly dropping off. Despite having woody stems these are herbaceous. The plant increases outwards, rather than upwards, and has a neat, broad, bushy habit. New shoots emerge from the bottom of each woody stem. Intersectional peonies are easy to grow and establish, and flower at the same time as other herbaceous peonies.

FLOWER SHAPE

Peony flowers come in four shapes. The following terms are used in the descriptions:
- **Single** Flowers have a single or double row of petals
- **Japanese** These have outer 'guard' petals and a centre of staminodes (*see* box)
- **Semi-double** Flowers have three or more rows of petals
- **Double** These have lots of petals and form a 'powder-puff' or domed crown

Single-flowered *Paeonia* 'Roselette'

Semi-double flowered *Paeonia* 'Zuzu'

Japanese-type *Paeonia* 'Barrington Belle'

Double *Paeonia* 'Elsa Sass'

PEONY TERMS USED

CARPELS The centre 'pod' where the seeds are produced

GUARD PETALS The outer petals

PETALOIDS These look like slender petals, but are sepals or bracts

STAMINODES Resembling very thin, central petals, these sterile stamens are usually a feature of Japanese peony flowers

FLOWERING PERIOD

As with all perennials, flowering depends on where you live in the country. At our nursery, located in the middle of the UK, peonies tend to flower from the last week of May to the third week of June, with each variety blooming very early, early, mid-season, or late within this period.

PEONIES FOR CUTTING

Most peonies make good cut flowers. I recommend these particular varieties, which last for a long time (up to 10 days) in water.

'Barbara'
'Bowl of Beauty'
'Bridal Icing'
'Coral Charm'
'Duchesse de Nemours'
'Edulis Superba'
'Festiva Maxima'
'Kansas'
'Myrtle Gentry'
'Nancy Nora'
'Pillow Talk'
'Sarah Bernhardt'
'Shirley Temple'

SCENT

Many peonies are fragrant. In some varieties the scent is light; in others it is released only after the flowers have been picked and placed in a vase. Scent depends on the time of day, where in the garden the plant is grown (a warm spot for instance) and, of course, your nose! Some good scented varieties are listed below, but there are many others. Information about fragrance is given in each plant's description.

'Alexander Fleming'
'Auguste Dessert'
'Bartzella'
'Bouquet Perfect'
'Bowl Of Cream'
'Bridal Icing''
'Claire de Lune'
'Duchesse de Nemours'
'Edulis Superba'
'Festiva Maxima'
'Helen Hayes'
'Honey Gold'
'Krinkled White'
'Monsieur Jules Elie'
'Myrtle Gentry'
'Nancy Nora'
'Pillow Talk'
'Raspberry Sundae'
'Tom Eckhardt'

GROWING PEONIES

Peonies need a soil that does not become waterlogged at any time during the year. A good, well-drained loam is ideal, but they are just as happy in a clay soil provided it does not stay wet. These are plants of open grassland so prefer full sun, although they will tolerate a light, shady spot.

Peonies can take up to three years to flower, but once established can live for more than 50 years. As with roses, try not to plant peonies where other peonies have been grown in the past.

Planting time

A peony's roots grow once the leaves have died-back in autumn, so the best time to plant is between October and March. Although some advise against putting peonies in the ground after December, I've had no problem planting them in spring.

Dividing

Contrary to received wisdom, peonies really do not mind being moved, especially if they are not divided. However, if a plant has become too large and needs to be divided, make sure the transplanted clumps have at least three 'eyes' (leaf buds).

Planting distances

After five years, each peony plant will have grown to take up approximately one square metre, so they should be planted about 75cm to 90cm apart.

The leaves of intersectional peonies are thick, leathery, and disease-free. In autumn they drop off neatly and cleanly

Planting

It is important to plant herbaceous peonies with the eyes no more than 2cm below the soil. If they are buried any deeper, they may not flower.

Maintaining

If you want to feed peonies put only a ring of very well-rotted manure around the dormant plant in winter. Be sure not to cover the plant as the 'eyes' may rot as they grow.

Top growth can be removed when it dies back. If you have intersectional peonies, you can cut the woody stems back to the ground to tidy up the plant. This is optional, but it won't harm the plant.

PROBLEMS AND SOLUTIONS

The most common ailment peonies suffer from is botrytis, a fungal disease that is more prevalent during warm, damp weather. Evidence of it can be found at the base of the stem or on the buds, which become brown and mouldy. Remove infected foliage and spray the plant with a fungicide.

Failure to flower

I am frequently asked why a peony has not flowered and there are usually three main reasons:

- The peony has been planted too deeply. Lift the plant in autumn and replant at the correct depth.
- If the plant has become too dry during the spring growing season, the buds will fail to swell and look dried up.
- The plant is growing in a very shady spot, which can lead to dry roots.

Leaves

Brown spots may appear on leaves later in the summer, usually in August, just before the plant starts to enter the dormant state. There is no need to worry about them.

Ants

I have been asked how to get rid of ants on peony flower buds. The answer is: don't. In my experience, ants do no harm. Appearing as the bud swells, they feed on the sugary substance it exudes, and may even help the bud to open properly. As soon as the buds start to open, the ants disappear.

Peony shoots are known as 'eyes'

Red shoots of *Paeonia* 'Shirley Temple' emerging in April

Paeonia 'Shirley Temple', fully grown in May

PEONIES IN THE GARDEN

Peonies are easy to grow amongst other perennials. The roots go deep into the ground, which means they don't have to compete for space. I have two rules when placing peonies in a border. One is to put them with small-flowered plants and the other (unless your border is devoted to just peonies) is to plant them as a single specimen. Peony flowers are large and can easily dominate other plants in bloom, making a border look too fussy. However, if the neighbouring flowers are small, the peony will take centre stage for the three or four weeks it is in bloom. Once the flowers have faded, the clump of handsome leaves will enhance other flowering plants. As autumn approaches, peony leaves often turn attractive shades of red or orange before dying right back in winter.

The following perennials look particularly good with peonies:

Achillea	*Iris* (Sibirica types)
Aquilegia	*Nepeta*
Astrantia	*Potentilla*
Campanula	*Salvia*
Centaurea	*Stachys*
Digitalis	*Veronica*
Geranium	
Geum	

Intersectional *Paeonia* 'Cora Louise' with *Papaver orientale* 'Türkenlouis'

Paeonia 'Suruga' creates a focal point in the border and needs no staking

Paeonia 'Moonrise' in May

Paeonia 'Lilac Time' in early June with *Campanula*, *Iris* 'Fond Kiss' and *Geranium* 'Brookside'

Paeonia 'Adolphe Rousseau'

Paeonia 'Alexander Fleming'

'Adolphe Rousseau' Easy to grow, this peony has double, deep cerise-red flowers. Revealing yellow stamens as they open fully, the blooms are carried on strong, upright stems with dark green foliage. Mid. **H** 90cm

'Alexander Fleming' The sweetly scented, double, rich-pink flowers are touched at the edges with silver. When open, the shallow-domed flowers have a loose, swirling centre of petals. Early to mid. **H** 87cm

'Angel Cheeks' The large, ruffled, double, pale-pink flowers are infused with cream and pale to blush-pink as they age. They are mildly fragrant and borne on sturdy stems. Mid. **H** 85cm

'Auguste Dessert' Scented and semi-double, this variety has deep rose-pink flowers with petals that fade to silver-pink around the edges. The flowers open flat revealing a small ring of deep yellow stamens. Good autumn foliage. Mid. **H** 90cm

'Barbara' Great for cutting but not scented. The deep-pink flowers form a tight ball that is surrounded by large guard petals. It has grey leaves and very strong stems. Mid. **H** 90cm

'Bartzella' An excellent intersectional peony with large, lemon- scented, soft-yellow flowers. The petals form a perfect, frilly rosette around delicate, yellow stamens, which have magenta flares at the base. Mid. **H** 90cm

'Bouquet Perfect' This lovely, rose-scented peony has perfectly shaped, bright-pink flowers. A swirling ball of petals is circled by a saucer of large guard petals. As it ages, the centre pales in colour around the edges. Mid to late. **H** 90cm

Paeonia 'Angel Cheeks'

Paeonia 'Auguste Dessert'

Paeonia 'Barbara'

Paeonia 'Bartzella'

Paeonia 'Bouquet Perfect'

Paeonia 'Bowl of Beauty'

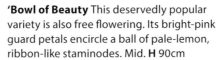

Paeonia 'Bowl of Cream'

Paeonia 'Bridal Icing'

Paeonia 'Buckeye Belle'

'Bowl of Beauty' This deservedly popular variety is also free flowering. Its bright-pink guard petals encircle a ball of pale-lemon, ribbon-like staminodes. Mid. **H** 90cm

'Bowl of Cream' Each smooth, creamy-white petal curves inwards, forming a bowl-like centre. The flowers are double and scented; the leaves are large and grey-green. Early. **H** 78cm

'Bridal Icing' At the centre of the scented, open flower, a ball of slender, cream and white petals looks rather like a scoop of ice cream. As the flower ages, the white petals extend out into a pompom. The flower stems are strong. Mid. **H** 75cm

'Buckeye Belle' This early-blooming plant has fabulous, cupped flowers with velvety, deep-red petals. These are tinged with brown and purple and open around a ring of stamens. Early. **H** 75cm

'Callie's Memory' The underlying colour of the large sumptuous, semi-double flowers of this intersectional peony is cream. The petals seem flushed with peach owing to the magenta flares that stain the base of each. The generous number of side buds on this wide bush make this is a long-flowering peony. Mid. **H** 75cm

'Claire de Lune' An absolutely beautiful plant. The single, sweetly scented, pale-lemon flowers have a central boss of golden yellow stamens. It has red stems and large, deep-green leaves. Very early. **H** 90cm

'Cora Louise' An intersectional peony, this bears glistening, white, semi-double flowers with yellow stamens. At the base of each petal is a striking magenta flare. Mid. **H** 75cm

Paeonia 'Callie's Memory'

Paeonia 'Claire de Lune'

Paeonia 'Cora Louise'

Paeonia 'Coral Charm'

Paeonia 'Cytherea'

Paeonia 'Dinner Plate'

Paeonia 'Doreen'

Paeonia 'Duchesse de Nemours'

Paeonia 'Early Windflower'

'Coral Charm' Impressive for the size of the semi-double, scented, coral flowers alone. They open into deep goblets with loose, golden stamens, the flower colour softening to orange. The long, red stems need staking but the flowers are excellent for cutting, lasting ten days or longer. The leaves are large, deep-green, and shiny. Early to mid. **H** 90cm or more

'Cytherea' The semi-double, bright rose-pink flowers have three or four rows of petals. Goblet-shaped when first open, the blooms age to form a relaxed cup. The flowers are held on short, strong stems with mid-green leaves. Early. **H** 75cm

'Dinner Plate' Aptly named, the large soft-pink flowers open into flat rosettes, their soft, silky petals paler along the edges. Although they are carried on strong, thick stems with thick, leathery, dark green leaves, the flower heads may need staking. Late. **H** 110cm.

'Doreen' This Japanese peony has bright-pink guard petals that fade to paler pink as the flower opens. They are ranged round a pompom-like centre of frilly, ribbon-like, cream staminodes. It blooms over a long period. Mid. **H** 81cm

'Duchesse de Nemours' The double, white flowers of this old yet reliable variety are beautifully scented and excellent for cutting. The loose petals are tinted yellow at the base. Mid. **H** 90cm

'Early Windflower' One of the loveliest early flowering peonies. The small, cupped, pure-white flowers are carried on branched stems and open just above a mound of beautiful, deeply divided leaves. Creates a dense and upright clump. Early. **H** 71cm

Paeonia 'Edulis Superba'

Paeonia 'Eliza Lundy'

Paeonia 'Festiva Maxima'

Paeonia 'First Arrival'

Paeonia 'Garden Treasure'

Paeonia 'Gay Paree'

'Edulis Superba' Among the oldest surviving varieties still grown, this has heavily scented, deep rose-pink blooms that form shallow domes. Despite having rather weak stems, the flowers are great for cutting. Early to mid. **H** 85cm

'Eliza Lundy' A low-growing plant with short stems, it produces small, rich-red, double flowers with ruffled petals held in a ball by larger, outer guard petals. The glossy, mid-green leaves create a generally upright mound that may flop over at the edges. Early to mid. **H** 71cm

'Festiva Maxima' Loosely formed and scented, the double, white flowers display a few red streaks and have large guard petals. A free-flowering variety that is good for cutting. Mid. **H** 90cm

'First Arrival' A delightful intersectional peony with large, semi-double, glossy, lavender-pink flowers that soften to pink with age. Each bloom opens at even intervals across an open, spreading bush with deeply divided leaves that turn red in autumn. Early. **H** 80cm

'Garden Treasure' My first intersectional peony, this superb plant was given to me by the breeder. The large, semi-double, primrose-yellow flowers are fragrant, their petals forming a ruff around a ring of golden stamens and distinctive, green carpels. Large, mid-green, divided leaves create a handsome rounded, broad mound. Mid. **H** 90cm

'Gay Paree' The dainty flowers have rich rose-pink guard petals and a large centre of ribbon-like, cream staminodes that are stained pink along the edges. The flowers are held upright. Mid. **H** 90cm

Paeonia 'Goldilocks'

Paeonia 'Helen Hayes'

Paeonia 'Hillary'

Paeonia 'Honey Gold'

Paeonia 'Inspecteur Lavergne'

Paeonia 'Jan van Leeuwen'

Paeonia 'Julia Rose'

'Goldilocks The nicely scented, ball-shaped, soft-yellow flower has intertwined petals and large guard petals. It might take a few years to produce the most glamorous blooms. Mid. **H** 75cm

'Helen Hayes' Carried on strong stems with dark green, glossy leaves the scented, double, deep-pink flowers have notched petal edges. The head forms a high dome with the shorter inner petals creating a central bowl. Mid. **H** 90cm

'Hillary' This may not be the most shapely of intersectional peonies, but it carries a great profusion of shaggy, semi-double, raspberry red-stained, cream flowers. Mid to late. **H** 90cm

'Honey Gold' Pure-white guard petals encase long, fringed, yellow staminodes on this long-flowering and very fragrant variety. These fill out to form a dome, sometimes with extra flutes of petals in the centre. Early. **H** 76cm

'Inspecteur Lavergne' A classic peony with long stems of ball-shaped, double, rich-red flowers that have silver-lined, frilly edged petals. Mid. **H** 90cm

'Jan van Leeuwen' One of the most perfect white peonies. The cupped, pristine flowers are filled with golden staminodes and carried on evenly sized, upright stems to form a neat mound. Mid. **H** 90cm

'Julia Rose' A stunning intersectional peony with large, silky, semi-double blooms. These start out red then quickly fade to a rose-pink, warmed by gold tones at the base of the petals. The thick, long, deeply divided foliage is burnished with pewter in autumn. Mid. **H** 80cm

Paeonia 'Kansas'

Paeonia 'Karl Rosenfield'

Paeonia 'Krinkled White'

Paeonia 'Lemon Chiffon'

Paeonia 'Magical Mystery Tour'

Paeonia 'Mai Fleuri'

'Kansas' The compact, frilly flowers are large doubles and the colour is a clear yet rich shade between pink and red. They sit above a robust clump of leaves on upright stems, which makes this a good variety for cutting. Early to mid. **H** 90cm

'Karl Rosenfield' On this free-flowering plant, the petals of the bright-crimson blooms curl inwards and are notched along the edges. The flowers are borne on strong stems with dark green leaves and the plant forms a neat, self-supporting clump. Mid. **H** 91cm

'Krinkled White' Resembling crêpe paper, the petals of this heavily scented, single, pure-white flower surround a boss of yellow stamens. The straight stems rise above shiny, light green leaves. Early. **H** 81cm

'Lemon Chiffon' The lovely, large, soft-lemon flowers are semi-double. They open into a wide cup showing off a small mound of golden stamens. Depending on the wind strength, the strong stems will stay upright. Mid. **H** 86cm

'Magical Mystery Tour' The colour of the semi-double flowers, which form shaggy rosettes, changes from soft peach to pale yellow with age. Each bloom has a centre of small stamens and red flares stain the base of the petals. When mature, this is a neat mounding plant. Mid. **H** 60cm

'Mai Fleuri' The deeply cupped, single, soft-pink flowers have translucent petals and a centre of fine, yellow stamens. This variety may not flower for long, but the large, bright-green leaves are very handsome. Early. **H** 75cm

Paeonia 'Marie Lemoine'

Paeonia 'Midnight Sun'

Paeonia mlokosewitschii

Paeonia 'Monsieur Jules Elie'

Paeonia 'Moonrise'

Paeonia 'Mr G. F. Hemerik'

Paeonia 'Myrtle Gentry'

'Marie Lemoine' A classic peony of long standing with fragrant, double, pure-white blooms that open out to reveal shorter, frilly inner petals just touched with lemon. A fairly short plant with deep green leaves. Late. **H** 70cm

'Midnight Sun' Elegant, cupped, dark red flowers with silky petals are filled with gold-edged staminodes. The blooms are scented and carried on stiff, upright stems. Mid. **H** 91cm

mlokosewitschii I find this fleeting beauty difficult to grow, as it needs warm, well-drained soil. The soft-lemon, cupped flowers are carried on upright stems above large, glaucous leaves. Very early. **H** 85cm

'Monsieur Jules Elie' Strongly rose-scented, the large, double, rose-pink flowers open into a high dome. The petals curve inwards and are edged with silver. Mid. **H** 90cm

'Moonrise' Big ball-like, soft green buds open into scented, single, soft-yellow blooms filled with yellow stamens. The flowers pale to cream with age. The big leaves are glossy, light green. Very early. **H** 90cm

'Mr G. F. Hemerik' Deep-pink petals, fading slightly with age, surround a perfect dome of broad, cream staminodes. This Japanese peony has distinctive, crinkled leaves. Mid. **H** 90cm

'Myrtle Gentry' Very beautiful, like a perfect old rose, the large, double, scented, blush-pink flowers fade to white with age. They are carried on stiff stems above matt, mid-green leaves. Excellent for cutting. Mid. **H** 90cm

Paeonia 'Nancy Nora'

Paeonia 'Nellie Saylor'

Paeonia 'Nosegay'

'Nancy Nora' The large, scented, pale blush-pink flowers have equal-sized petals and a dipped centre, rather like a lovely old rose. Upright stems with soft-green leaves make this variety good for cutting. Mid. **H** 90cm

'Nellie Saylor' Piled high on the broad, ruffled, pink-red guard petals is a dense mound of broad, white petaloids that are heavily and unevenly stained with magenta. A tuft of red petals emerges from the centre of the sweetly scented flower. Mid to late. **H** 90cm

'Nosegay' Although not very long-lasting, the single, delicate shell-pink flowers with petals like silk, are beautiful. They are carried above deeply divided, mid-green leaves. Early. **H** 65cm

'Nymphe' A free-flowering plant with upward-facing, strongly scented, single blooms in deep pink. Upright stems rise above a neat mound of dark green leaves. This always sets seed. Late. **H** 90cm

officinalis **'Anemoniflora Rosea'** This Japanese peony is an absolute delight when mature. The shallowly domed, bright pink flowers are carried on stiff stems with grey-green leaves. Early. **H** 75cm

officinalis **'Rubra Plena'** A traditional double, red cottage-garden peony. The ball-shaped, scented, deepest-crimson flowers have frilly petals that form small rosettes. The blooms are carried on long, rather lax stems above lush, deep-green leaves. Early. **H** 75cm

Paeonia 'Nymphe'

Paeonia officinalis 'Anemoniflora Rosea'

Paeonia officinalis 'Rubra Plena'

Paeonia 'Paul M. Wild'

Paeonia 'Paula Fay'

'Paul M. Wild' Definitely one of the best reds we have grown, this variety has luxurious, double, richest-red flowers with velvety petals that form a neat dome. The leaves are bright green. Mid. **H** 90cm

'Paula Fay' The fragrant, vivid-pink, single flowers are really lovely, even when they are in bud. Opening into deep, tulip-shaped cups, they are carried on thick stems that remain firmly upright, with shiny, light green leaves. Early. **H** 88cm

***peregrina* 'Otto Froebel'** A fleeting but handsome peony bearing goblet-shaped vermilion flowers with a ring of golden stamens. They are carried singly on long stems with attractive, large, shiny, mid-green leaves. Early. **H** 80cm

'Picotee' A lovely, rather brief-flowering variety with single, white flowers tinted a soft pink that darkens to magenta at the petal edges. Ruffled leaves form an attractive mound. Early. **H** 60cm

'Pillow Talk' Like perfect powder-puffs, the clear-pink, scented flowers are freely produced on strong stems above dark green leaves. This is great for cutting. Mid. **H** 90cm

'Raspberry Sundae' Large and high-domed, these fragrant flowers consist of rings of cream petaloids and soft pink-flushed, white petals. The flower grows into a true ice-cream sundae on long, rather relaxed stems. Mid. **H** 90cm

'Red Charm' This excellent plant has double, glossy-red flowers that are long-lasting. Held on stiff stems, the blooms form a domed ball of serrated petals within large guard petals. Early. **H** 81cm

Paeonia peregrina 'Otto Froebel'

Paeonia 'Picotee'

Paeonia 'Pillow Talk'

Paeonia 'Raspberry Sundae'

Paeonia 'Red Charm'

Paeonia 'Sarah Bernhardt'

Paeonia 'Scarlet O'Hara'

Paeonia 'Shirley Temple'

Paeonia 'Sword Dance'

Paeonia 'Tom Eckhardt'

Paeonia 'Vogue'

Paeonia wittmanniana (pink form)

'Sarah Bernhardt' The scented, double, pure-pink flowers of this classic variety are tinted with silver around the edges. Long stems make the flowers excellent for cutting. Late. **H** 90cm

'Scarlet O'Hara' Each lightly scented flower, which looks like a big, scarlet poppy, lasts for up to ten days. As the flowers age, the petals get bigger and fade to deep pink. Early. **H** 90cm

'Shirley Temple' A free-flowering plant with big, glamorous balls of double, white flowers with pink-tinged guard petals. Long flower stems make this an excellent flower for cutting. Mid. **H** 86cm

'Sword Dance' A stunning Japanese peony with a ruff of silky, bright-red guard petals surrounding a large, loose dome of red-tinged, yellow staminodes. Late. **H** 87cm

'Tom Eckhardt' The scented flowers have fuchsia-pink guard petals, a large dome of cream staminodes and may produce a few more pink inner petals. The whole flower pales with age and sits above very large, bright-green leaves. Late. **H** 90cm

'Vogue' Excellent for cutting, the beautiful flowers are large, scented, and double. When they open, the blooms are soft pink and fade to white with age. Mid. **H** 89cm

wittmanniana I grow the pink form of this usually white-flowered peony in the semi-shade of trees. The petals are almost translucent with undertones of yellow and the big, shiny, green leaves form a neat mound. Early. **H** 85cm

Panicum virgatum 'Warrior'

PANICUM

(Switch grass) Creating a graceful fountain, the tops of the slender, upright, mid-green leaves tip over towards the top. Late in the summer, slender stems carry a cloud of tiny purple flowers.

Needs Well-drained soil in sun
Great for Middle of the border
Bees & Butterflies No
For Cutting No
Care Cut the leaves back in spring

virgatum **'Shenandoah'** Blue-grey leaves turn shades of red from the tips downwards. July to September. **H × S** 120cm × 60cm. AGM

virgatum **'Warrior'** From late summer to autumn the purple-tinged green leaves take on shades of red to yellow. July to September. **H × S** 120cm × 105cm

PAPAVER (Oriental poppy)

Among the most opulent of perennial flowers, the very large, often cupped blooms of poppies really draw the eye into a border. At the centre of the papery petals, the distinctive, knob-shaped seed pod turns fluffy with stamens. The tall, hairy stems rise above a thick clump of long, rough, mid-green leaves.

Needs Well-drained soil in sun

Great for Middle of the border

Bees & Butterflies Bees

For Cutting Yes, but the stems have a milky sap so need to be sealed in hot water

Care Foliage dies back after flowering, re-emerging from late summer onwards, so think about what to plant near them as a temporary measure to cover up the gap. I use later-flowering asters such as *Aster* 'Little Carlow'. Poppy roots can be difficult to eradicate. When you lift the plant, any pieces left in the ground will re-grow. Some oriental poppy varieties need staking.

orientale **'Burning Heart'** A fairly new variety with perfectly shaped, semi-double, deep reddish-pink flowers. This needs no staking. May to June. **H × S** 75cm × 70cm

orientale **Goliath Group 'Beauty of Livermere'** Held at the top of stiff stems are big, silky, vibrant, rich-red blooms with black spots at each petal's base. May not come true if grown from seed. May to June. **H × S** 105cm × 80cm

orientale **'Mrs Perry'** An old, but reliable variety with delicate, deeply cupped, soft salmon-pink flowers with black 'thumb prints' at the base of each petal. May need staking. May to June. **H × S** 90cm × 80cm

Papaver orientale 'Burning Heart'

Panicum virgatum 'Shenandoah'

Papaver orientale Goliath Group 'Beauty of Livermere'

Papaver orientale 'Mrs Perry'

Papaver orientale 'Patty's Plum'

Papaver orientale 'Snow Goose'

orientale 'Patty's Plum' During the 1990s this was THE poppy to grow owing to its glamorous, ruffled, deep plum-mauve flowers. The tall stems might need some staking. May to June. **H × S** 90cm × 80cm

orientale 'Snow Goose' Perfectly shaped, ruffled, and pure-white, the flowers have dark maroon blotches at the base of each petal. May to June. **H × S** 80cm × 70cm

orientale 'Türkenlouis' With its large, vibrant-red flowers fringed along the edges, this is beautiful and eye-catching. May need support. May to June. **H × S** 90cm × 80cm

PENSTEMON

These free-flowering plants drip with colourful foxglove-like flowers. I find most of them difficult to blend with other flowering perennials, therefore I have chosen just two that will fit any style of border.

Needs Well-drained soil in sun
Great for Middle of the border; containers
Bees & Butterflies Bees
For Cutting Yes

Care Can be tender in cold areas of the country and may not thrive in soil that remains wet over winter. Prune the woody stems to a leaf joint in spring

'Andenken an Friedrich Hahn' This handsome plant is covered with long, slim, bright-crimson trumpets. It forms an open, upright bush with red stems and slender, mid-green leaves. July to September. **H × S** 80cm × 50cm. AGM

digitalis 'Husker Red' I would grow this plant for the deep-red leaves alone, although the spikes of slender, white, lilac-tinged trumpets round things off nicely. July to September. **H × S** 75cm × 60cm

Papaver orientale 'Türkenlouis'

Penstemon digitalis 'Husker Red'

Penstemon 'Andenken an Friedrich Hahn'

Persicaria affinis 'Darjeeling Red'

Persicaria amplexicaulis 'Blackfield'

Persicaria amplexicaulis 'Alba'

Persicaria amplexicaulis 'Fat Domino'

Persicaria amplexicaulis 'Inverleith'

PERSICARIA (Bistort)

Although bistorts may not be the most 'flowery' of perennials, they are among the longest-blooming. Great quantities of flower spikes packed with tiny stars or bell-shaped flowers are carried with enormous grace, over many months. The stems are slender and rise above a mound or carpet of weed-excluding leaves.

Needs Soil that remains moist in sun or partial shade
Great for All parts of the border
Bees & Butterflies Bees
For Cutting Yes
Care Trouble free and easy to grow in the right soil. *P. amplexicaulis* hybrids will self-seed freely

affinis **'Darjeeling Red'** Long 'pokers' of tiny, soft-pink flowers are carried just above a thick carpet of slim, mid-green leaves. These turn brick-red as they age, creating interesting mixed tones. Other very similar varieties include *P. affinis* 'Superba' and 'Donald Lowndes'. June to September. **H × S** 30cm × 90cm. AGM

amplexicaulis **'Alba'** Thread-thin spikes of white flowers open from bronze buds and rise elegantly from a mound of big, oval leaves. Very effective when planted against a background of dark foliage. July to September. **H × S** 90cm × 90cm

amplexicaulis **'Blackfield'** A plant with rich-red flowers opening from very dark buds, giving the spikes a dark red tinge. The leaves are big, oval, and mid-green. July to September. **H × S** 105cm × 90cm

amplexicaulis **'Fat Domino'** On this very open and upright plant, the long, fat spikes of rich-red flowers make a big impact. It has slender stems and large, mid-green leaves. July to October. **H × S** 90cm × 75cm

amplexicaulis **'Inverleith'** Stumpy and profuse spikes of tiny, pink-red flowers tumble from a dense mound of mid-green leaves. July to October. **H × S** 60cm × 75cm

amplexicaulis **'Jo and Guido's Form'** Slim flower spikes in a pretty shade of bright pink cover a mound of big, dark green leaves. July to September. **H × S** 90cm × 90cm

amplexicaulis **'Orange Field'** A handsome plant with upright spikes of coral-pink flowers sitting proudly above a mound of large, oval, mid-green leaves. July to October. **H × S** 90cm × 90cm

amplexicaulis **'Rosea'** Slender, soft-pink spikes seem to hang in the air like strings of beads on this gently coloured plant with big, mid-green leaves. July to September. **H × S** 90cm × 90cm

Persicaria amplexicaulis
'Jo and Guido's Form'

Persicaria amplexicaulis 'Orange Field'

Persicaria amplexicaulis 'Rosea'

Persicaria amplexicaulis 'Taurus'

Persicaria amplexicaulis 'White Eastfield' with
Anthemis 'E. C. Buxton'

amplexicaulis **'Taurus'** A continuous
stream of slender, bright-red spikes creates
a colourful swathe above large, handsome
leaves. *P. amplexicaulis* 'Firetail' is similar.
July to September. **H × S** 90 cm × 90cm

amplexicaulis **'White Eastfield'** Slim pure-
white flower spikes weave above leaves that
are narrower than others of the type. July to
September. **H × S** 90 cm × 60cm

bistorta **'Superba'** This spreading plant has
big, oval, soft-green leaves and pokers of
tiny, baby-pink flowers. Prefers damper soils.
May to June. **H × S** 90cm × 90cm. AGM

polymorpha Enormous, yet self-supporting,
this unassuming, bushy plant carries big
plumes of tiny, cream flowers that become
pink with age. The long, sturdy bronze
stems have large, mid-green leaves. July to
October. **H × S** 200cm × 150cm

Persicaria bistorta 'Superba'

Persicaria polymorpha

Phlomis tuberosa

PHLOMIS

This excellent, if very small, group of tough perennials has rough, heart-shaped leaves and hooded flowers carried in tiered whorls up rigidly straight stems. Over winter, the long-lasting stems of *P. russeliana* provide wonderful structure.

Needs Well-drained soil in sun or partial shade, including clay soils
Great for Front of the border
Bees & Butterflies Bees
For Cutting Yes
Care Can be slow to establish, otherwise trouble free

russeliana (Jerusalem sage) A plant with presence. The hooded, soft-yellow flowers are carried in thick rings all the way up the stems. Handsome, sage-green leaves sit in pairs just below the flowers and, at the base, form a weed-suppressing, evergreen carpet. June to August. **H × S** 90cm × 90cm. AGM

tuberosa An elegant plant with whorls of soft-mauve blooms set at intervals up dark red stems with rich-green leaves. June to August. **H × S** 120cm × 60cm

PHLOX

Bright-coloured, luxuriant, and very fragrant, phloxes come in shades of pink, white, and purple. The single flowers are flat and held in large, billowing clusters. They are carried on stiff stems that rarely need any staking. Within a few years, plants will grow into a big clump.

Needs Well-drained soil in sun or partial shade
Great for Front or middle of the border
Bees & Butterflies Yes
For Cutting Yes

Phlomis russeliana with *Geranium psilostemon*

Phlox × *arendsii* 'Hesperis'

Phlox × *arendsii* 'Luc's Lilac' with *Persicaria amplexicaulis* 'Jo and Guido's Form'

Care When lifting *P. paniculata* types, ensure you clear all roots to prevent re-growth. In damp summers *P. paniculata* can suffer from leaf spot and sometimes powdery mildew

× *arendsii* **'Hesperis'** One of the last phlox to bloom. Tall heads of small, lilac, heavily scented flowers rise from an open clump. July to September. **H × S** 105cm × 75cm

× *arendsii* **'Luc's Lilac'** The heads of delicate pink, magenta-eyed flowers form shallow domes and an airy clump. July to September. **H × S** 90cm × 60cm. AGM

glaberrima **'Bill Baker'** A trailing phlox that is ideal for the front of a border. The lavender-pink flowers with tiny, white eyes are held in open clusters on red stems. June to July. **H × S** 30cm × 45cm. AGM

Phlox maculata (Meadow phlox) *There are only a few varieties and all flower before the more dramatically coloured Phlox paniculata. Their slender columns of small, flat flowers and slim, mid-green leaves form elegant clumps.*

maculata **'Alpha'** A lovely, strongly scented variety with fine, tall heads of small, rich-pink flowers. July to August. **H × S** 90cm × 75cm. AGM

maculata **'Natascha'** Borne in tapering spikes, the heavily scented white flowers have starry, pink centres. July to August. **H × S** 90cm × 75cm. AGM

maculata **'Omega'** White flowers with small, pale pink-ringed eyes stand tall on neat, upright clumps. July to August. **H × S** 90cm × 75cm. AGM

Phlox glaberrima 'Bill Baker'

Phlox maculata 'Alpha'

Phlox maculata 'Natascha'

Phlox maculata 'Omega'

Phlox paniculata 'Blue Boy'

Phlox paniculata 'Blue Paradise'

Phlox paniculata 'Brigadier'

Phlox paniculata 'Bright Eyes'

Phlox paniculata 'David'

Phlox paniculata 'Discovery'

Phlox paniculata (Border phlox) *Often richly coloured, the individual flowers are quite large, their clusters forming towering or shallow domes. The flowers continue to open over a long period and are carried on stiff stems with, usually, mid-green leaves. There are many, many varieties in this very popular group. In our garden, they look their best during August.*

paniculata **'Blue Boy'** A short plant with heavily scented, lilac-blue flowers. July to September. **H × S** 60cm × 60cm

paniculata **'Blue Paradise'** Single, vivid lilac-blue flowers are carried in neatly domed clusters on dark purple stems. July to September. **H × S** 90cm × 75cm

paniculata **'Brigadier'** The domed heads of bright pink-red flowers borne by this old variety have a lovely scent. July to September. **H × S** 75cm × 75cm

paniculata **'Bright Eyes'** This soft-coloured variety bears domed clusters of pale-pink flowers with bright-pink eyes. July to September. **H × S** 90cm × 75cm

paniculata **'David'** A sturdy and disease-resistant plant with large, tall heads of pure-white flowers. The bright green of the smooth leaves is distinctive. July to September. **H × S** 90cm × 75cm. AGM

paniculata **'Discovery'** More delicate than many *P. paniculata* types, it has shallow heads of soft-pink flowers with magenta eyes. July to September. **H × S** 90cm × 75cm

paniculata **'Eva Cullum'** A heavily scented plant, this bears clusters of bright-pink flowers with darker pink eyes. July to August. **H × S** 90cm × 75cm. AGM

paniculata **'Sweet Summer Dream'** One of a series of less-vigorous phloxes with scented, salmon-pink flowers on dark red stems. July to August. **H × S** 80cm × 50cm

paniculata **'Sweet Summer Fantasy'** Loose heads of very fragrant, pink-purple flowers display large white centres. July to August. **H × S** 80cm × 50cm

paniculata **'Sweet Summer Surprise'** Forming a neat, short mound over time, this plant bears clusters of rose-purple flowers. July to August. **H × S** 80cm × 50cm

paniculata **'Uspekh'** The most strongly scented phlox I have grown, this variety has big, rosy-purple flowers with large, white eyes. Sometimes listed as 'Laura'. July to August. **H × S** 75cm × 60cm. AGM

paniculata **'White Admiral'** A free-flowering plant with towering heads of heavily scented, pure-white flowers that are more star-shaped than round. July to August. **H × S** 90cm × 75cm. AGM

Phlox paniculata 'Eva Cullum'

Phlox paniculata 'Sweet Summer Dream'

Phlox paniculata 'Sweet Summer Surprise'

Phlox paniculata 'Sweet Summer Fantasy'
with Stachys officinalis 'Hummelo' and
Eryngium 'Pen Blue'

Phlox paniculata 'Uspekh'

Phlox paniculata 'White Admiral'

Phuopsis stylosa

Physostegia virginiana 'Summer Snow'

Physostegia virginiana var. *speciosa* 'Variegata'

Physostegia virginiana 'Vivid'

Pimpinella major 'Rosea'

PHUOPSIS

stylosa The short stems of this rather untidy, but useful, ground-covering plant are topped by fluffy, bright-pink flowers like pom-poms. These are carried in profusion above whorls of scented, crisp, light green leaves. May to June. **H × S** 23cm × 60cm

Needs Well-drained soil in sun or partial shade
Great for Front of the border
Bees & Butterflies Bees
For Cutting No
Care Neaten straggly plants by cutting back after flowering; otherwise trouble free

PHYSOSTEGIA (Obedient plant)

Upright, elegant but not showy, this perennial resembles a short foxglove. Tapering spires of small, tubular flowers – the lips extending outwards – cover a straight stem with long leaves. If you give a flower a gentle push to one side, it will stay put for a while, hence the common name.

Needs Well-drained soil in sun or partial shade
Great for Middle of the border
Bees & Butterflies Bees
For Cutting Yes
Care Trouble free

virginiana var. *speciosa* 'Variegata' The flowers are a pretty shade of soft mauve, but the attractive cream-edged foliage also looks good on its own. July to September. **H × S** 80cm × 60cm

virginiana 'Summer Snow' A clean-looking plant carrying stems of purest-white flowers. July to September. **H × S** 80cm × 60cm. AGM

virginiana 'Vivid' A softly coloured, upright clump, this has pale-mauve flowers. July to September. **H × S** 80cm × 60cm. AGM

PIMPINELLA

major 'Rosea' (Great burnet saxifrage) Resembling our native cow parsley, but in pink, this bears flat heads of tiny, bright-pink flowers that fade with age. These are carried on branched, upright stems above a loose mound of deeply divided, rich-green leaves. July to August. **H × S** 60cm × 50cm

Needs Soil that remains moist but not wet in sun
Great for Front of a border and wild gardens
Bees & Butterflies Bees
For Cutting No
Care Trouble free in the right soil

POLEMONIUM (Jacob's ladder)

Clusters of bell-shaped flowers are ranged all the way up the stems and the attractive divided leaves resemble the rungs of a ladder.

Needs Well-drained soil in sun or partial shade
Great for Front or middle of the border
Bees & Butterflies Bees
For Cutting No
Care These can be very short-lived in a soil that does not drain well. Prefers a cooler spot in the garden.

caeruleum subsp. *caeruleum* f. *albiflorum*
This white form of *P. caeruleum* (which is usually blue) self-seeds freely. It produces leafy, upright stems topped with sprays of silky, pure-white flowers. June to August. **H × S** 60cm × 45cm

'Heaven Scent' A compact, free-flowering, mounding plant with chocolate-brown tinged green leaves. Against this pretty backdrop, soft-blue, bell-shaped flowers held on slender stems emerge in a continuous flow just above the mound. June to August. **H × S** 45cm × 30cm

'Lambrook Mauve' A charming, very early flowering variety with sprays of open, soft mauve-pink flowers carried above a broad, relaxed clump of mid-green leaves. May to June. **H × S** 60cm × 75cm

'Northern Lights' Free-flowering and bushy, this plant carries sprays of lilac-blue flowers on straight stems with ladder-like mid-green leaves. June to September. **H × S** 45cm × 30cm. AGM

reptans **'Stairway To Heaven'** A native North American woodland plant included for its vigour and determination to thrive. The variegated leaves are mid-green, prettily edged with cream and flushed deep pink. Sprays of palest blue flowers add further colour to this unusual form. May to July. **H × S** 30cm × 30cm

yezoense var. *hidakanum* **'Bressingham Purple'** On this upright plant, clusters of violet bells stand out against almost-black stems. The dark green leaves are tinged with red. May to July. **H × S** 60cm × 45cm

Polemonium caeruleum subsp. *caeruleum* f. *albiflorum*

Polemonium 'Heaven Scent'

Polemonium 'Lambrook Mauve'

Polemonium 'Northern Lights'

Polemonium repans 'Stairway to Heaven'

Polemonium yezoense var. *hidakanum* 'Bressingham Purple'

Potentilla × *hopwoodiana* in the middle of an August border

POLYGONATUM (Solomon's seal)

× hybridum This noble plant prefers shady parts of the garden. Structurally different to many perennials, it has long, arching stems with offset pairs of wing-like, pleated, mid-green leaves. Below them dangle clusters of small, green-rimmed, cream bells. The stems bend gracefully over the ground, forming a canopy. May to June. **H × S** 105cm × 75cm. AGM

Needs Cool, shady spot with moist soil
Great for Woodland or by a north wall
Bees & Butterflies No
For Cutting Yes
Care Although they won't kill it, the larvae of Solomon's seal sawfly can attack the plant in late spring. Pick off the little grey caterpillars when you see them.

POTENTILLA (Cinquefoil)

Individually, the blooms of this charming, easy-to-grow group may not be dramatic, but they are produced in great quantity. Most varieties have a relaxed shape, the slender, long stems forming a waterfall of colour that makes them useful for edging borders. They resemble strawberries, and have very similar, large leaves.

Needs Well-drained soil in sun or partial shade
Great for Front and middle of the border
Bees & Butterflies Bees
For Cutting No
Care Some potentillas are so lax in habit they will fall forwards. To encourage them to stand taller, plant in the middle of a border among upright plants and the stems will sneak upwards

'Arc-en-ciel' The semi-double, red flowers, highlighted with flecks of yellow, are carried on long, arching stems. June to August. **H × S** 45cm × 45cm

'Esta Ann' A vividly coloured plant. The long, arching stems terminate in sprays of startling bright-yellow flowers with contrasting red flares in the centre. June to August. **H × S** 45cm × 45cm

'Gibson's Scarlet' Among the most vivid of the red-flowered varieties. Blooms are carried on long, lax stems over many weeks. June to August. **H × S** 45cm × 75cm. AGM

× hopwoodiana (left) A lovely, long-flowering plant with white-edged, soft salmon-pink flowers and long, arching stems. May to August. **H × S** 45cm × 60cm

nepalensis 'Miss Willmott' This seed-raised variety flowers very freely. Its rich-pink, raspberry-centred blooms pale with age. June to August. **H × S** 45cm × 60cm

Polygonatum × hybridum

Potentilla 'Arc-en-ciel'

Potentilla 'Esta Ann'

Potentilla 'Gibson's Scarlet'

Potentilla nepalensis 'Miss Willmott'

Potentilla recta var. *sulphurea*

Potentilla rupestris

recta var. sulphurea Upright, well-branched stems are topped with upward-facing, soft primrose-yellow flowers. The jagged, mid-green leaves are carried all the way down the stems. Comes true from seed. June to August. **H × S** 60cm × 45cm

rupestris An early-flowering, rather frothy plant. Pretty, pure-white flowers with yellow centres are held on slender, well-branched stems. May to June. **H × S** 60cm × 75cm

'William Rollisson' The eye-catching, semi- double flowers are vermilion at first with flares of yellow. As they age, the blooms turn orange. June to August. **H × S** 60cm × 75cm. AGM

PRIMULA (Primrose)

Of the thousands of primulas available to gardeners, only a limited number are suitable for bigger borders. Those listed below work well and are perfect for damp ground. The primrose family is a charming group of plants with simply shaped flowers, which are often scented, springing from a rosette of long, broad, mid-green leaves.

Needs Soil that remains reliably moist in partial shade or shade
Great for Suitable for pond edges and any damp soil
Bees & Butterflies Bees
For Cutting No
Care Given the right site and soil, they will not only thrive but seed around

bulleyana Rings of single, yellow-orange flowers are carried in tiers up the stiff, mid-green stems above a rosette of slightly crinkled, long leaves. June to July. **H × S** 45cm × 23cm. AGM

florindae This heavily scented plant likes wetter soils. Drooping, primrose-yellow flowers form a cluster at the top of tall, light-green stems above soft-green leaves. June to July. **H × S** 60cm × 30cm. AGM

japonica 'Miller's Crimson' A really colourful candelabra primula with whorls of single, pink-crimson flowers carried at intervals up straight, felted, grey stems. June to July. **H × S** 60cm × 30cm. AGM

japonica 'Postford White' The simply shaped, white flowers with yellow rings around the centres are carried in whorls up straight stems. At the base sits a rosette of long, mid-green leaves. May to July. **H × S** 80cm × 23cm. AGM

pulverulenta Carrying whorls of wine-red flowers in tiers, the stiffly upright stems rise from a rosette of light green leaves. June to July. **H × S** 60cm × 30cm. AGM

Primula bulleyana

Potentilla 'William Rollisson'

Primula florindae

Primula japonica 'Miller's Crimson'

Primula japonica 'Postford White'

Primula pulverulenta

Prunella grandiflora 'Alba'

PRUNELLA (Self heal)

These free-flowering, ground-cover plants are useful for the front of a shady border. Stumpy spikes of large, hooded flowers bloom above a carpet of mid-green leaves.

Needs Well-drained soil that remains moist in sun, partial shade, or shade
Great for Front of the border
Bees & Butterflies Bees
For Cutting No
Care Trouble free

grandiflora **'Alba'** A white-flowered variety. June to August. **H × S** 15cm × 45cm

grandiflora **'Altenberg Rosa'** Rose-pink flowers. June to August. **H × S** 23cm × 60cm

grandiflora **'Loveliness'** A pretty carpet of soft-lilac flowers. June to August. **H × S** 15cm × 45cm

Prunella grandiflora 'Loveliness'

Prunella grandiflora 'Altenberg Rosa'

Pulmonaria 'Blue Ensign'

Pulmonaria 'Diana Clare'

Pulmonaria mollis

Pulmonaria 'Opal'

PULMONARIA (Lungwort)

A spring delight and one of the earliest perennial to bloom. Sprays of funnel-shaped flowers cluster on top of stout stems above a thick, flat rosette or mound of large, often spotted, decorative leaves. As the season progresses, the leafy clump fills out.

Needs Well-drained soil that remains moist in sun, partial shade, or shade
Great for Front of the border
Bees & Butterflies Bees
For Cutting No
Care Trouble free

'Blue Ensign' Bright violet-blue flowers set in almost-black bracts are carried above smooth, deep-green leaves. March to April. **H × S** 25cm × 23cm. AGM

'Diana Clare' A flat rosette of long, silvery-green leaves is topped with small clusters of violet-blue flowers on lax stems. March to May. **H × S** 30cm × 30cm. AGM

mollis An easy plant to grow. Clusters of funnel-shaped, violet-blue flowers open from pink buds, forming a mist above a mound of smooth, mid-green leaves. March to April. **H × S** 45cm × 45cm

'Opal' A big, upright clump of long, broad, evenly spotted leaves throws up strong stems of soft sky-blue flowers. March to April. **H × S** 25cm × 30cm. AGM

***rubra* 'Bowles's Red'** This short, spreading plant has evergreen, plain-green leaves and small clusters of attractive, coral-red flowers. March to April. **H × S** 30cm × 30cm

***saccharata* 'Leopard'** Reddish-pink bells fading to mauve are held on short stems above fresh-green leaves, spotted with silver. March to April. **H × S** 30cm × 30cm

Pulmonaria rubra 'Bowles's Red'

Pulmonaria saccharata 'Leopard'

Pulmonaria saccharata 'Mrs Moon'

saccharata **'Mrs Moon'** A free-flowering variety with pure-blue flowers that emerge from pink buds. It forms a neatly rounded mound of silver-spotted, mid-green leaves. March to April. **H × S** 30cm × 30cm

'Sissinghurst White' Pure-white flowers sit in airy clusters above silver-splashed, pale-green leaves on this slowly spreading plant. Can be slow to establish. March to April. **H × S** 30cm × 30cm. AGM

'Trevi Fountain' Dense clusters of large, open, mid-blue flowers emerge from violet buds. These are carried well above silver-splashed, dark green leaves. April to May. **H × S** 35cm × 30cm. AGM

RANUNCULUS

aconitifolius These charming plants are valuable for a shady spot with soil that does not dry out. The double white variety is more widely available than this pretty, single-flowered form with numerous, small white flowers carried on long, slender, well-branched stems. The basal leaves are deeply, divided and dark green. April to June. **H × S** 90cm × 40cm

Needs Soil that remains moist in sun or partial shade
Great for moist borders
Bees & Butterflies Bees
For Cutting No
Care Trouble free in the right soil

RHODIOLA (Rose root)

rosea Looking something like a sedum, this handsome little plant evolves through the season. In early spring hummocks of short stems are thickly clothed with evenly spaced, fleshy, grey leaves that resemble scales. These terminate in a cluster of tiny, lime-green flowers that will later become fluffy with stamens. The stems then stretch upwards forming a loose mound. It is easily tucked among other perennials. May to June. **H × S** 30cm × 30cm

Needs Well-drained soil in sun
Great for Front of the border
Bees & Butterflies Bees
For Cutting No
Care Extremely tolerant of a wide variety of conditions. Plant and leave it alone.

Pulmonaria 'Sissinghurst White'   *Pulmonaria* 'Trevi Fountain'

Ranunculus aconitifolius

Rhodiola rosea

Rodgersia sambucifolia

Rudbeckia laciniata 'Herbstsonne'

RODGERSIA

sambucifolia A striking plant for damp spots. Curling sprays of tiny, cream flowers are carried on side branches down tall, strong, red stems. The bold leaves resemble those of the horse-chestnut tree. July. **H × S** 90cm × 80cm

Needs Moist soil in sun or partial shade
Great for Damp soils: bogs, pond edges, or by a stream
Bees & Butterflies Bees
For Cutting No
Care Trouble free in the right soil

RUDBECKIA (Black-eyed Susan)

Brightly coloured, easy to grow, and cheerful, these daisies have distinctive cone-shaped centres. They are invaluable for late-summer and autumn colour, forming broad mounds or upright clumps covered with flowers for many weeks.

Needs Well-drained soil in sun
Great for Middle and back of the border
Bees & Butterflies Yes
For Cutting Yes
Care Trouble free and needs no staking

fulgida var. *sullivantii* **'Goldsturm'** Large, black-centred, golden-yellow flowers are carried on a broad, upright dome. July to October. **H × S** 90cm × 80cm. AGM

laciniata **'Herbstsonne'** Ideal for the back of a border, this tall, imposing plant has green-centred, citrus-yellow flowers. August to September. **H × S** 180cm × 105cm. AGM

triloba An airy, upright plant with smallish, round, black-centred, rich-yellow flowers on slender, leafy, branched stems. August to October. **H × S** 90cm × 75cm. AGM

Rudbeckia fulgida var. *sullivantii* 'Goldsturm'

Rudbeckia triloba

SALVIA (Sage)

There really should be a place in every garden for these long- and free-flowering plants. Neat and mounding, then getting bigger as the season trundles on, they are perfect for mixing with other perennials. The tiny flowers are carried in slender spikes up stems that are sparingly covered with leaves. These look distinctly sage-like, but their fragrance is not as pleasant when they are crushed between the fingers.

Needs Well-drained soil in sun
Great for Front or middle of the border
Bees & Butterflies Bees
For Cutting Yes
Care Trouble free. Cut back after blooming to encourage further flowers

forsskaolii A handsome, if rather coarse-looking plant. Large, hairy, mid-green leaves form a flat rosette from which tall stems ending in well-branched and spaced spires of large, open, deep-blue flowers emerge. July to August. **H × S** 80cm × 80cm

glutinosa Not all plants need to be 'in your face' and this salvia creates a more subtle effect. A large, rather retiring plant, it produces a mound of soft-green, heart-shaped leaves and sends up stems of large, buff-yellow flowers. July to August. **H × S** 120cm × 80cm

nemorosa **'Amethyst'** An upright plant with slim, rather wavy spikes of tiny, amethyst-pink flowers and mid-green leaves. June to August. **H × S** 60cm × 45cm. AGM

nemorosa **'Caradonna'** The slender, firmly upright, purple stems carry spikes of small, blue-purple flowers and grey-green leaves. This makes an attractive and quite airy plant. June to August. **H × S** 50cm × 45cm. AGM

nemorosa **'Ostfriesland'** A bushy plant with spikes of violet flowers emerging from mauve calyces. June to August. **H × S** 60cm × 45cm. AGM

× sylvestris **'Blauhügel'** This is a shorter, compact variety with lavender-blue flower spikes, and is ideal for planting at the front of the border. June to August. **H × S** 45cm × 45cm. AGM

Salvia forsskaolii

Salvia glutinosa

Salvia nemorosa 'Amethyst'

Salvia nemorosa 'Caradonna'

Salvia nemorosa 'Ostfriesland'

Salvia × sylvestris 'Blauhügel'

Salvia × sylvestris 'Schneehügel'

Salvia verticillata 'Hannay's Blue'

Salvia verticillata 'Purple Rain'

Sanguisorba 'Blackthorn'

Sanguisorba hakusanensis

Sanguisorba 'Cangshan Cranberry'

× *sylvestris* 'Schneehügel' A short plant with spikes of white flowers and light-green leaves. It blooms for many weeks. June to August. **H × S** 45cm × 45cm

***verticillata* 'Hannay's Blue'** Whorls of lilac-blue flowers are carried on long stems above spreading, mid-green leaves that are rough to the touch. June to August. **H × S** 60cm × 45cm

***verticillata* 'Purple Rain'** The small purple flowers are carried in even whorls up the stem. They rise above mid-green, deeply serrated leaves and the plant makes a spreading clump. June to August. **H × S** 60cm × 60cm

SANGUISORBA (Burnet)

With their slim stems topped by poker-like flowers, burnets are graceful plants with a 'see-through' quality that makes them invaluable mixers in the border. Some flowers change as the stamens emerge and turn fluffy, like catkins or bottle brushes. The deeply divided leaves are highly decorative.

Needs Well-drained soil that remains moist in sun or partial shade
Great for Front, middle, or back of the border
Bees & Butterflies Bees
For Cutting Yes
Care Cut back to the first set of leaves after blooming to encourage more flowers.
S. tenuifolia types die back early, so cut them right to the ground

'Blackthorn' A lovely upright plant with straight pokers of tiny, fluffy flowers that open from dark red buds. These are borne on stiff stems above a mound of deeply cut, mid-green leaves. August to October. **H × S** 120cm × 75cm

***Sanguisorba* 'Cangshan Cranberry'** Dark burgundy-red in colour, the small, egg-shaped flowers are elegantly carried on tall, very slender, but sturdy stems above a low mound of mid-green, pinnate leaves. July to October. **H × S** 150cm × 80cm

hakusanensis A plant for injecting drama. Long, fluffy, soft-pink, tassel-like flowers tumble forward on slender stems above lovely, bluish-grey leaves that are serrated around the edges. July to August. **H × S** 90cm × 80cm

menziesii A handsome plant with fat spikes of maroon flowers that soften in colour as the stamens appear. The lovely grey-green leaves are tinted red. July to September. **H × S** 75cm × 60cm. AGM

obtusa Long, shaggy, bright-pink 'catkins' arch gently at the top above a clump of deeply divided, mid-green leaves. July to September. **H × S** 75cm × 60cm

officinalis (Great burnet) A very tall, elegant plant with compact, burgundy flower spikes carried above long, deeply divided leaves. It sometimes suffers from mildew. July to September. **H × S** 150cm × 30cm

***officinalis* 'Red Thunder'** Small, dense heads of rich-red flowers are held above a carpet of small, mid-green leaves. July to September. **H × S** 30cm × 60cm

'Pink Tanna' Above a spreading mound of deeply divided leaves, long, pink 'pokers' rise up on elegant, willowy stems. July to September. **H × S** 60cm × 75cm

tenuifolia* var. *alba Emerging on upright stems, the long, slender, white flower spikes arch slightly as they age. They are carried above a dense mound of soft-green leaves. July to September. **H × S** 150cm × 75cm

Sanguisorba menziesii

Sanguisorba obtusa

Sanguisorba officinalis

Sanguisorba officinalis 'Red Thunder'

Sanguisorba 'Pink Tanna'

Sanguisorba tenuifolia var. *alba*

Saxifraga × *urbium*

Scabiosa 'Butterfly Blue'

Scabiosa caucasica 'Clive Greaves'

Scabiosa caucasica 'Miss Willmott'

Scabiosa columbaria subsp. *ochroleuca*

Scabiosa lucida

SAXIFRAGA (London pride)

× *urbium* Grown in gardens for around 300 years, this robust plant often lines the edges of paths. With pretty, pale-pink flowers and evergreen foliage that slowly forms a broad mat of round, mid-green leaves, it is a faultless ground-covering plant. May to June. **H × S** 45cm × 60cm. AGM

Needs Well-drained soil in sun or partial shade
Great for Very front of the border
Bees & Butterflies Bees
For Cutting Yes
Care Trouble free

SCABIOSA (Scabious)

A disc-like centre surrounded by a frill of petals gives the flowers a rather dignified look. Nectar-rich, they are carried on slender stems, above a clump of deeply divided, mid-green leaves, over a long period.

Needs Well-drained soil in sun
Great for Front, middle, or back of the border
Bees & Butterflies Yes
For Cutting Yes
Care Cut back after blooming to encourage further flowers. Very floriferous, so may be short-lived, and can also suffer from mildew

'Butterfly Blue' A good variety for containers, with short stems of soft-blue flowers that attract butterflies. June to September. **H × S** 30cm × 30cm

caucasica **'Clive Greaves'** At one time, this was a popular plant in the cut-flower industry. The large, soft-blue flowers are carried on long, slender stems. June to September. **H × S** 60cm × 30cm. AGM

caucasica **'Miss Willmott'** The large, milk-white flowers with pin-cushion centres are wonderful for cutting. June to September. **H × S** 60cm × 30cm. AGM

columbaria **subsp. *ochroleuca*** This free-flowering variety with small, lemon blooms makes bushy swathes. An excellent plant for the wilder garden, it seeds freely. June to September. **H × S** 45cm × 60cm

lucida Possessing similar qualities to *S. columbaria*, this variety is more suited to a drier soil. The flowers are small and lavender-blue and the leaves silver-green. June to September. **H × S** 60cm × 30cm

Sedum (Herbstfreude Group) 'Herbstfreude' in July

Sedum 'José Aubergine'

Sedum 'Mr Goodbud'

SEDUM (Ice plant)

Succulent by nature and in appearance, the border varieties of this easily grown, bee- and butterfly-attracting group need little attention. Plate-like flower heads are borne on stout stems that, when dry, give handsome structure to the winter border. These are now listed by the Royal Horticultural Society under the new name of *Hylotelephium*.

Needs Well-drained soil in sun
Great for Front or middle of the border
Bees & Butterflies Yes
For Cutting Yes
Care Trouble free. Some varieties with broad heads may topple over, especially in richer soils. Cut back the stems in late spring to create a shorter, more compact plant.

(Herbstfreude Group) 'Herbstfreude' The pale-green foliage is topped with broad, gently domed heads of tiny, lime-green buds that open coral-pink, then dark pink stars. August to October. **H × S** 60cm × 45cm. AGM

'José Aubergine' Small heads of tiny, starry, reddish-pink flowers, dusky-pink in bud, are carried on grey-purple stems and leaves. August to October. **H × S** 45cm × 45cm

'Matrona' Upright stems in eye-catching deep maroon bear broad heads of small, soft rose-pink flowers on this very handsome plant. The dark green leaves are also tinted maroon. August to October. **H × S** 60cm × 45cm. AGM

'Mr Goodbud' The domed heads of large, flowers open pink-mauve and deepen to rich red-mauve. The blue-green of the stems and leaves makes a wonderful contrast. July to October. **H × S** 30cm × 30cm. AGM

Sedum 'Matrona' with *Persicaria amplexicaulis* 'Firetail'

Sedum 'Mr Goodbud' (front) and *Sedum* (Herbstfreude Group) 'Herbstfreude' (behind) with
Persicaria affinis 'Darjeeling Red' and *Echinacea purpurea* 'White Swan'

Sedum 'Red Cauli'

Sedum spectabile

Sedum 'Stewed Rhubarb Mountain'

'Red Cauli' This richly coloured variety bears small, domed heads of flowers in an intense shade of red. Both stems and leaves are dark red. July to October. **H × S** 30cm × 30cm. AGM

spectabile Held in small, flat clusters, the soft-pink flowers become fluffy as they age. The foliage is a pale green and forms a sturdy, upright mound. August to October. **H × S** 45cm × 45cm. AGM

'Stewed Rhubarb Mountain' Neatly domed heads of soft-pink flowers are held on sturdy stems and form a compact tower. The succulent, oval leaves are grey-green and edged with red. August to September. **H × S** 50cm × 45cm

telephium **(Atropurpureum Group) 'Gooseberry Fool'** Broad, shallow-domed, heads of tiny, star-shaped, greenish-white flowers are carried on red stems with round, grey-green leaves. Forms a neat, rounded mound. July to September. **H × S** 60cm × 45cm

telephium **(Atropurpureum Group) 'Purple Emperor'** The upright, purple-brown stems and leaves are topped with small, rounded clusters of pale-pink flowers. The darker bracts remain after the flowers fade. August to October. **H × S** 60cm × 45cm. AGM

telephium **(Atropurpureum Group) 'Xenox'** An excellent variety, this creates a neat, dusky-purple mound that looks good all season. Flat heads of tiny, red flowers bloom above the foliage. August to October. **H × S** 30cm × 30cm. AGM

Sedum telephium (Atropurpureum Group) 'Gooseberry Fool'

Sedum telephium (Atropurpureum Group) 'Purple Emperor'

Sedum telephium (Atropurpureum Group) 'Xenox'

Selinum wallichianum

Senecio polyodon

Sidalcea candida

Sidalcea 'Elsie Heugh'

Stachys byzantina

SELINUM

wallichianum Beautifully structured with broad heads of tiny, white flowers, this plant looks similar to our native cow parsley. The dusky-red stems emerge from a dense mound of deeply divided, mid-green leaves that, although large, have a delicate quality. July to September. **H × S** 120cm × 90cm. AGM

Needs Well-drained soil in sun or partial shade
Great for Middle of the border
Bees & Butterflies Bees
For Cutting No
Care Prefers a soil that does not dry out, otherwise easy to grow and will self-seed

SENECIO

polyodon Grow this charming plant between perennials with dense foliage, where its wispiness will have a softening effect. The small, bright-pink daisies rise above a rosette of fresh-green leaves. June to September. **H × S** 30cm × 30cm

Needs Well-drained soil; sun or partial shade
Great for Front of the border
Bees & Butterflies Bees
For Cutting Yes
Care Likely to be short-lived, but may seed around. Otherwise trouble free

SIDALCEA (Prairie mallow)

Paper-thin flowers are carried around the stems of these pretty plants that resemble a short hollyhock. The flower spikes vary in height, eventually growing into a neat, uneven, upright clump with delicate, shiny, deeply divided leaves.

Needs Well-drained soil in sun
Great for Front or middle of the border
Bees & Butterflies Yes
For Cutting Yes
Care Trouble free. Just cut back after flowering to increase longevity

candida Pure-white flowers sometimes with gaps between the petals, are loosely spaced along the spikes of this attractive variety. It is usually seed grown, so forms may vary. July to August. **H × S** 90cm × 45cm

'Elsie Heugh' A very pretty plant with soft-pink flowers that are neatly fringed around the edges of the petals. July to August. **H × S** 90cm × 45cm. AGM

STACHYS

Within this group there are two distinct types: one has semi-evergreen, woolly, silver-grey foliage that is soft to the touch, the other has plain, mid-green leaves. The woolly-leaved varieties add texture and make extremely useful ground-cover at the front of a border. Those with green leaves are more upright in habit and better for the middle of a border. All have funnel-shaped flowers with large lower lips.

Needs Well-drained soil in sun or partial shade
Great for Front or middle of the border
Bees & Butterflies Bees
For Cutting Yes
Care Trouble free, but *S. byzantina* types will benefit from a trim to get rid of the old woody stems. In warm summers the leaves may get a mild attack of mildew

byzantina (Lamb's ears) From a carpet of silver-grey, furry leaves, numerous soft, grey stems bear tiny, pink flowers, which emerge from woolly buds. June to August. **H × S** 45cm × 60cm

byzantina **'Big Ears'** As the name suggests, the felted, silver-grey leaves of this variety are very big. The long, leafy stems carry woolly whorls of tiny, lilac-pink flowers. June to August. **H × S** 60cm × 60cm

byzantina **'Silver Carpet'** Rarely producing any flowers, this plant forms a perfect carpet of furry, silver leaves that is so dense, weeds find it almost impossible to penetrate. June to August. **H × S** 30cm × 60cm

macrantha **'Superba'** (Big-sage) Big spikes of large, purple, trumpet-shaped flowers are carried on thick, upright stems, but soon fade. The foliage forms rounded clumps, which contrast well with frothy plants. July to August. **H × S** 70cm × 45cm. AGM

officinalis **'Alba'** (White betony) Pokers of white flowers bloom on straight stems with a few bright-green leaves. More foliage forms a basal clump. July to August. **H × S** 85cm × 30cm

officinalis **'Hummelo'** (Betony) The tightly packed spikes of this compact, upright plant are an unusual shade of rosy-purple. They are carried on straight, sparsely leaved stems above a rosette of long, serrated, mid-green leaves. July to August. **H × S** 75cm × 30cm. AGM

officinalis **'Rosea'** Very neat and upright in habit, this pretty variety has stiff stems that carry short, stumpy spikes of little, pale-pink flowers above mid-green leaves. July to August. **H × S** 40cm × 30cm

Stachys byzantina 'Big Ears'

Stachys byzantina 'Silver Carpet'

Stachys macrantha 'Superba'

Stachys officinalis 'Alba'

Stachys officinalis 'Hummelo'

Stachys officinalis 'Rosea'

Stemmacantha centaureoides

Stipa calamagrostis

Stipa gigantea

Stokesia laevis

Stokesia laevis 'Alba'

STEMMACANTHA

centaureoides This striking plant may at first prove difficult to establish. Once settled, it produces globular heads of fluffy lilac flowers set in scaly, bronze cups. Long, serrated-edged, silver leaves form a basal clump. Formerly listed as *Centaurea* 'Pulchra Major', it has now been reclassified as *Rhaponticum*. July to August. **H × S** 90cm × 60cm

Needs Well-drained, fairly moist soil, in sun
Great for Middle of the border
Bees & Butterflies Yes
For Cutting Yes
Care Once established, trouble free

STIPA

Handsome and deservedly popular, these grasses send up thick tufts of fine leaves and fountains of elegant flowers that last for months and are easy to blend into a border.

Needs Well-drained soil in a warm spot in sun
Great for Front or back of a border
Bees & Butterflies No
For Cutting Yes
Care Reasonably trouble free. Shorter varieties may seed about once established

calamagrostis White flowers in soft, silky, feathery plumes emerge from a clump of mid-green leaves. Reliable, even in poor soils. June to October. **H × S** 90cm × 75cm. AGM

gigantea Very tall and very handsome, the stiff stems of soft-beige, oat-like flowers form airy plumes that catch the light. August to September. **H × S** 180cm × 120cm. AGM

STOKESIA (Stokes's aster)

When these plants get their roots down and start to bloom, the big, flat, flowers with fringed petals are really eye-catching. Their stiff stems spring from a rosette of long, leathery, evergreen leaves.

Needs Well-drained soil that does not dry out in sun or partial shade
Great for Front of the border
Bees & Butterflies Yes
For Cutting Yes
Care May take a little while to establish. Trouble free, especially in a slightly acid soil

laevis Lilac-blue flowers bloom over several weeks. July to October. **H × S** 60cm × 50cm

***laevis* 'Alba'** A plant with creamy-white flowers, often flushed with very pale lilac. July to October. **H × S** 60cm × 50cm

STROBILANTHES (Hardy Persian shield)

wallichii This handsome, free-flowering, late blooming plant carries purple-blue, funnel-shaped flowers on well-branched, upright stems with fresh green leaves. An airy plant that perfectly complements many other late-flowering perennials. September to October. **H × S** 90cm × 75cm

Needs Well-drained soil that does not dry out in sun or partial shade
Great for Middle of a border
Bees & Butterflies Yes
For Cutting No
Care Will self-seed but is not invasive

SUCCISA (Devil's bit scabious)

pratensis This very free-flowering plant is a magnet for bees and butterflies. Forming a 'see-through' network, the fine, branched stems terminate in a compact ball of lilac-blue flowers, like bright pom-poms. July to October. **H × S** 120cm × 90cm

Needs Well-drained soil in sun or partial shade
Great for Middle of a border
Bees & Butterflies Yes
For Cutting Yes
Care Will self-seed once established but is not invasive

SYMPHYTUM (Comfrey)

Although its rough foliage may look rather coarse, comfrey will shade the ground so thoroughly that weeds get smothered. The flowers are carried in small clusters on long stems. Some varieties spread rapidly and uncontrollably; others are well behaved.

Needs Any soil that does not dry out in sun, partial shade, or shade
Great for Wild areas
Bees & Butterflies Bees
For Cutting No
Care Trouble free

azureum The intense colour of its bright sky-blue flowers is very desirable, but this creeping variety should be grown with caution. May to July. **H × S** 45cm × 90cm

'Hidcote Pink' Short stems of nodding, soft-blue and pale-pink flowers sit above a well-behaved, dense carpet of leaves. May to July. **H × S** 45cm × 90cm

'Rubrum' A handsome, non-invasive plant with crimson flowers and dark green leaves. May to June. **H × S** 30cm × 45cm

× uplandicum (Russian comfrey) Clusters of blue, purple, or violet flowers are carried on long, leafy stems. Robust and long flowering, it is generally grown from seed. May to September. **H × S** 90cm × 90cm

Strobilanthes wallichii

Succisa pratensis

Symphytum azureum

Symphytum 'Hidcote Pink'

Symphytum 'Rubrum'

Symphytum × uplandicum

Tellima grandiflora Rubra Group

Thalictrum 'Black Stockings'

Thalictrum delavayi

Thalictrum delavayi 'Album'

Thalictrum delavayi 'Hewitt's Double'

TELLIMA (Fringe cups)

***grandiflora* Rubra Group** Unassuming yet invaluable for ground-cover, this evergreen plant bears slender spikes of dainty, green bells, fringed around the edges with pink. The vine-like foliage starts out bright green; by autumn it is burnished with bronze. May to July. **H × S** 60cm × 45cm

Needs Well-drained soil in partial shade
Great for Shady spots
Bees & Butterflies Bees
For Cutting Yes
Care Trouble free

THALICTRUM (Meadow rue)

Tall and very elegant, these delightful perennials will light up a shady part of the garden for weeks with their delicate sprays of tiny, cup-shaped flowers. The individual blooms are single or semi-double and are borne on the side branches of straight stems. They are held well above deeply divided, fern-like foliage that remains attractive right through to late autumn.

Needs Soil that remains moist in partial sun or dappled shade
Great for Borders and woodland
Bees & Butterflies Bees
For Cutting Yes
Care Trouble free in the right soil. Although sturdy, *T. delavayi* and *T. flavum* may need staking in a windy spot

'Black Stockings' Aptly named, this plant has particularly dark, long, purple-black stems. In spring, they rise up from a clump of delicate, mid-green leaves and carry heads of fluffy, rose-purple flowers in summer. June to July. **H × S** 90cm × 75cm. AGM

delavayi Open sprays of small flowers in a delicate lavender with cream stamens are carried on soft-mauve stems. June to August. **H × S** 150cm × 75cm

***delavayi* 'Album'** Pure-white flowers with long stamens create delicate open spires. These are carried on stiff stems above deeply divided, mid-green leaves. June to August. **H × S** 120cm × 60cm

***delavayi* 'Hewitt's Double'** As the name suggests, this is a double form, but it can be tricky to establish. Once settled, the airy sprays of small, mauve, pom-pom flowers are both long-lasting and exquisite. June to August. **H × S** 150cm × 75cm

Thalictrum rochebruneanum

Thalictrum 'Splendide White'

Thermopsis lanceolata

Tiarella cordifolia

Thalictrum 'Elin'

'Elin' In spring, the handsome, blue-grey foliage of this variety displays a red tint, which has faded by the time the open sprays of lilac flowers emerge. This beautiful giant of a plant needs no staking. June to August. H × S 180cm × 90cm . AGM

rochebruneanum A robust, tall variety with sprays of open, shallow-cupped, lavender flowers with pale-yellow stamens. These are carried on soft-purple stems above handsome, deeply divided, mid-green leaves. June to August. H × S 150cm × 75cm. AGM

'Splendide White' Tall stems with bright-green leaves carry clouds of little, cupped, downward-facing flowers that are pure-white with long cream stamens. There is also a lilac form. Said to be good for cutting. July to September. H × S 170cm × 80cm. AGM

THERMOPSIS (False lupin)

lanceolata Resembling a slender, yellow lupin, this neat, clump-forming plant has similar pea-shaped flowers. They are carried in open spikes on almost-black stems with green foliage that is reminiscent of the leaves of false indigo (*Baptisia*). May to June. H × S 90cm × 75cm

Needs Well-drained soil in sun
Great for Middle of the border
Bees & Butterflies No
For Cutting No
Care Slow to establish, but can be left undisturbed for years

TIARELLA (Foam flower)

cordifolia This pretty woodlander forms domes of evergreen, vine-like foliage that will, in time, creep over the ground to form a dense mat. The starry, white flowers are borne in airy spikes just above the mound of leaves, which turn shades of red in autumn. April to May. H × S 30cm × 60cm. AGM

Needs Humus-rich, moist soil in partial shade
Great for Shady areas
Bees & Butterflies No
For Cutting Yes
Care Can suffer attack by vine weevil

Tradescantia (Andersoniana Group) 'Concord Grape'

Tradescantia (Andersoniana Group) 'J. C. Weguelin'

Tradescantia (Andersoniana Group) 'Osprey'

Tradescantia (Andersoniana Group) 'Perrine's Pink'

Tricyrtis formosana 'Dark Beauty'

Tricyrtis hirta 'Miyazaki'

TRADESCANTIA (Spiderwort)

A thicket of grassy leaves is topped, in early summer, with clusters of flat, three-petalled blooms that flower over a long period. In the centre is a fluffy tuft from which the long, pollen-tipped stamens protrude.

Needs Moist soil in sun or partial shade
Great for Front of the border
Bees & Butterflies No
For Cutting Yes
Care The leaves can be prone to leaf spot in the sun. If they become marked, trim them back, which also promotes more flowers

(Andersoniana Group) 'Concord Grape'
The combination of soft-purple flowers and disease-resistant, grey-green leaves is lovely. June to August. **H × S** 45cm × 60cm. AGM

(Andersoniana Group) 'J. C. Weguelin'
A free-flowering plant with blooms of soft violet-blue and fresh-green leaves. June to August. **H × S** 45cm × 60cm

(Andersoniana Group) 'Osprey' Pure-white flowers are enhanced by a centre of fluffy, blue stamens. June to August. **H × S** 45cm × 60cm

(Andersoniana Group) 'Perrine's Pink' A taller variety with a pretty mix of lilac-pink flowers and grey-green, disease-resistant leaves. June to August. **H × S** 60cm × 70cm

TRICYRTIS (Toad lily)

Exotic and intriguing, these very late-flowering woodland plants will, given the right soil, slowly spread. At each leaf joint, the upright or arching stems carry a smallish, star-shaped flower, often spotted inside. Its six waxy petals are cupped around a raised 'mast' that looks rather like the blades of a helicopter and bristles with tiny beads of nectar.

Needs Soil that remains moist in partial shade or shade
Great for Shady areas
Bees & Butterflies No
For Cutting No
Care Trouble free if planted where they are not competing with other border plants

formosana **'Dark Beauty'** The many forms of *T. formosana* have mid-green leaves and their white flowers are heavily dotted with purple. On this tall plant, the spots are so closely set the petals look almost mauve. September to October. **H × S** 90cm × 50cm

hirta **'Miyazaki'** Lightly speckled with purple, the eye-catching white flowers appear at the upper leaf joints on upright stems. The leaves are large, dark green, and deeply grooved. September to October. **H × S** 75cm × 70cm *hirta* **'Taiwan Atrianne'** The white flowers of this upright, leafy plant are sparsely speckled with maroon. Given a shady spot with really moist soil, this will grow tall and add autumn impact. September to October. **H × S** 105cm × 60cm

'Tojen' A sprawling plant with long, arching stems of white flowers. The petal edges are delicately tinged with lilac. August to September. **H × S** 75cm × 60cm

TRIFOLIUM (Clover)

Although clovers can be invasive, these upright bushy forms are not. They are wonderful for the front of a border but can be short-lived, so look out for seedlings emerging around the base of the plants.

Needs Well-drained soil that stays moist in sun or partial shade
Great for Front of the border. Works well in containers
Bees & Butterflies Bees
For Cutting No
Care Cut back to keep tidy and to encourage a few more flowers

ochroleucon Balls of creamy-yellow flowers sit above a tidy, upright plant with soft-green clover-shaped leaves. June to July. **H × S** 60cm × 40cm

rubens The pink-red flowers form neat, tapering 'towers' that look fluffy when the individual blooms emerge. These are carried on sturdy, bright-green stems with long leaves. June to August. **H × S** 60cm × 45cm

TRILLIUM (Wake robin)

These select, slow-growing plants are best suited to dappled shade beneath deciduous trees and large shrubs. Their structure is very unusual, but beautiful: petals, bracts, and leaves are all in groups of three.

Needs Soil that remains moist in partial shade
Great for Woodland
Bees & Butterflies Bees
For Cutting No
Care Slow to get going. If possible, buy big plants, which will establish better

luteum (Yellow trillium) Carried on thick stems, the long, soft-lemon, scented flowers sit on top of large leaves that are heavily mottled with khaki. It will not thrive in acid soils. April to May. **H × S** 30cm × 30cm. AGM

sessile (Sessile trillium) A mounding plant with large, mid-green leaves, slightly blotched with darker tones. These form a 'plate' for the upright, burgundy flowers. Will flourish under trees where the soil is rich in leaf mould. April to May. **H × S** 30cm × 30cm

Tricyrtis hirta 'Taiwan Atrianne'

Tricyrtis 'Tojen'

Trifolium ochroleucon

Trifolium rubens

Trillium luteum

Trillium sessile

Uvularia grandiflora

Valeriana phu 'Aurea'

Valeriana officinalis

Verbascum chaixii 'Album'

Verbascum olympicum

UVULARIA (Merrybells)

grandiflora An attractive plant for a lightly shaded spot with slender, soft-yellow bells that droop from branched stems. A little slow to get going, but will slowly spread. April to May. **H × S** 60cm × 30cm. AGM

Needs Soil that remains moist in partial shade
Great for Woodland
Bees & Butterflies Bees
For Cutting No
Care Prefers ground rich in leaf mould

VALERIANA (Valerian)

Flat heads of beautifully, scented, tiny, white flowers are held on upright stems that rise from a thick clump of attractive foliage. A good choice for a naturalistic planting.

Needs Soil that remains moist in sun or partial shade
Great for Middle or back of the border
Bees & Butterflies Bees
For Cutting No
Care Trouble free, but cats will roll in it

officinalis (Common valerian) Tall and very upright stems with deeply divided foliage bear domed sprays of tiny, white flowers. July to August. **H × S** 150cm × 60cm

***phu* 'Aurea'** A tufted clump of bright-yellow leaves turns green by summer, when domed sprays of small, white, honey-scented flowers appear. May to June. **H × S** 60cm × 45cm

VERBASCUM (Mullein)

For flowers with impact and vertical structure, few plants can match mulleins. Tall, elegant spikes of usually single flowers open over many weeks and are carried above a rosette of broad leaves.

Needs Well-drained soil in sun or partial shade
Great for Middle or back of the border
Bees & Butterflies Bees
For Cutting Yes
Care These short-lived perennials self-seed and germinate easily. If you want to keep numbers down and aid longevity, remember to dead-head them

***chaixii* 'Album'** A plant reliably raised from seed, it bears slim spikes of pure-white flowers with purple stamens. Carried on sturdy stems above a rosette of mid-green leaves, they bloom for many weeks. June to August. **H × S** 90cm × 55cm

olympicum A dramatic and defiant plant that throws up candelabras of bright-yellow flowers. The stiff stems have many side branches and large, soft-green leaves. July to August. **H × S** 180cm × 75cm

VERBENA

The slender, branched stems add height to the border and create a lovely 'see-through' effect. Although rather short-lived, they produce masses of tiny, bright flowers that are loved by insects.

Needs Well-drained soil in sun
Great for Middle or back of the border
Bees & Butterflies Yes
For Cutting Yes
Care Easy to grow. Allow the plant to seed around and hope for seedlings

bonariensis A tall, elegant plant with rigid, sparsely leaved, well-branched stems. These are topped with small clusters of tiny, violet flowers over a long period. There is also a much smaller version named *Verbena* 'Lollipop'. This grows to 60cm and is good for containers. June to October. **H × S** 120cm × 45cm. AGM

hastata* f. *rosea Tiny pink flowers emerge from deep-pink buds at the top of stems that branch profusely towards the top. Easier to establish than *V. bonariensis*. June to October. **H × S** 110cm × 45cm

VERONICA (Speedwell)

These charming plants form either a neat mound or a spreading carpet and send up masses of short flower spikes. The simply shaped blooms add welcome colour, with *spicata* types flowering over a long period.

Needs Well-drained soil in sun or partial shade
Great for Front or middle of the border
Bees & Butterflies Bees
For Cutting Yes
Care *Gentianoides* types prefer soil that does not dry out. Cut back flowering stems of the others to encourage better growth

gentianoides Slender, open spikes of lovely, sky-blue flowers appear in late spring. They are carried above a tight, spreading carpet of shiny, deep-green leaves. May to June. **H × S** 45cm × 60cm

'Shirley Blue' A domed mound of mid-green leaves is covered with short spikes of flowers in a vivid shade of blue. May to July. **H × S** 30cm × 30cm. AGM

***spicata* 'Icicle'** A short, broad, mounding plant with neat spikes of clean, pure-white flowers and long, grey-green leaves. June to September. **H × S** 30cm × 45cm

***spicata* 'Rotfuchs'** The bright red-pink spikes are carried above a slowly creeping mound of long, mid-green leaves. June to September. **H × S** 30cm × 30cm

Verbena bonariensis

Verbena hastata f. *rosea*

Veronica gentianoides

Veronica 'Shirley Blue'

Veronica spicata 'Icicle'

Veronica spicata 'Rotfuchs'

Veronicastrum sibiricum 'Red Arrows'

Veronicastrum virginicum 'Lavendulturm'

Veronicastrum virginicum 'Album'

Waldsteinia ternata

Veronicastrum virginicum f. *roseum* 'Pink Glow'

VERONICASTRUM (Culver's root)

Perfectly architectural in form, these perennials look stunning when planted in drifts, adding graceful linear structure to the border. Very tall, slender, tapering flower spikes of tiny, bell-shaped flowers are carried in layers, rather like a candelabra. Below each, right down to the bottom of the stem, are whorls of long, pointed leaves. The 'scaffolding' of spikes is so slim that these perennials won't hide anything planted behind them.

Needs Soil that remains moist in sun or partial shade
Great for Back of a border
Bees & Butterflies Bees
For Cutting No
Care Trouble free in the right soil

sibiricum **'Red Arrows'** Spikes of tiny, deep-lilac flowers open from red-purple buds in tiers up stems also tinged with red. July to September. **H × S** 150cm × 90cm

virginicum **'Album'** This beautiful variety carries long spikes of white flowers on bronze stems with dark green leaves. July to September. **H × S** 150cm × 90cm. AGM

virginicum **'Fascination'** Wands of rich-lilac flowers are held in branched tiers, rather like a candelabra, on this handsome, eye-catching plant. These become paler in colour as the blooms fade. July to September. **H × S** 150cm × 90cm

virginicum **'Lavendulturm'** Early to bloom, this variety has pale-lilac flower spikes and mid-green leaves. It finishes flowering before others have really got going. July to August. **H × S** 150cm × 90cm. AGM

virginicum f. *roseum* **'Pink Glow'** A lovely and rather subtle plant with spikes of palest pastel-pink flowers and dark green leaves. It creates a gentle, bushy structure. July to September. **H × S** 120cm × 90cm

WALDSTEINIA (Golden strawberry)

ternata Excellent for ground-cover, this spreading evergreen bears single, golden-yellow flowers, like those of a strawberry. These are scattered in sprays above a clump of round, shiny, dark green leaves. April to May. **H × S** 15cm × 50cm

Needs Well-drained soil in partial shade
Great for Ground-cover
Bees & Butterflies No
For Cutting No
Care Trouble free in the right soil

Veronicastrum virginicum 'Fascination' with *Thalictrum* 'Elin' and *Persicaria polymorpha* behind

Author's acknowledgments

Thanks to the following for their help: my husband Ric for taking on the extra nursery duties while I buried my head in this book, and for his encouragement. To Andrea Jones for her generosity in letting me use her photograph. And many thanks to Anna Kruger for her knowledge, advice and enthusiastic input.